Terry Moore
Story & Art

Robyn Moore
Publisher

Brian Miller
Cover Color

Strangers In Paradise: TATTOO

ISBN 1-892597-33-0

Published by
Abstract Studio, Inc.
P. O. Box 271487
Houston, Texas 77277
www.StrangersInParadise.com

Printed In Canada

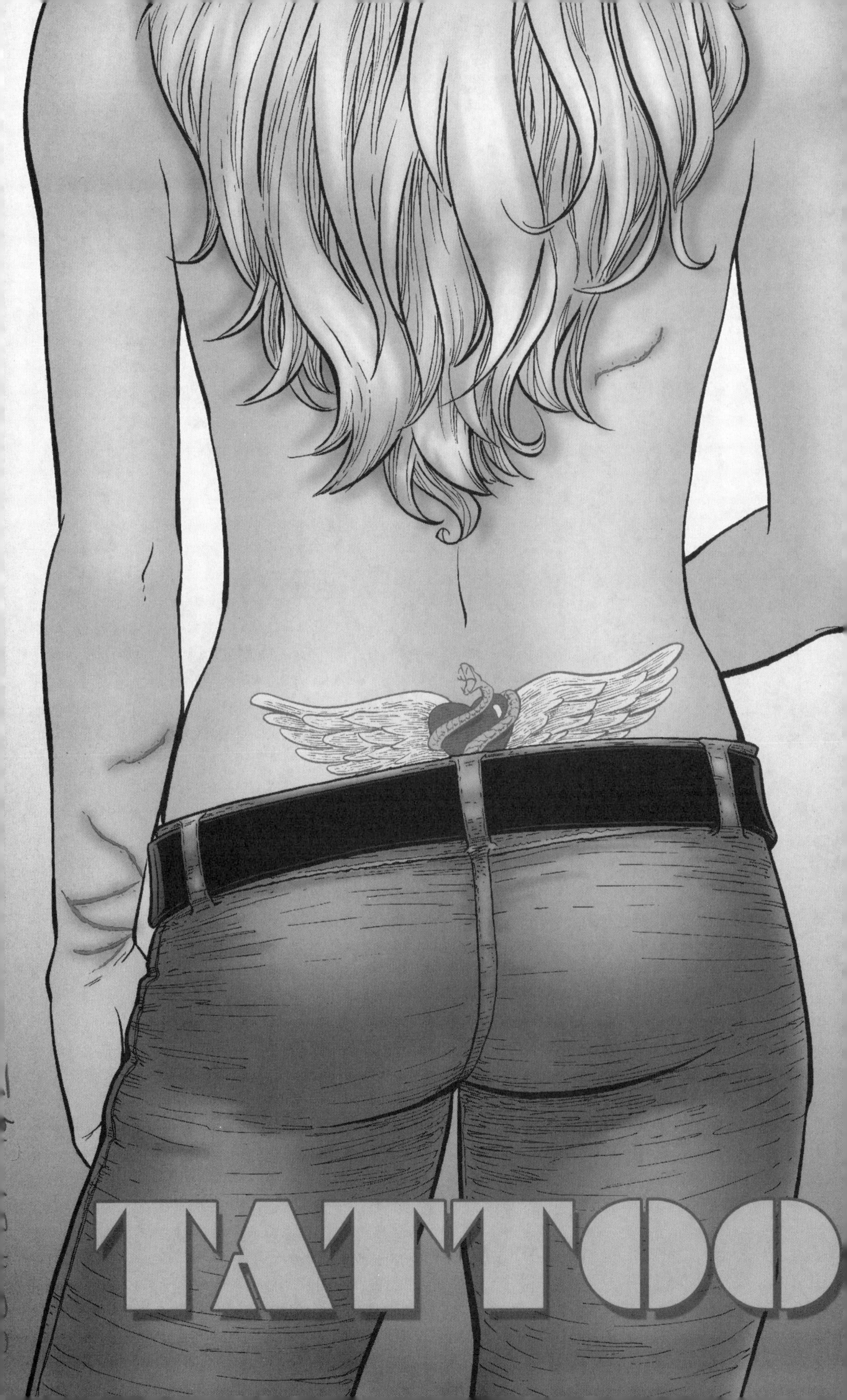
TATTOO

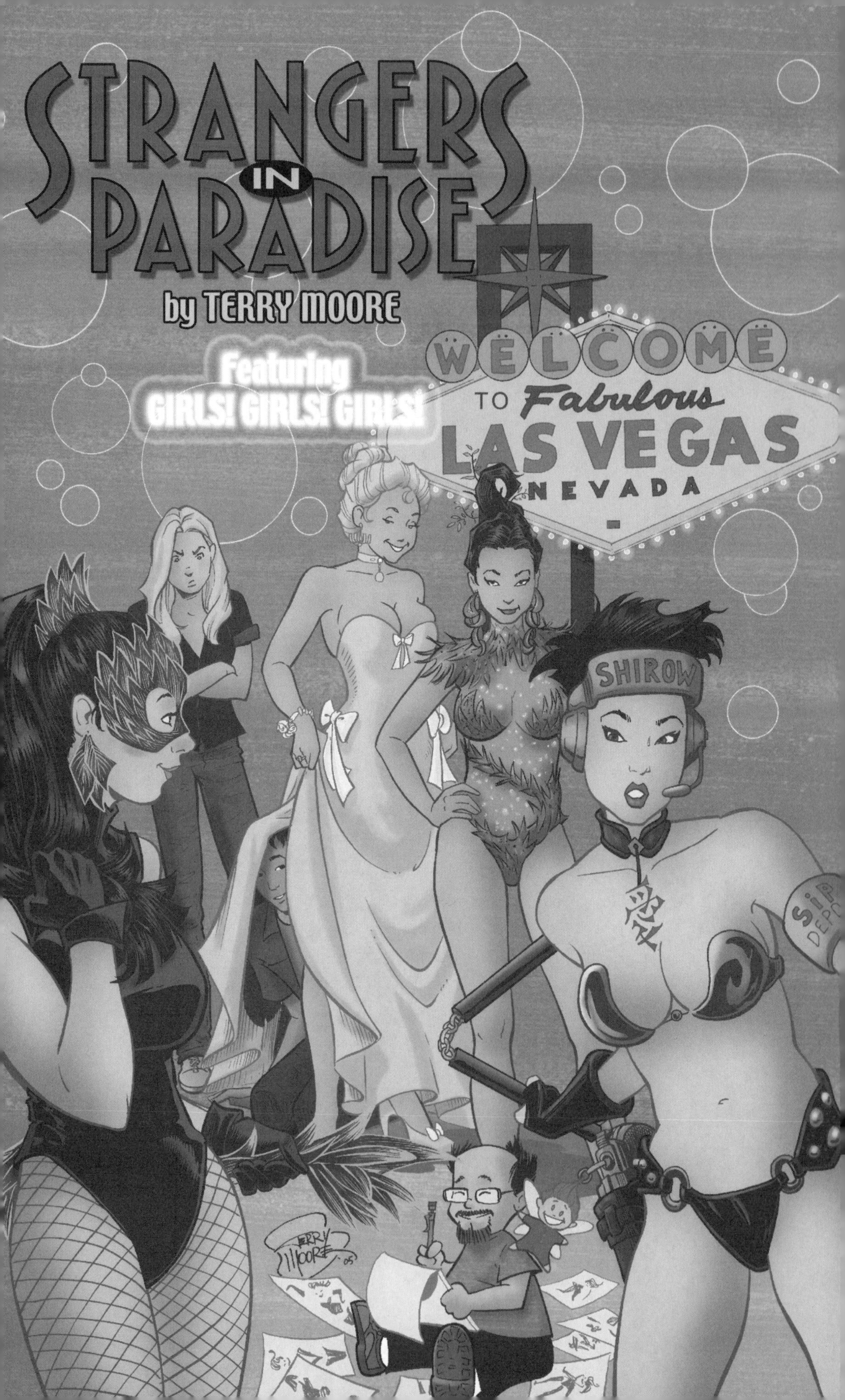
STRANGERS IN PARADISE
by TERRY MOORE
Featuring
GIRLS! GIRLS! GIRLS!
WELCOME
TO Fabulous
LAS VEGAS
NEVADA
SHIROW
TERRY MOORE '05

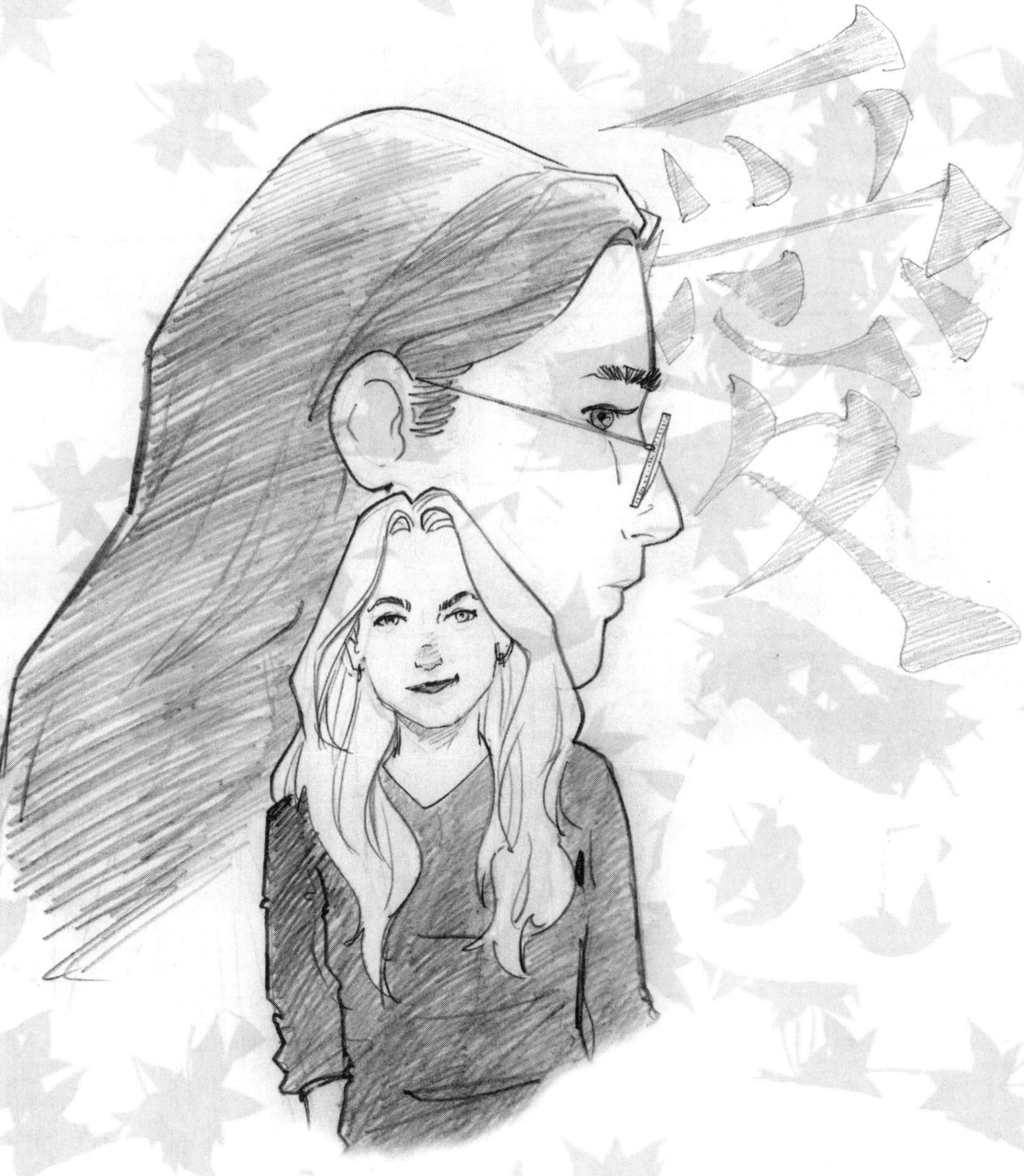
愛

Perfection is achieved, not when there is nothing left to add,
but when there is nothing left to take away.
—Antoine de St. Exupery

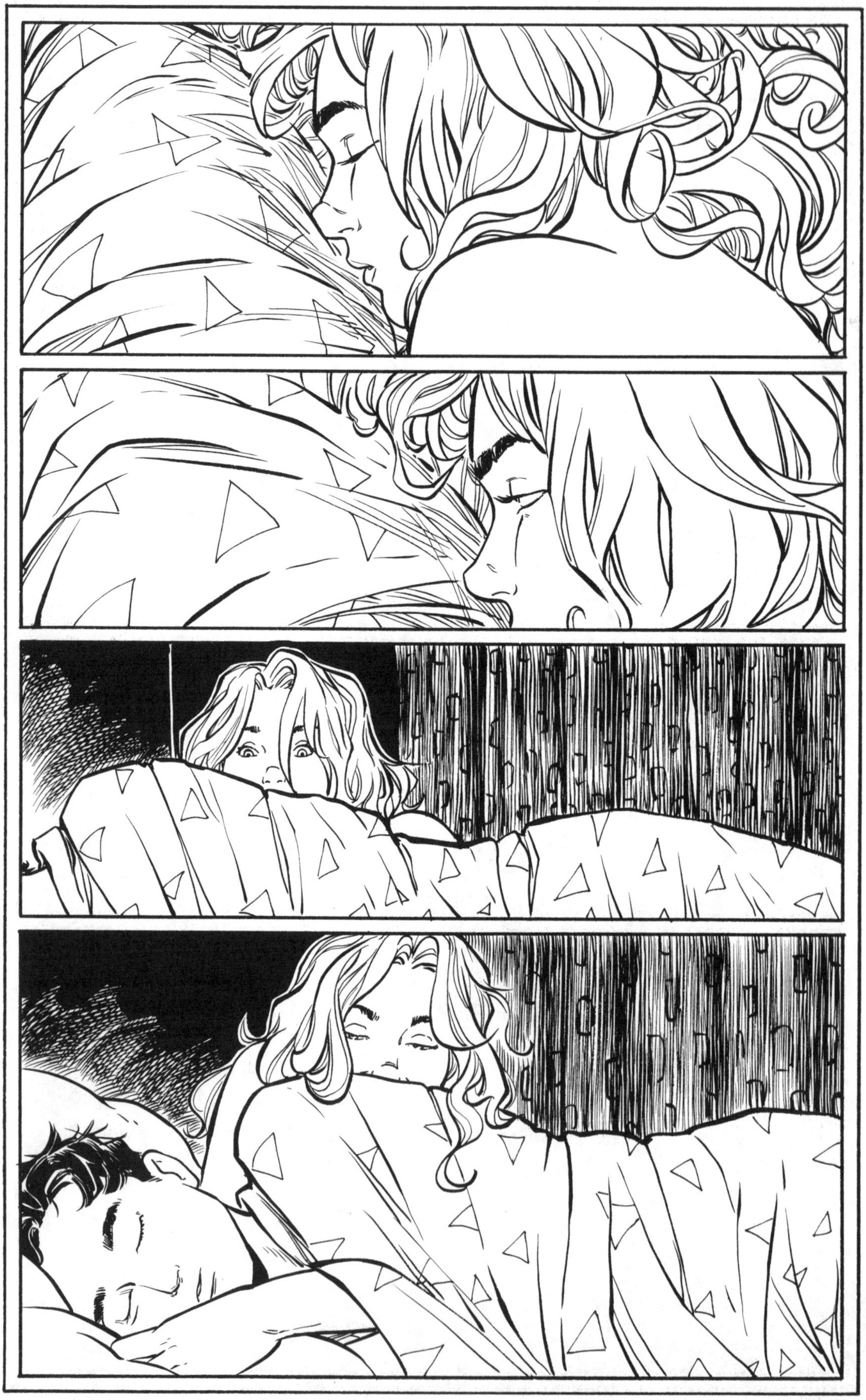

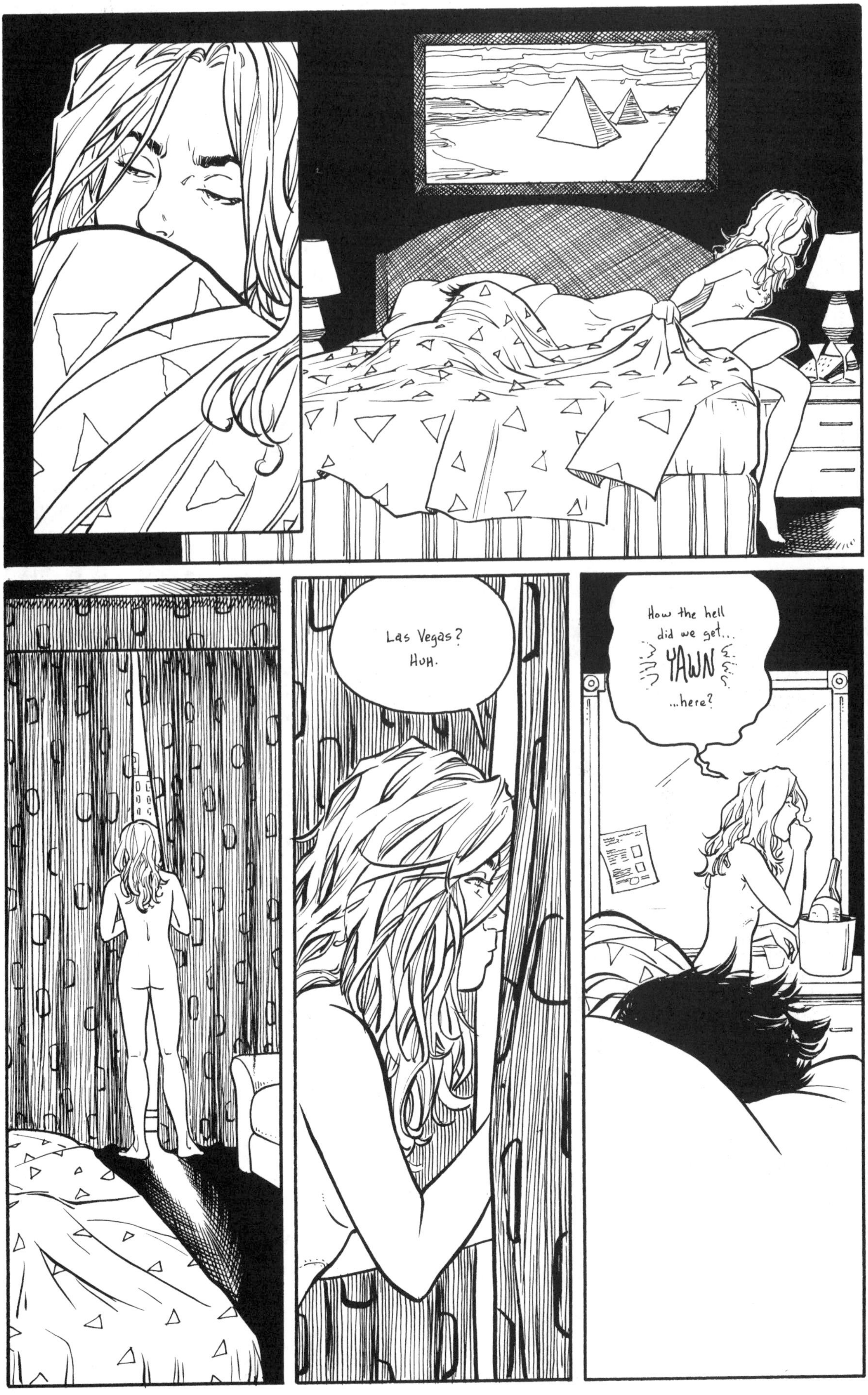
Las Vegas? Huh.
How the hell did we get... YAWN ...here?

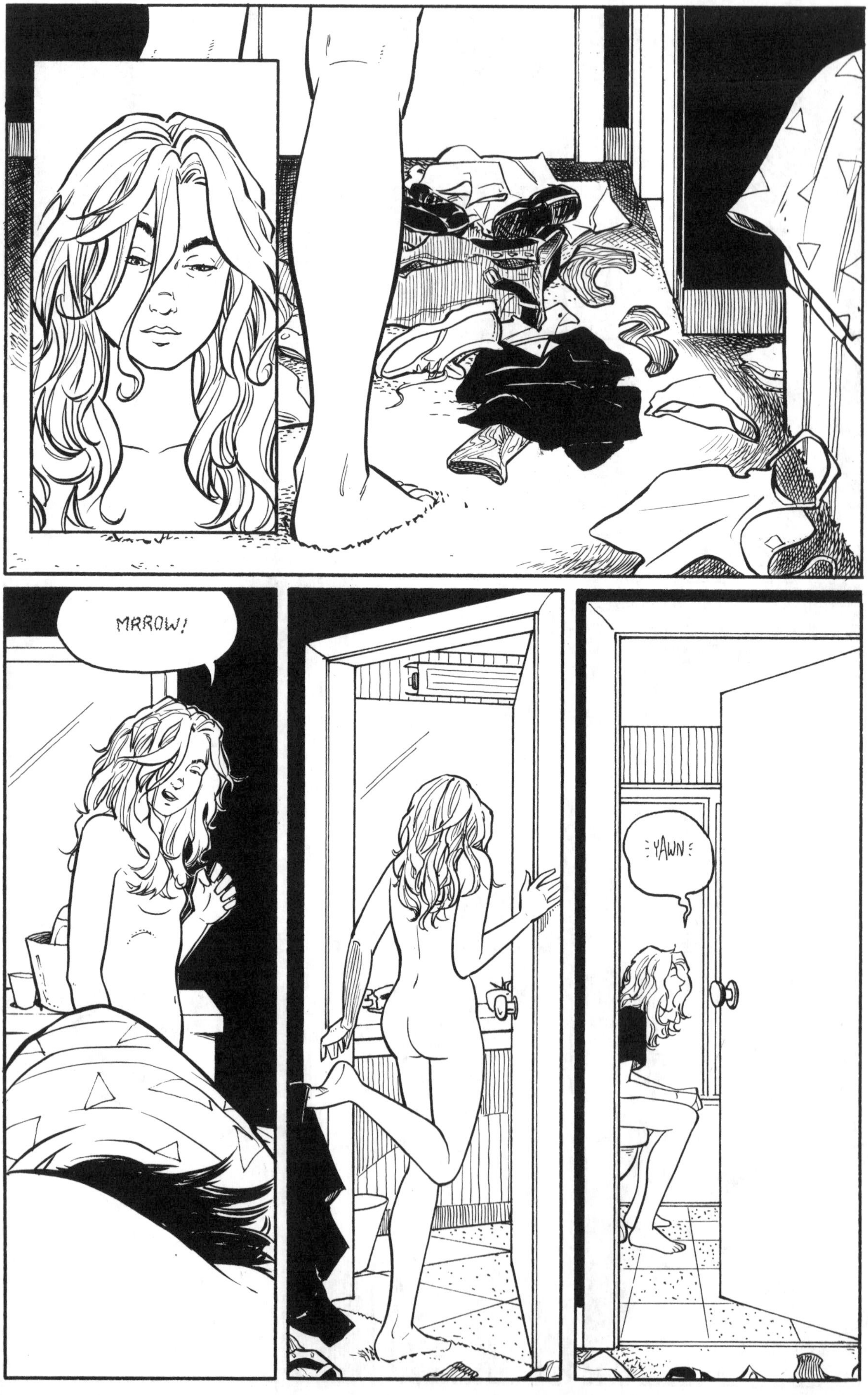
MRROW!
YAWN

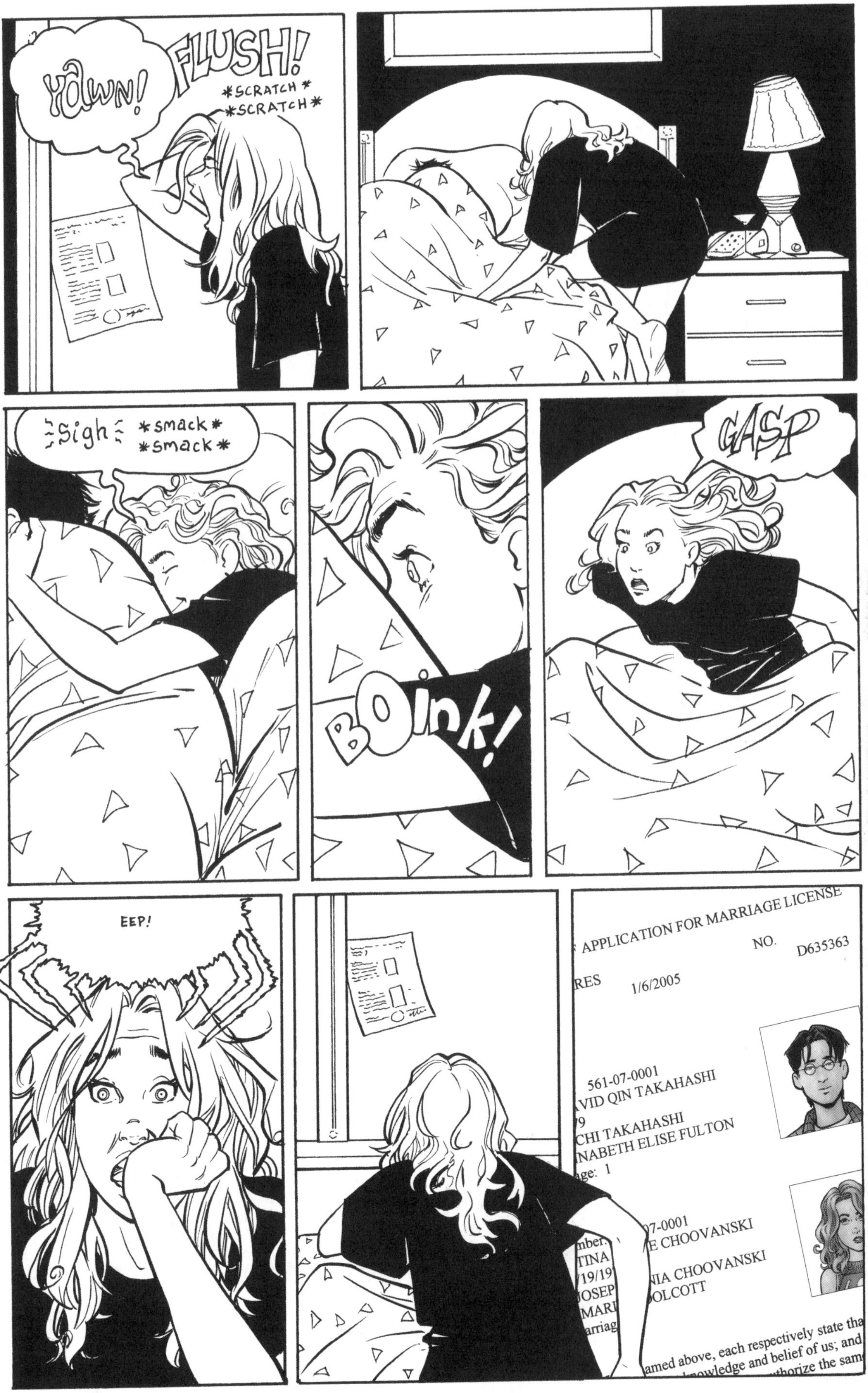
YAWN!
FLUSH!
SCRATCH
SCRATCH
SIGH
smack
smack
BOINK!
GASP
EEP!
F APPLICATION FOR MARRIAGE LICENSE
NO. D635363
RES 1/6/2005
561-07-0001
AVID QIN TAKAHASHI
79
CHI TAKAHASHI
NABETH ELISE FULTON
age: 1
07-0001
E CHOOVANSKI
NIA CHOOVANSKI
OLCOTT
amed above, each respectively state tha
knowledge and belief of us; and
uthorize the sam

AFFIDAVIT OF APPLICATION FOR MARRIAGE LICENSE

State of Nevada } ss: County Clerk	EXPIRES 1/6/2005	NO. D635363

GROOM
Social Security Number: 561-07-0001
Name: YOUSAKA DAVID QIN TAKAHASHI
Date of Birth: 1/16/1979
Father's Name: KENICHI TAKAHASHI
Mother's Name: ANNABETH ELISE FULTON
Number of this marriage: 1

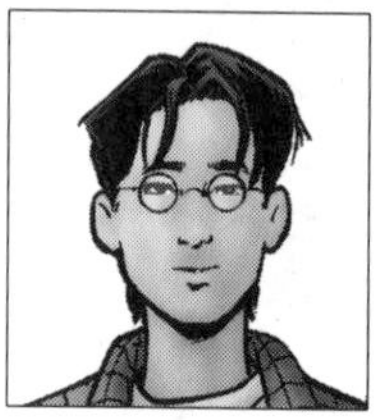

BRIDE
Social Security Number: 561-07-0001
Name: KATINA MARIE CHOOVANSKI
Date of Birth: 11/19/1976
Father's Name: JOSEPH SONIA CHOOVANSKI
Mother's Name: MARIE WOOLCOTT
Number of this marriage: 1

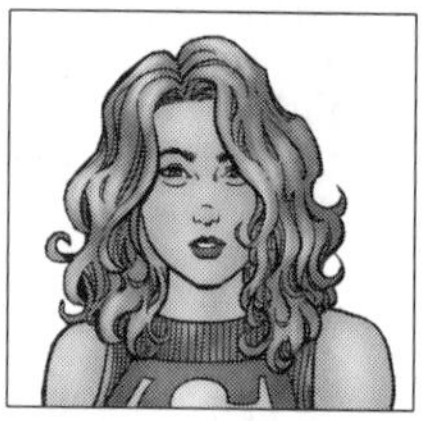

We, the bride and groom named above, each respectively state that the foregoing information is correct to the best knowledge and belief of us; and that no legal objections to the marriage nor the issuance of a license to authorize the same is known to us.

Groom Bride

Subscribed and sworn to before me this 1st day of January, 20____

UNITED STATES OF AMERICA OF THE SEAL COUNTY OF CLARK STATE OF NEVADA

MARY B. SHARRON, COUNTY OF CLARK

By: Linda Rochester
Linda Rochester Deputy

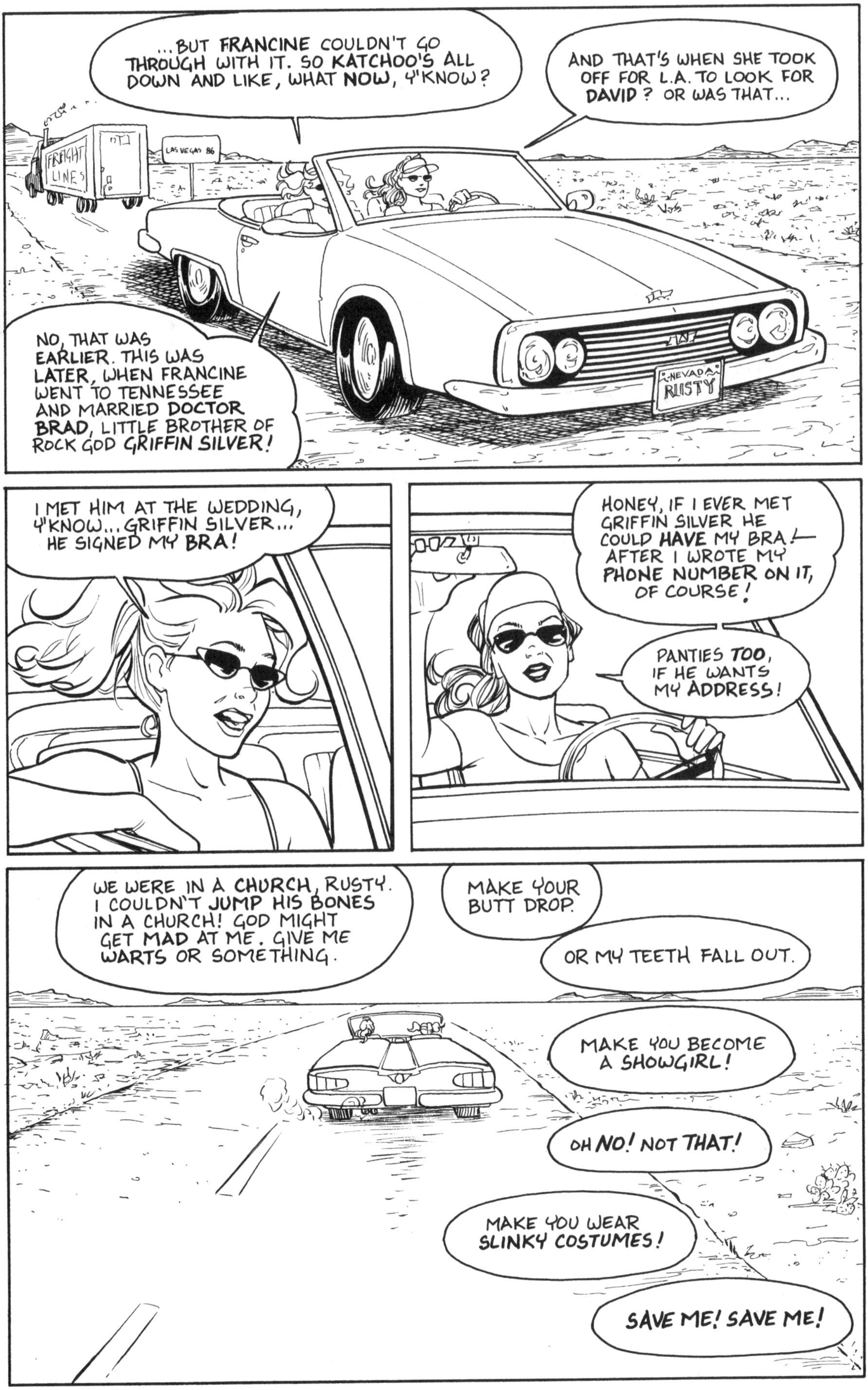
...BUT FRANCINE COULDN'T GO THROUGH WITH IT. SO KATCHOO'S ALL DOWN AND LIKE, WHAT NOW, Y'KNOW?
AND THAT'S WHEN SHE TOOK OFF FOR L.A. TO LOOK FOR DAVID? OR WAS THAT...
FREIGHT LINES
LAS VEGAS 86
NO, THAT WAS EARLIER. THIS WAS LATER, WHEN FRANCINE WENT TO TENNESSEE AND MARRIED DOCTOR BRAD, LITTLE BROTHER OF ROCK GOD GRIFFIN SILVER!
NEVADA
RUSTY
I MET HIM AT THE WEDDING, Y'KNOW... GRIFFIN SILVER... HE SIGNED MY BRA!
HONEY, IF I EVER MET GRIFFIN SILVER HE COULD HAVE MY BRA! AFTER I WROTE MY PHONE NUMBER ON IT, OF COURSE!
PANTIES TOO, IF HE WANTS MY ADDRESS!
WE WERE IN A CHURCH, RUSTY. I COULDN'T JUMP HIS BONES IN A CHURCH! GOD MIGHT GET MAD AT ME. GIVE ME WARTS OR SOMETHING.
MAKE YOUR BUTT DROP.
OR MY TEETH FALL OUT.
MAKE YOU BECOME A SHOWGIRL!
OH NO! NOT THAT!
MAKE YOU WEAR SLINKY COSTUMES!
SAVE ME! SAVE ME!

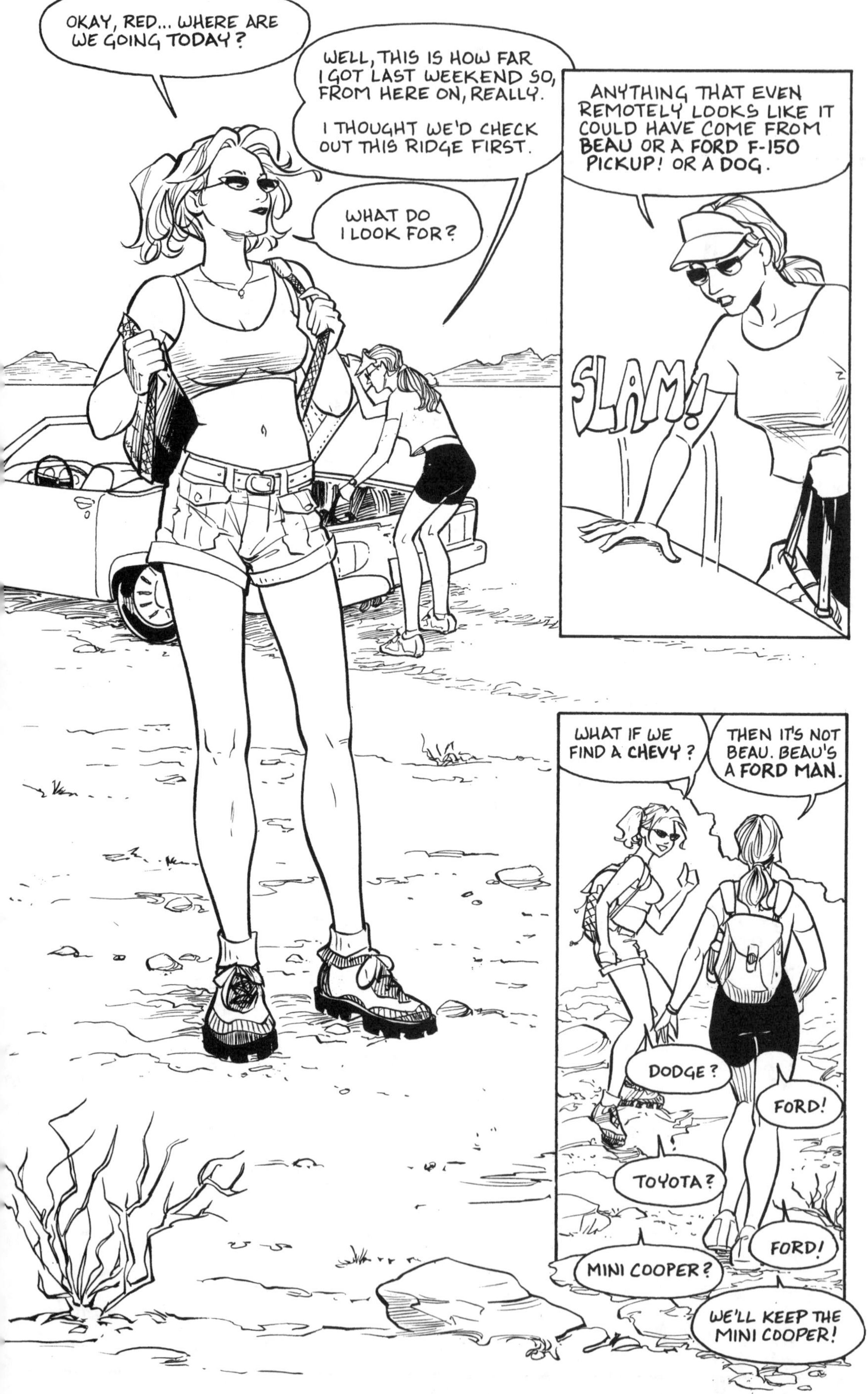
OKAY, RED... WHERE ARE WE GOING TODAY?
WELL, THIS IS HOW FAR I GOT LAST WEEKEND SO, FROM HERE ON, REALLY.
I THOUGHT WE'D CHECK OUT THIS RIDGE FIRST.
WHAT DO I LOOK FOR?
ANYTHING THAT EVEN REMOTELY LOOKS LIKE IT COULD HAVE COME FROM BEAU OR A FORD F-150 PICKUP! OR A DOG.
SLAM!
WHAT IF WE FIND A CHEVY?
THEN IT'S NOT BEAU. BEAU'S A FORD MAN.
DODGE?
FORD!
TOYOTA?
FORD!
MINI COOPER?
WE'LL KEEP THE MINI COOPER!

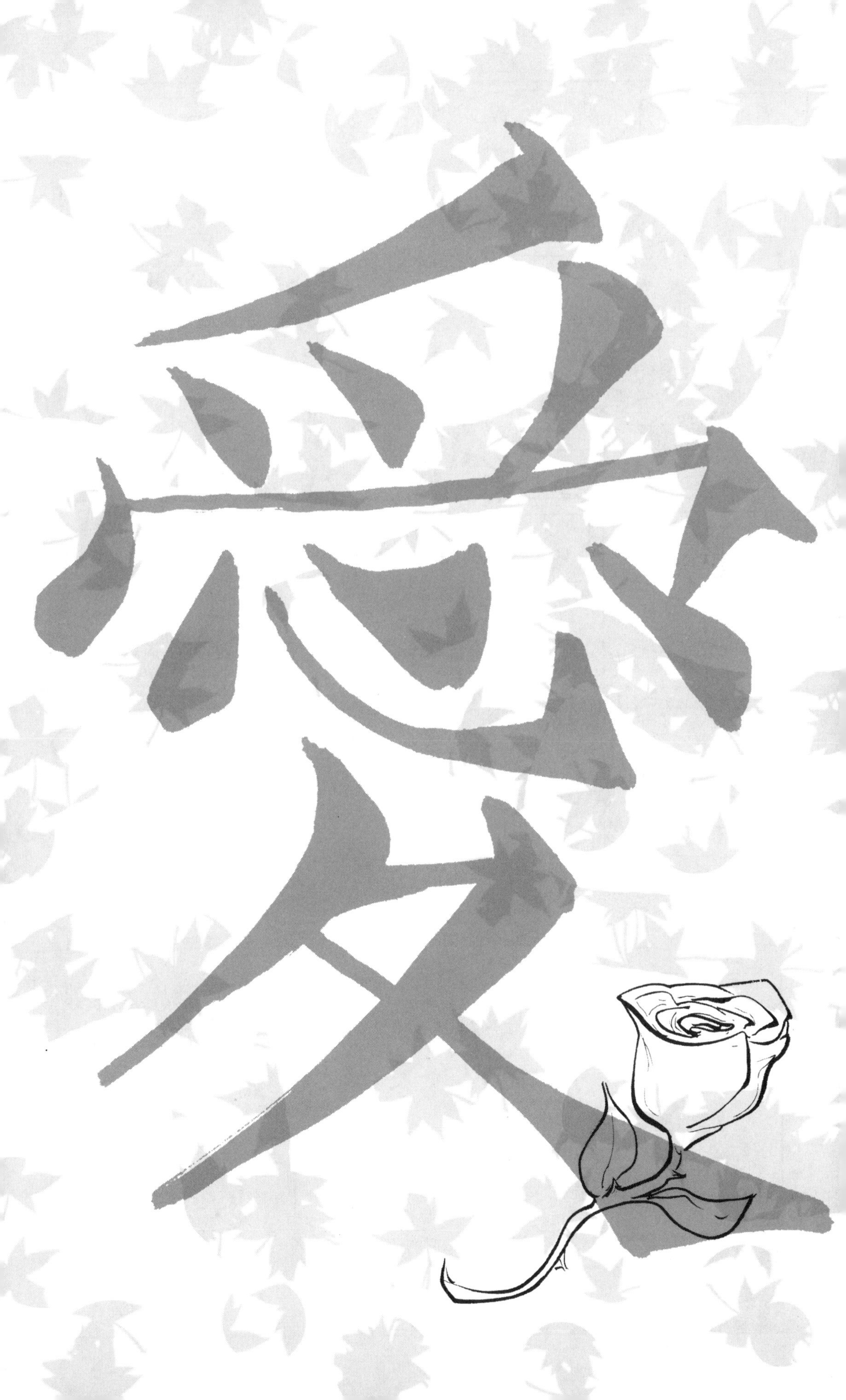
愛

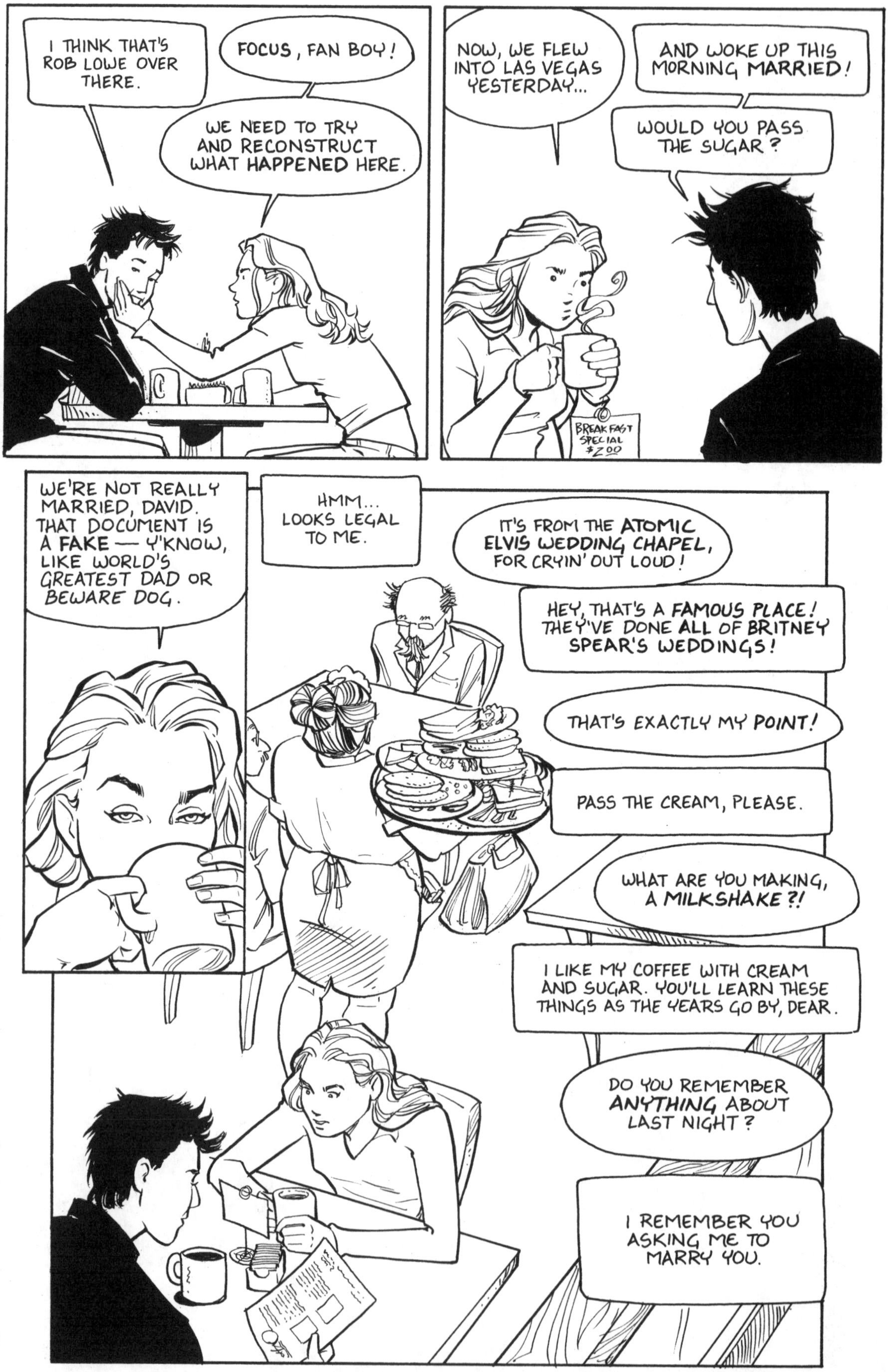
I THINK THAT'S ROB LOWE OVER THERE.
FOCUS, FAN BOY!
WE NEED TO TRY AND RECONSTRUCT WHAT HAPPENED HERE.
NOW, WE FLEW INTO LAS VEGAS YESTERDAY...
AND WOKE UP THIS MORNING MARRIED!
WOULD YOU PASS THE SUGAR?
BREAKFAST SPECIAL $2.00
WE'RE NOT REALLY MARRIED, DAVID. THAT DOCUMENT IS A FAKE — Y'KNOW, LIKE WORLD'S GREATEST DAD OR BEWARE DOG.
HMM... LOOKS LEGAL TO ME.
IT'S FROM THE ATOMIC ELVIS WEDDING CHAPEL, FOR CRYIN' OUT LOUD!
HEY, THAT'S A FAMOUS PLACE! THEY'VE DONE ALL OF BRITNEY SPEAR'S WEDDINGS!
THAT'S EXACTLY MY POINT!
PASS THE CREAM, PLEASE.
WHAT ARE YOU MAKING, A MILKSHAKE?!
I LIKE MY COFFEE WITH CREAM AND SUGAR. YOU'LL LEARN THESE THINGS AS THE YEARS GO BY, DEAR.
DO YOU REMEMBER ANYTHING ABOUT LAST NIGHT?
I REMEMBER YOU ASKING ME TO MARRY YOU.

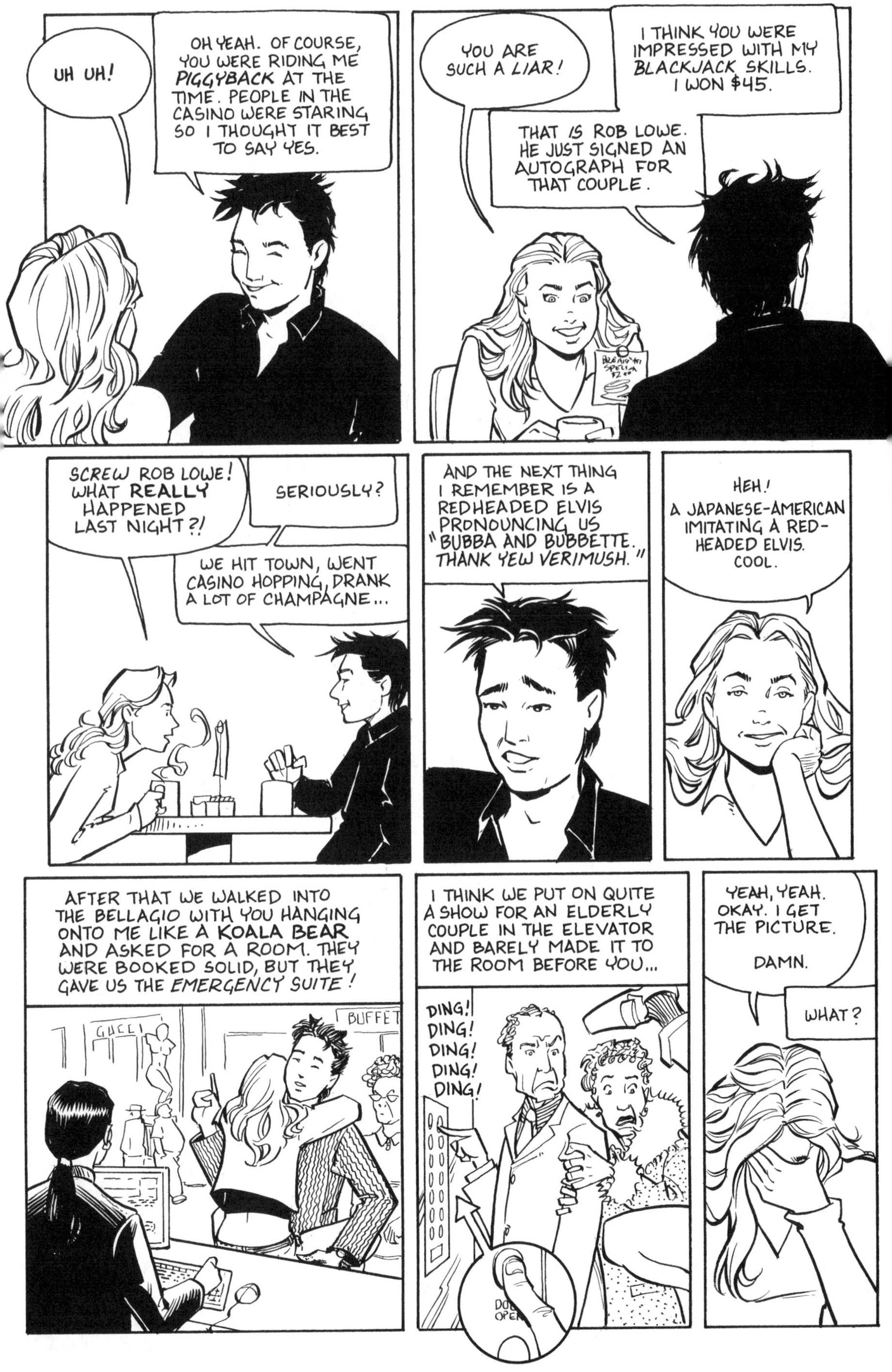
UH UH!
OH YEAH. OF COURSE, YOU WERE RIDING ME PIGGYBACK AT THE TIME. PEOPLE IN THE CASINO WERE STARING SO I THOUGHT IT BEST TO SAY YES.
YOU ARE SUCH A LIAR!
I THINK YOU WERE IMPRESSED WITH MY BLACKJACK SKILLS. I WON $45.
THAT IS ROB LOWE. HE JUST SIGNED AN AUTOGRAPH FOR THAT COUPLE.
SCREW ROB LOWE! WHAT REALLY HAPPENED LAST NIGHT?!
SERIOUSLY?
WE HIT TOWN, WENT CASINO HOPPING, DRANK A LOT OF CHAMPAGNE...
AND THE NEXT THING I REMEMBER IS A REDHEADED ELVIS PRONOUNCING US "BUBBA AND BUBBETTE. THANK YEW VERIMUSH."
HEH! A JAPANESE-AMERICAN IMITATING A RED-HEADED ELVIS. COOL.
AFTER THAT WE WALKED INTO THE BELLAGIO WITH YOU HANGING ONTO ME LIKE A KOALA BEAR AND ASKED FOR A ROOM. THEY WERE BOOKED SOLID, BUT THEY GAVE US THE EMERGENCY SUITE!
GUCCI
BUFFET
I THINK WE PUT ON QUITE A SHOW FOR AN ELDERLY COUPLE IN THE ELEVATOR AND BARELY MADE IT TO THE ROOM BEFORE YOU...
DING! DING! DING! DING! DING!
YEAH, YEAH. OKAY. I GET THE PICTURE.
DAMN.
WHAT?

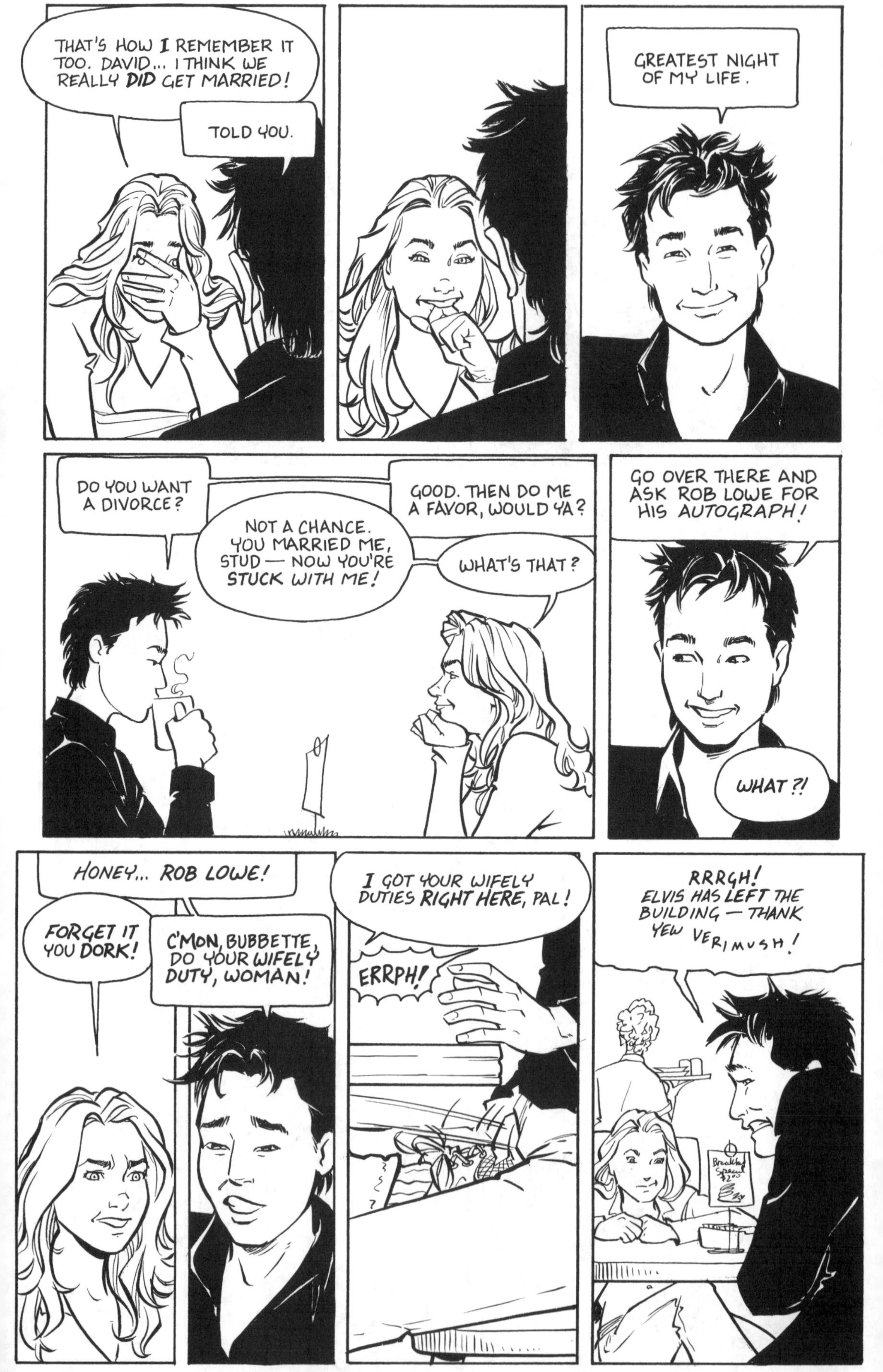
THAT'S HOW I REMEMBER IT TOO. DAVID... I THINK WE REALLY DID GET MARRIED!
TOLD YOU.
GREATEST NIGHT OF MY LIFE.
DO YOU WANT A DIVORCE?
NOT A CHANCE. YOU MARRIED ME, STUD — NOW YOU'RE STUCK WITH ME!
GOOD. THEN DO ME A FAVOR, WOULD YA?
WHAT'S THAT?
GO OVER THERE AND ASK ROB LOWE FOR HIS AUTOGRAPH!
WHAT?!
HONEY... ROB LOWE!
FORGET IT YOU DORK!
C'MON, BUBBETTE, DO YOUR WIFELY DUTY, WOMAN!
I GOT YOUR WIFELY DUTIES RIGHT HERE, PAL!
ERRPH!
RRRGH! ELVIS HAS LEFT THE BUILDING — THANK YEW VERIMUSH!

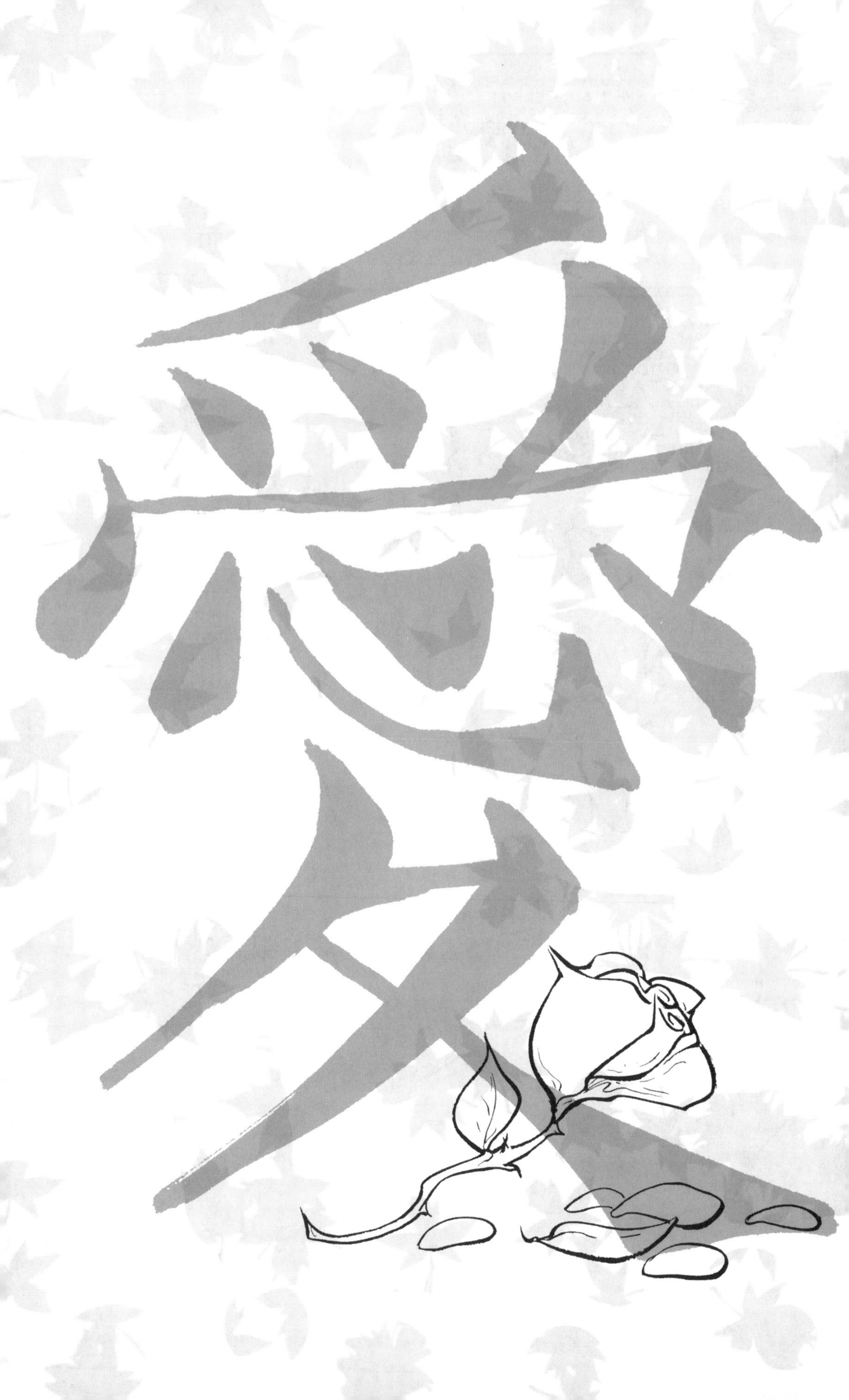
愛

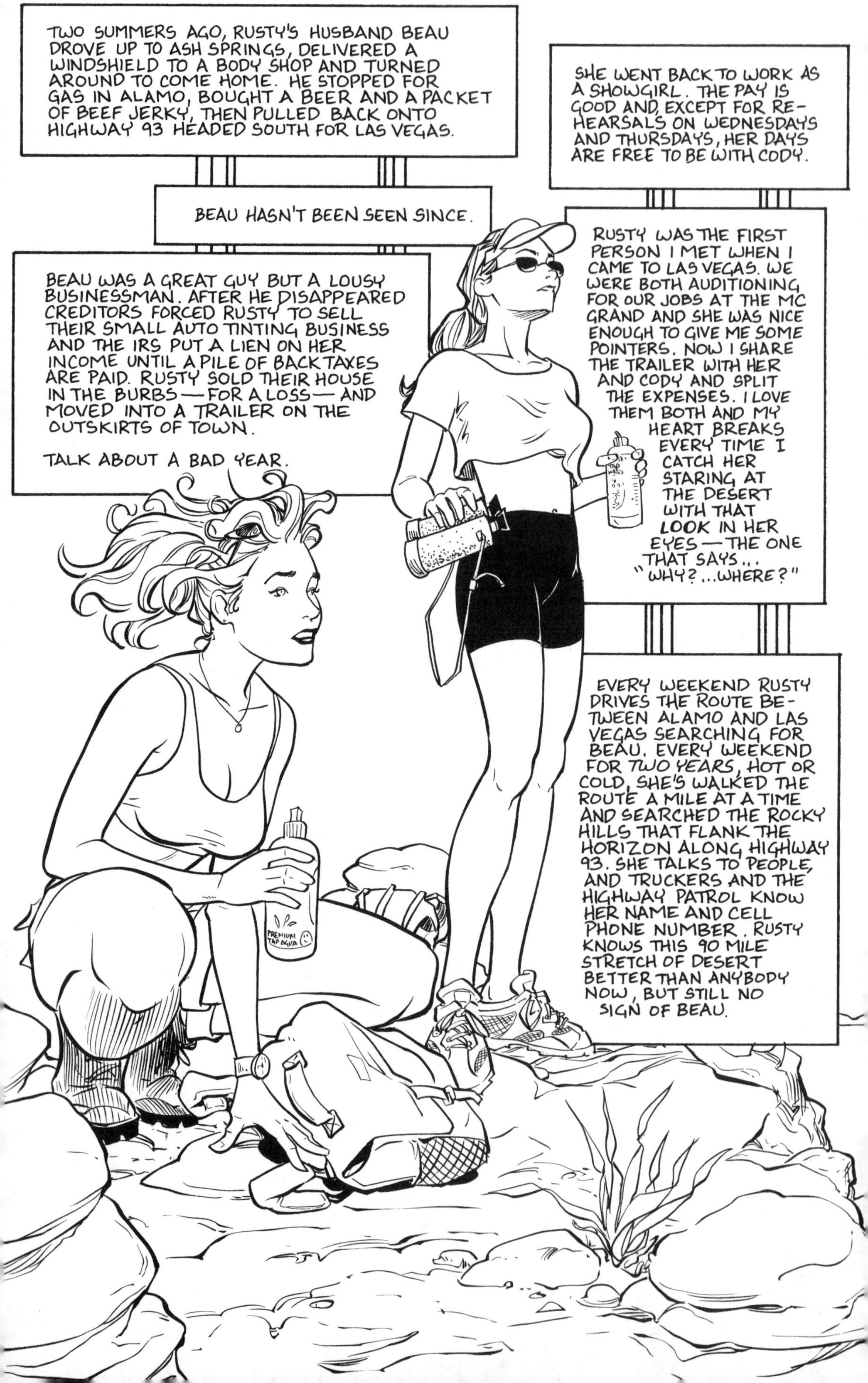
TWO SUMMERS AGO, RUSTY'S HUSBAND BEAU DROVE UP TO ASH SPRINGS, DELIVERED A WINDSHIELD TO A BODY SHOP AND TURNED AROUND TO COME HOME. HE STOPPED FOR GAS IN ALAMO, BOUGHT A BEER AND A PACKET OF BEEF JERKY, THEN PULLED BACK ONTO HIGHWAY 93 HEADED SOUTH FOR LAS VEGAS.
BEAU HASN'T BEEN SEEN SINCE.
BEAU WAS A GREAT GUY BUT A LOUSY BUSINESSMAN. AFTER HE DISAPPEARED CREDITORS FORCED RUSTY TO SELL THEIR SMALL AUTO TINTING BUSINESS AND THE IRS PUT A LIEN ON HER INCOME UNTIL A PILE OF BACK TAXES ARE PAID. RUSTY SOLD THEIR HOUSE IN THE BURBS — FOR A LOSS — AND MOVED INTO A TRAILER ON THE OUTSKIRTS OF TOWN.
TALK ABOUT A BAD YEAR.
SHE WENT BACK TO WORK AS A SHOWGIRL. THE PAY IS GOOD AND, EXCEPT FOR REHEARSALS ON WEDNESDAYS AND THURSDAYS, HER DAYS ARE FREE TO BE WITH CODY.
RUSTY WAS THE FIRST PERSON I MET WHEN I CAME TO LAS VEGAS. WE WERE BOTH AUDITIONING FOR OUR JOBS AT THE MC GRAND AND SHE WAS NICE ENOUGH TO GIVE ME SOME POINTERS. NOW I SHARE THE TRAILER WITH HER AND CODY AND SPLIT THE EXPENSES. I LOVE THEM BOTH AND MY HEART BREAKS EVERY TIME I CATCH HER STARING AT THE DESERT WITH THAT **LOOK** IN HER EYES — THE ONE THAT SAYS... "WHY?...WHERE?"
EVERY WEEKEND RUSTY DRIVES THE ROUTE BETWEEN ALAMO AND LAS VEGAS SEARCHING FOR BEAU. EVERY WEEKEND FOR *TWO YEARS*, HOT OR COLD, SHE'S WALKED THE ROUTE A MILE AT A TIME AND SEARCHED THE ROCKY HILLS THAT FLANK THE HORIZON ALONG HIGHWAY 93. SHE TALKS TO PEOPLE, AND TRUCKERS AND THE HIGHWAY PATROL KNOW HER NAME AND CELL PHONE NUMBER. RUSTY KNOWS THIS 90 MILE STRETCH OF DESERT BETTER THAN ANYBODY NOW, BUT STILL NO SIGN OF BEAU.
PREMIUM TAP AGUA

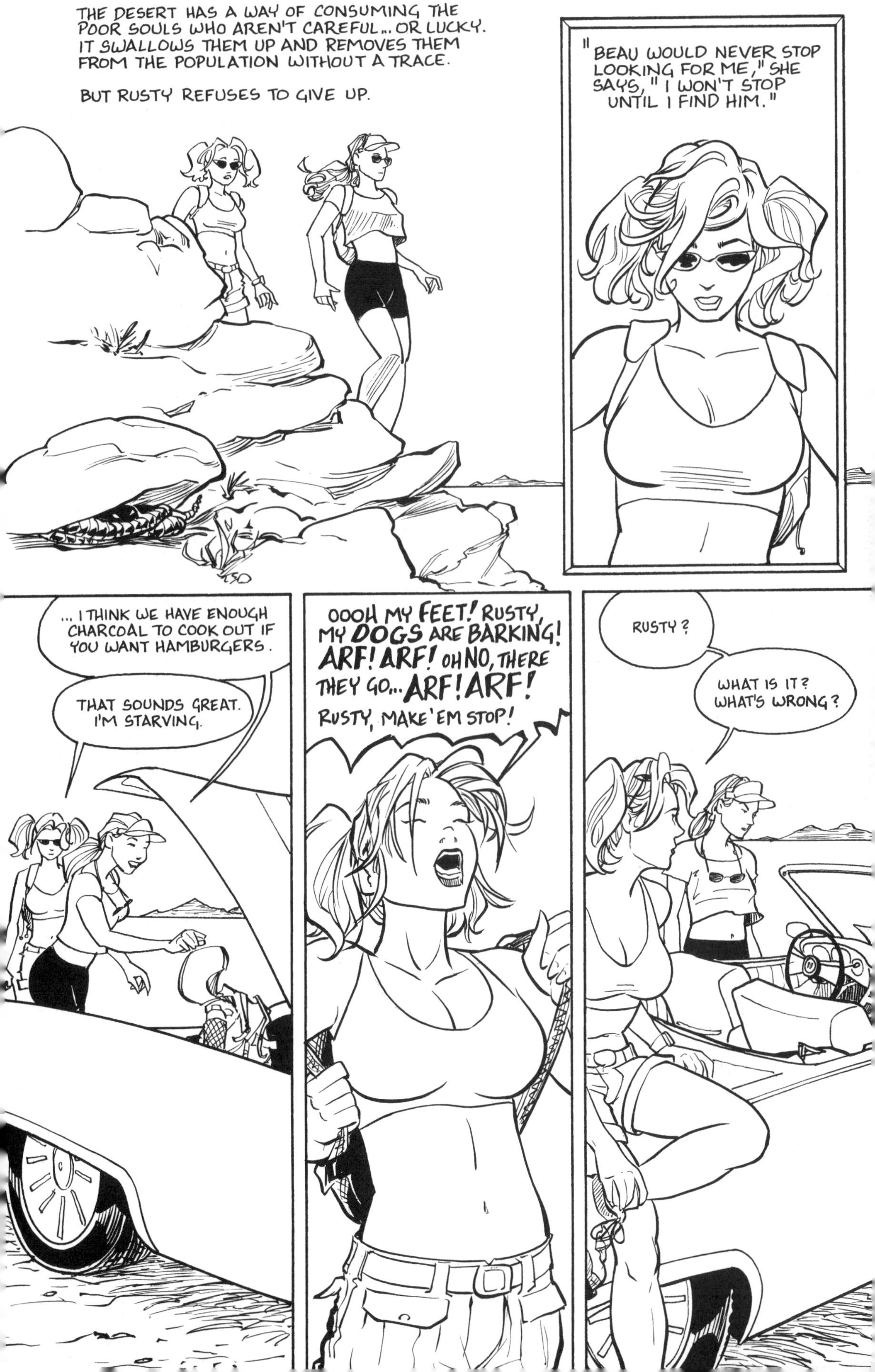
THE DESERT HAS A WAY OF CONSUMING THE POOR SOULS WHO AREN'T CAREFUL... OR LUCKY. IT SWALLOWS THEM UP AND REMOVES THEM FROM THE POPULATION WITHOUT A TRACE.
BUT RUSTY REFUSES TO GIVE UP.
"BEAU WOULD NEVER STOP LOOKING FOR ME," SHE SAYS, "I WON'T STOP UNTIL I FIND HIM."
... I THINK WE HAVE ENOUGH CHARCOAL TO COOK OUT IF YOU WANT HAMBURGERS.
THAT SOUNDS GREAT. I'M STARVING.
OOOH MY FEET! RUSTY, MY DOGS ARE BARKING! ARF! ARF! OH NO, THERE THEY GO... ARF! ARF! RUSTY, MAKE 'EM STOP!
RUSTY?
WHAT IS IT? WHAT'S WRONG?

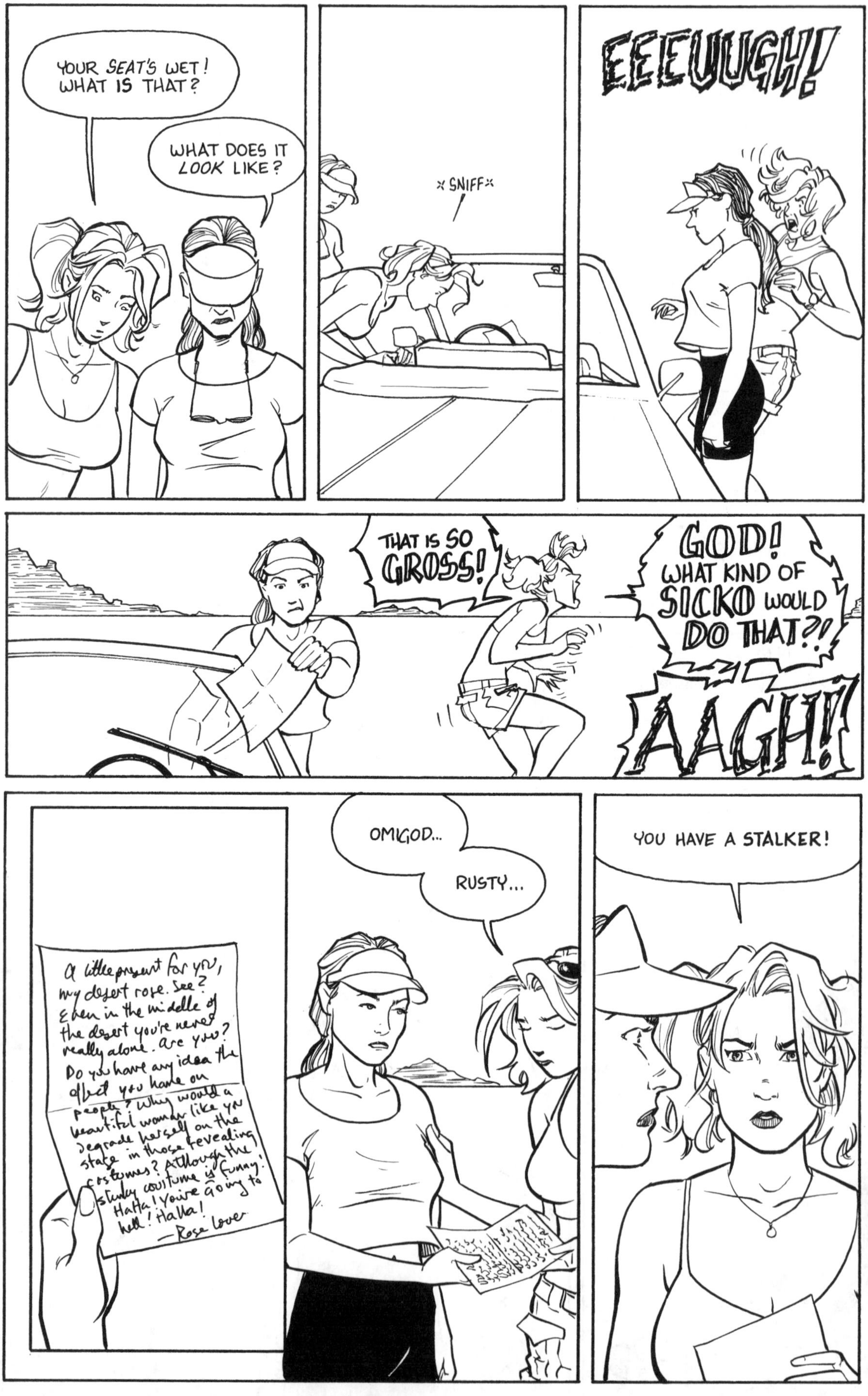
YOUR SEAT'S WET! WHAT IS THAT?
WHAT DOES IT LOOK LIKE?
SNIFF
EEEUUGH!
THAT IS SO GROSS!
GOD! WHAT KIND OF SICKO WOULD DO THAT?!
AAGH!
A little present for you, my desert rose. See? Even in the middle of the desert you're never really alone. Are you? Do you have any idea the effect you have on people? Why would a beautiful woman like you degrade herself on the stage in those revealing costumes? Although the stinky costume is funny! HaHa! You're going to hell! HaHa!
—Rose Lover
OMIGOD...
RUSTY...
YOU HAVE A STALKER!

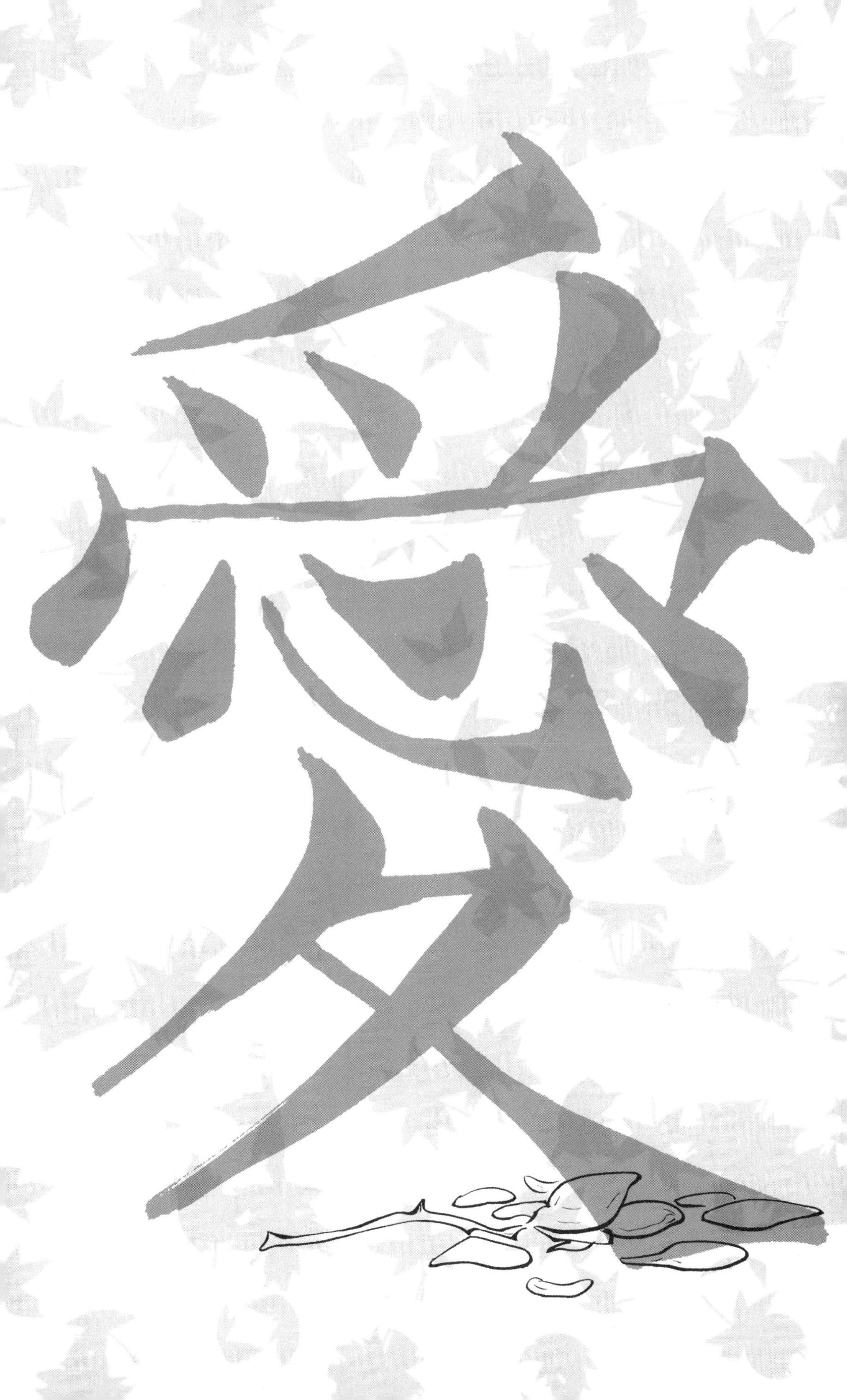
愛

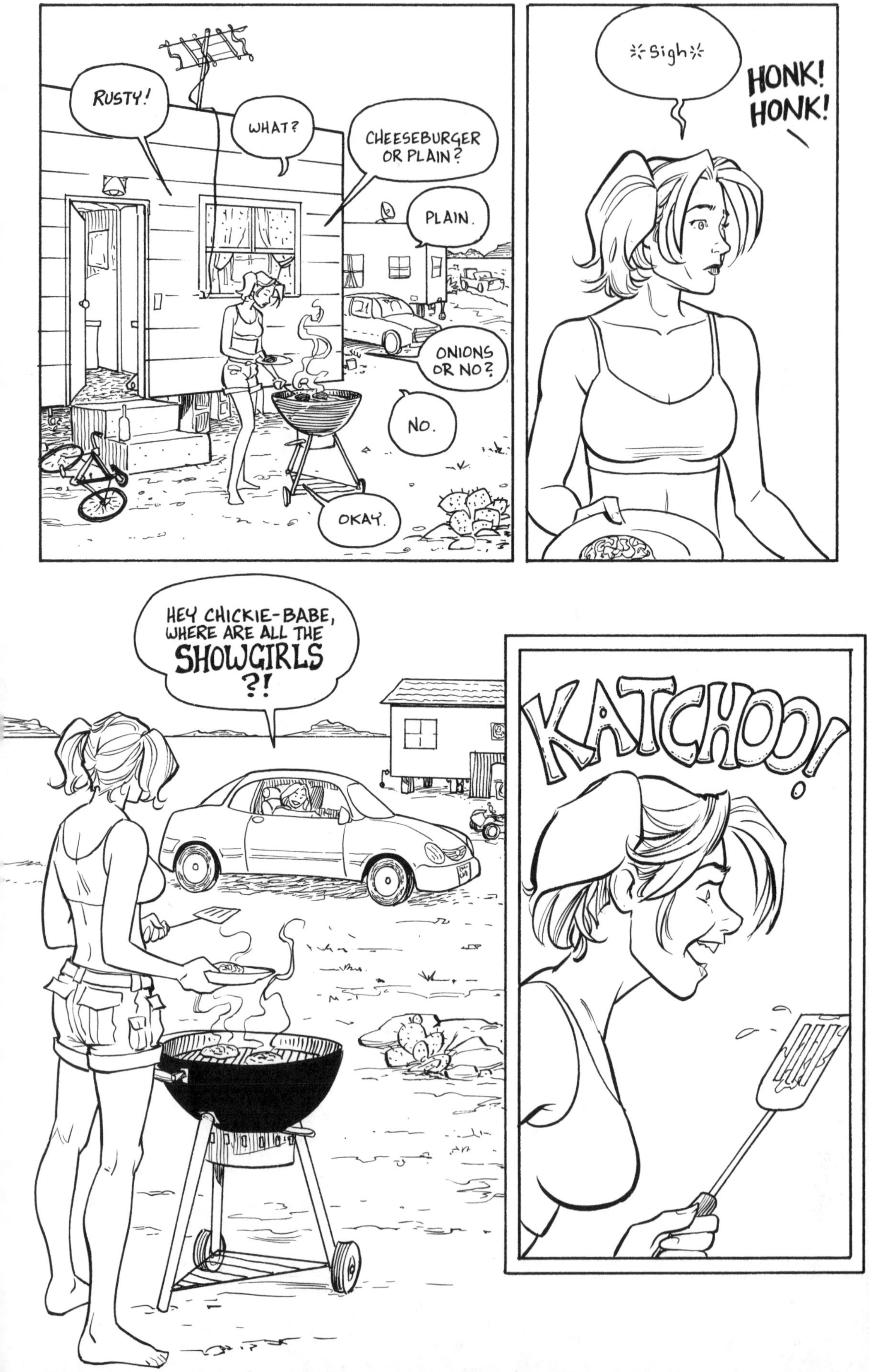
RUSTY!
WHAT?
CHEESEBURGER OR PLAIN?
PLAIN.
ONIONS OR NO?
NO.
OKAY.
SIGH
HONK! HONK!
HEY CHICKIE-BABE, WHERE ARE ALL THE SHOWGIRLS ?!
KATCHOO!

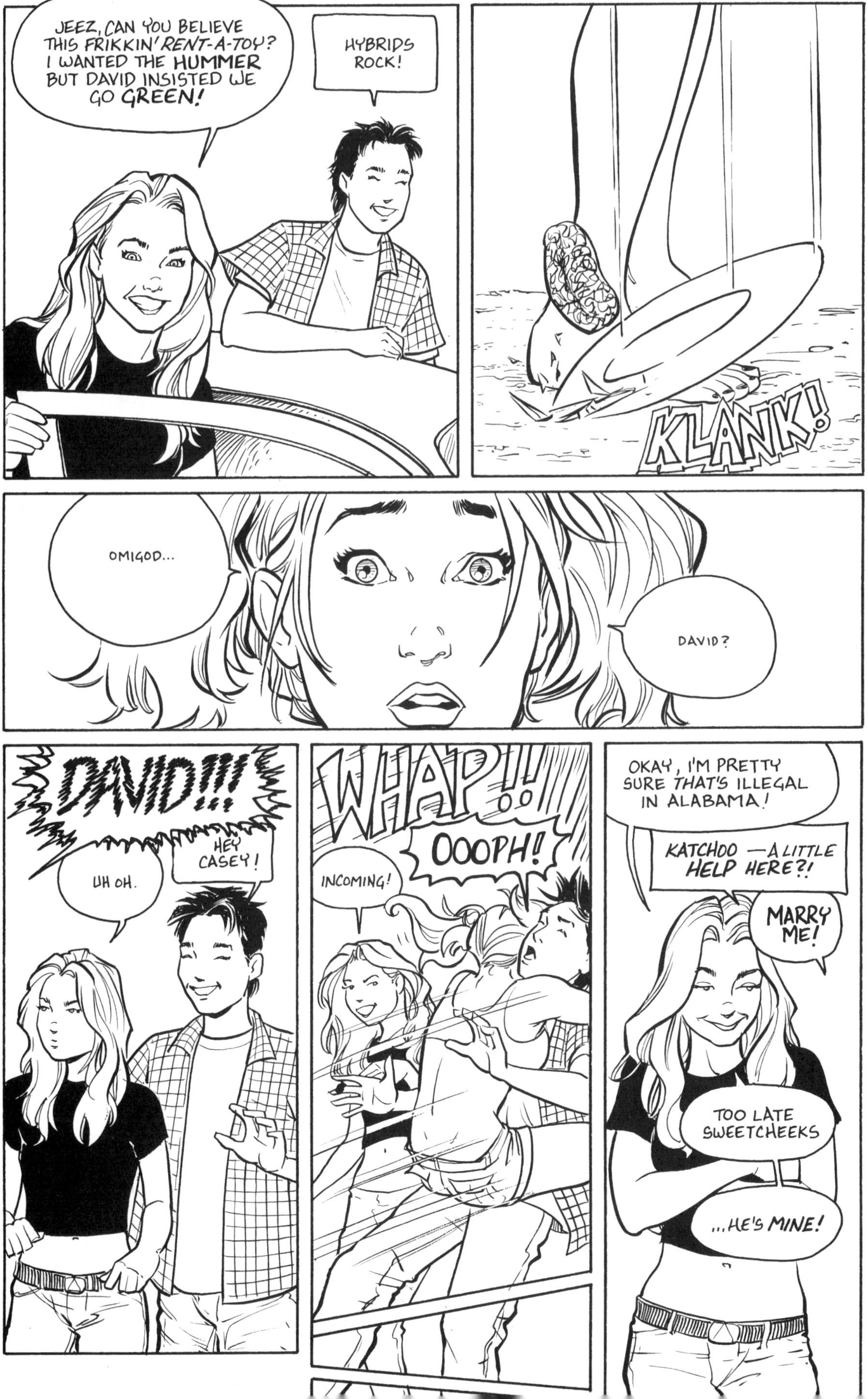
JEEZ, CAN YOU BELIEVE THIS FRIKKIN' RENT-A-TOY? I WANTED THE HUMMER BUT DAVID INSISTED WE GO GREEN!
HYBRIDS ROCK!
KLANK!
OMIGOD...
DAVID?
DAVID!!!
UH OH.
HEY CASEY!
WHAP!!
INCOMING!
OOOPH!
OKAY, I'M PRETTY SURE THAT'S ILLEGAL IN ALABAMA!
KATCHOO — A LITTLE HELP HERE?!
MARRY ME!
TOO LATE SWEETCHEEKS
...HE'S MINE!

FRANCINE LEARNS THE GREAT AMERICAN PASTIME.

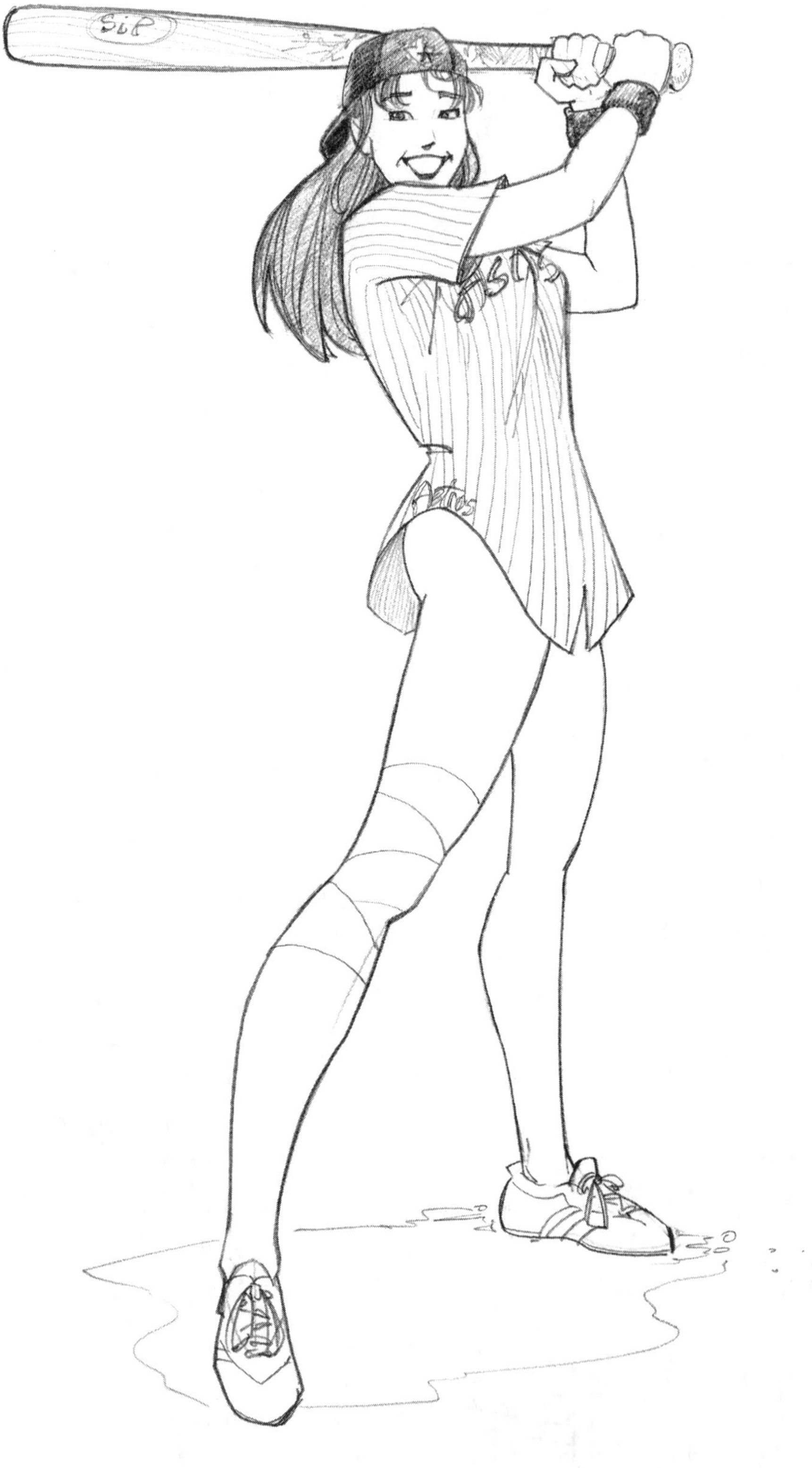

"I'VE NEVER BELIEVED IN MARRIAGE. I DON'T KNOW, I GUESS IT'S THAT WHOLE TIL DEATH DO US PART THING—IT'S TOO TEMPTING."

—KATCHOO

"MARRIAGE IS A BEAUTIFUL UNION BETWEEN TWO PEOPLE WHO WANT TO SHARE THE REST OF THEIR LIVES WITH EACH OTHER."

—DAVID

"MARRIAGE IS WHERE YOU SLEEP WITH THE SAME WOMAN EVERY NIGHT FOR THE REST OF YOUR LIFE, WHETHER YOU LIKE HER OR NOT."

—FREDDIE

"MARRIAGE IS THE MOST ROMANTIC THING TWO PEOPLE CAN DO...AS LONG YOU'RE BOTH HAPPY WITH THE PRE-NUPS, OF COURSE."

—CASEY

"I, YOUSAKA DAVID QIN TAKAHASHI, TAKE YOU, KATINA MARIE CHOOVANSKI, TO BE MY LAWFULLY WEDDED WIFE..."

—DAVID

"I DO."

—KATCHOO

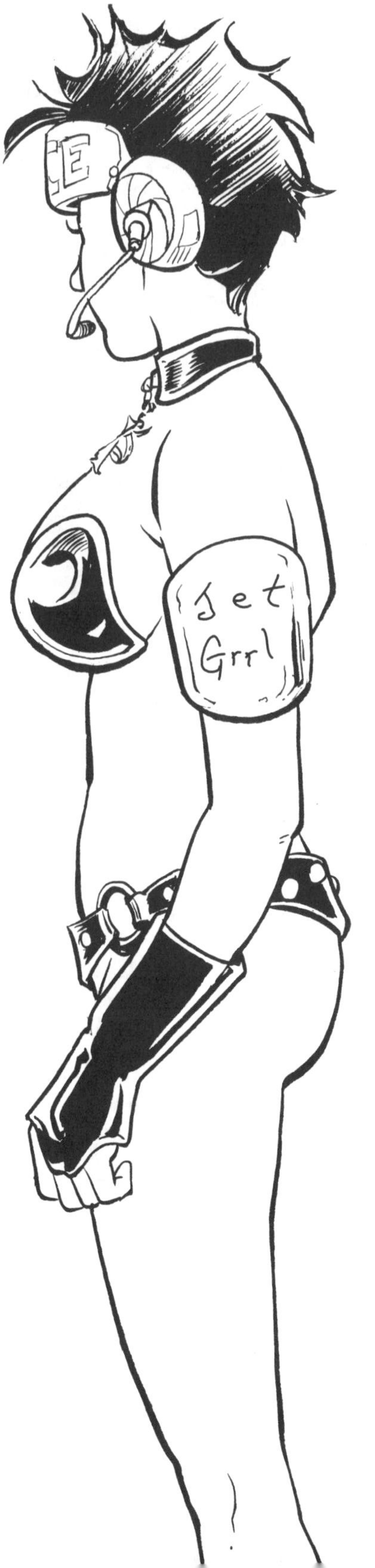
Jet
Grrl

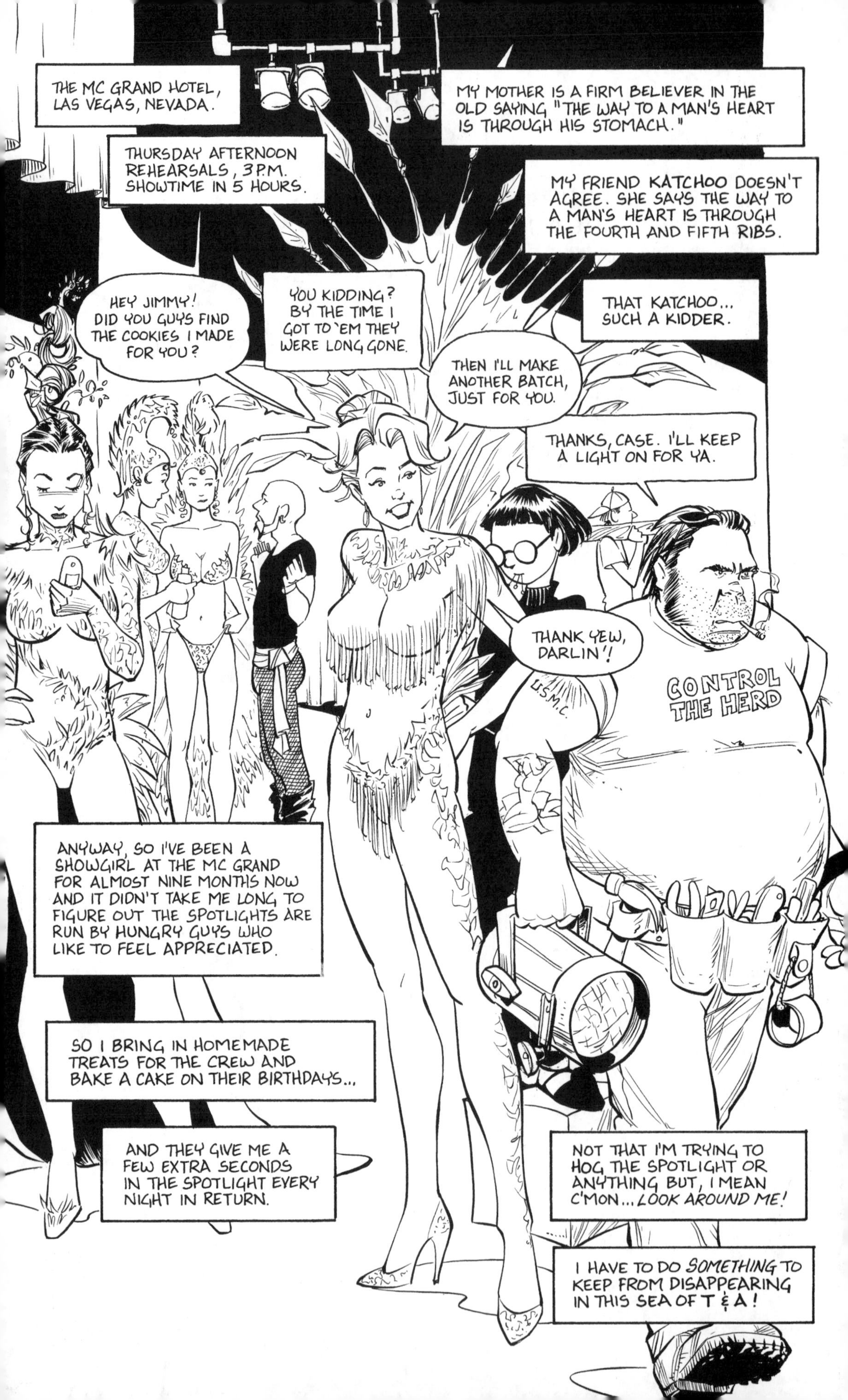
THE MC GRAND HOTEL, LAS VEGAS, NEVADA.
THURSDAY AFTERNOON REHEARSALS, 3 P.M. SHOWTIME IN 5 HOURS.
MY MOTHER IS A FIRM BELIEVER IN THE OLD SAYING "THE WAY TO A MAN'S HEART IS THROUGH HIS STOMACH."
MY FRIEND KATCHOO DOESN'T AGREE. SHE SAYS THE WAY TO A MAN'S HEART IS THROUGH THE FOURTH AND FIFTH RIBS.
HEY JIMMY! DID YOU GUYS FIND THE COOKIES I MADE FOR YOU?
YOU KIDDING? BY THE TIME I GOT TO 'EM THEY WERE LONG GONE.
THAT KATCHOO... SUCH A KIDDER.
THEN I'LL MAKE ANOTHER BATCH, JUST FOR YOU.
THANKS, CASE. I'LL KEEP A LIGHT ON FOR YA.
THANK YEW, DARLIN'!
CONTROL THE HERD
U.S.M.C.
ANYWAY, SO I'VE BEEN A SHOWGIRL AT THE MC GRAND FOR ALMOST NINE MONTHS NOW AND IT DIDN'T TAKE ME LONG TO FIGURE OUT THE SPOTLIGHTS ARE RUN BY HUNGRY GUYS WHO LIKE TO FEEL APPRECIATED.
SO I BRING IN HOMEMADE TREATS FOR THE CREW AND BAKE A CAKE ON THEIR BIRTHDAYS...
AND THEY GIVE ME A FEW EXTRA SECONDS IN THE SPOTLIGHT EVERY NIGHT IN RETURN.
NOT THAT I'M TRYING TO HOG THE SPOTLIGHT OR ANYTHING BUT, I MEAN C'MON... *LOOK AROUND ME!*
I HAVE TO DO *SOMETHING* TO KEEP FROM DISAPPEARING IN THIS SEA OF T & A!

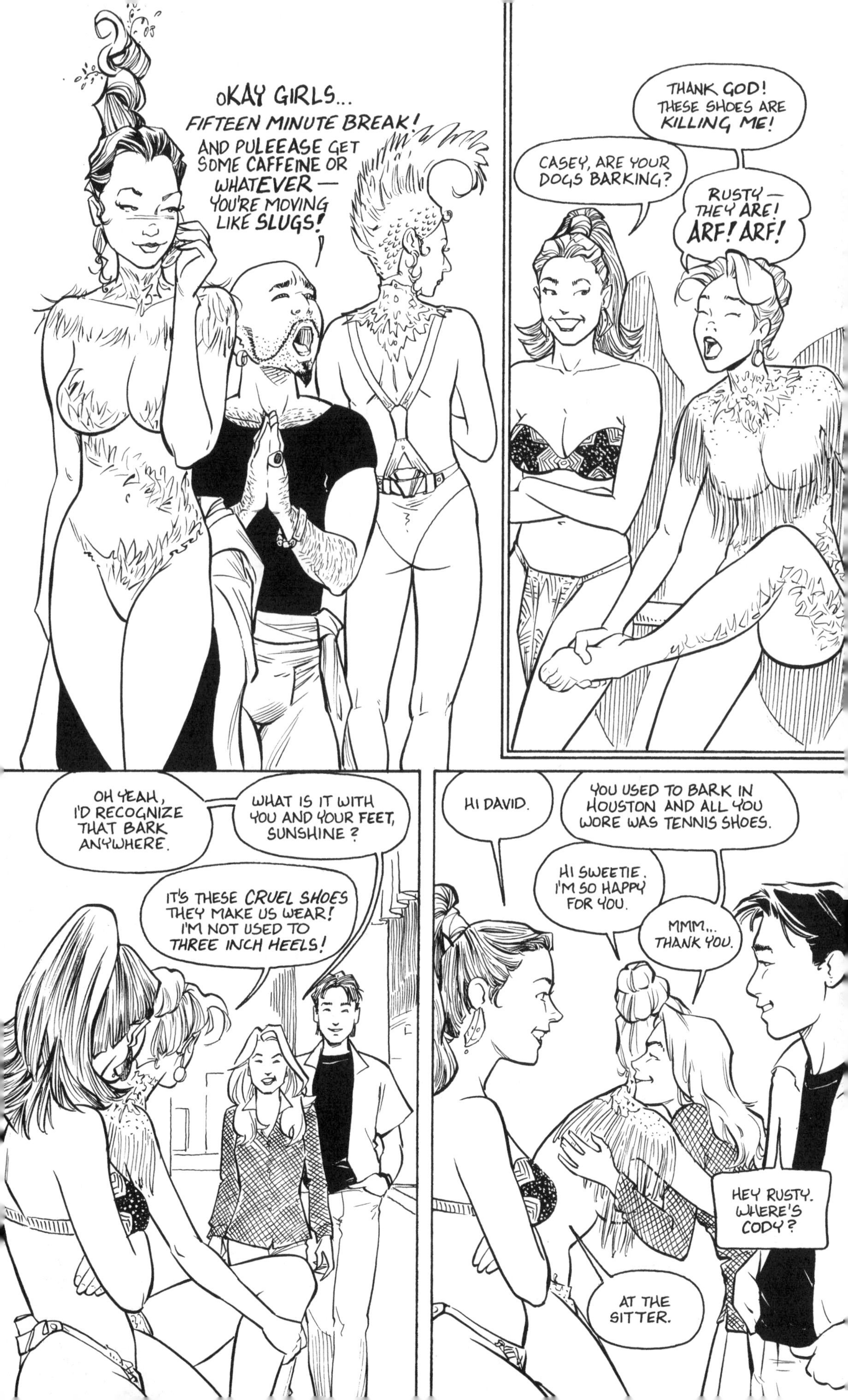
OKAY GIRLS...
FIFTEEN MINUTE BREAK! AND PULEEASE GET SOME CAFFEINE OR WHATEVER — YOU'RE MOVING LIKE SLUGS!
CASEY, ARE YOUR DOGS BARKING?
THANK GOD! THESE SHOES ARE KILLING ME!
RUSTY — THEY ARE! ARF! ARF!
OH YEAH, I'D RECOGNIZE THAT BARK ANYWHERE.
WHAT IS IT WITH YOU AND YOUR FEET, SUNSHINE?
IT'S THESE CRUEL SHOES THEY MAKE US WEAR! I'M NOT USED TO THREE INCH HEELS!
HI DAVID.
YOU USED TO BARK IN HOUSTON AND ALL YOU WORE WAS TENNIS SHOES.
HI SWEETIE. I'M SO HAPPY FOR YOU.
MMM... THANK YOU.
HEY RUSTY. WHERE'S CODY?
AT THE SITTER.

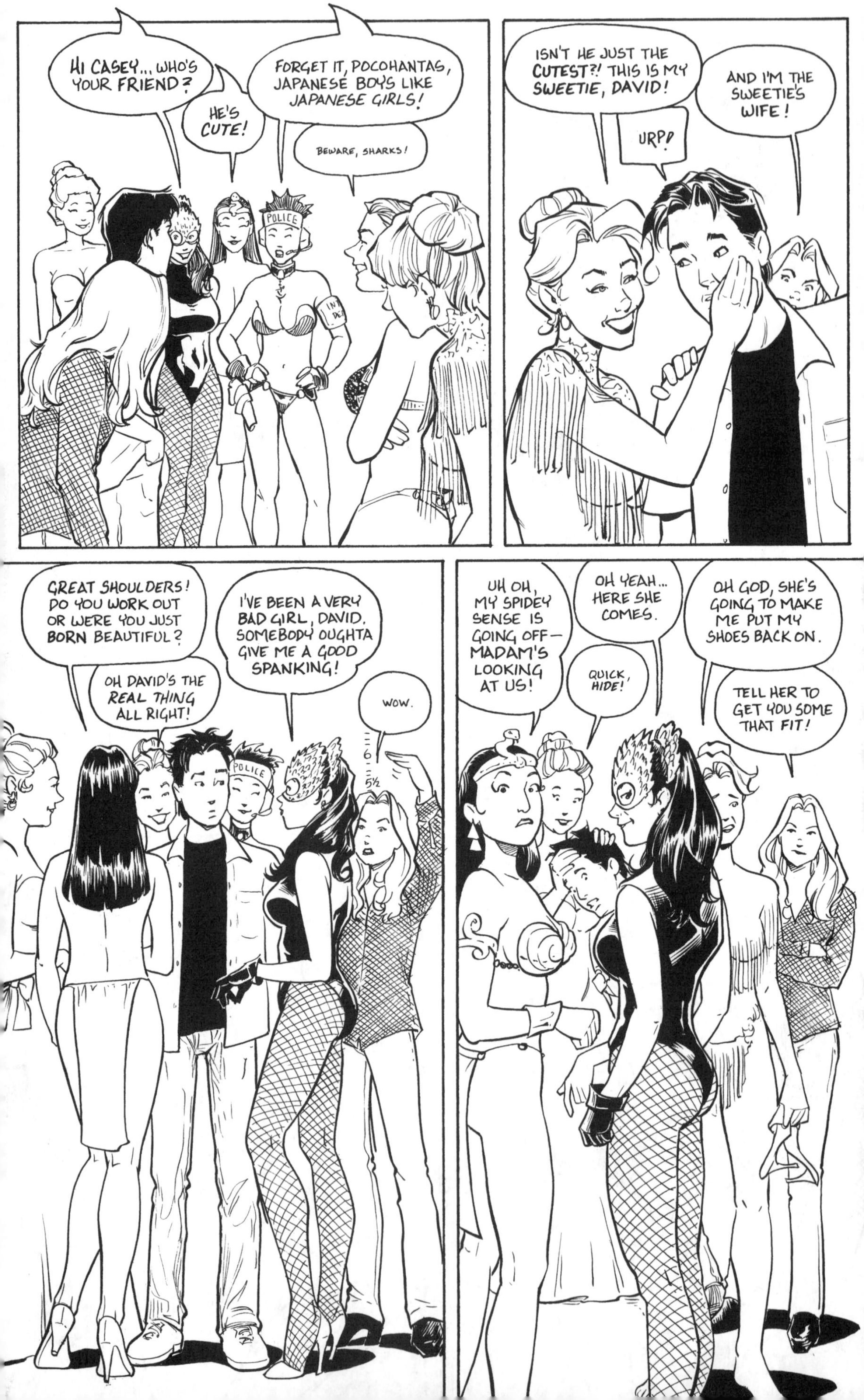

HI CASEY... WHO'S YOUR FRIEND?
HE'S CUTE!
FORGET IT, POCOHANTAS, JAPANESE BOYS LIKE JAPANESE GIRLS!
BEWARE, SHARKS!
POLICE
ISN'T HE JUST THE CUTEST?! THIS IS MY SWEETIE, DAVID!
URP!
AND I'M THE SWEETIE'S WIFE!
GREAT SHOULDERS! DO YOU WORK OUT OR WERE YOU JUST BORN BEAUTIFUL?
OH DAVID'S THE REAL THING ALL RIGHT!
I'VE BEEN A VERY BAD GIRL, DAVID. SOMEBODY OUGHTA GIVE ME A GOOD SPANKING!
WOW.
POLICE
6
5½
UH OH, MY SPIDEY SENSE IS GOING OFF— MADAM'S LOOKING AT US!
OH YEAH... HERE SHE COMES.
QUICK, HIDE!
OH GOD, SHE'S GOING TO MAKE ME PUT MY SHOES BACK ON.
TELL HER TO GET YOU SOME THAT FIT!

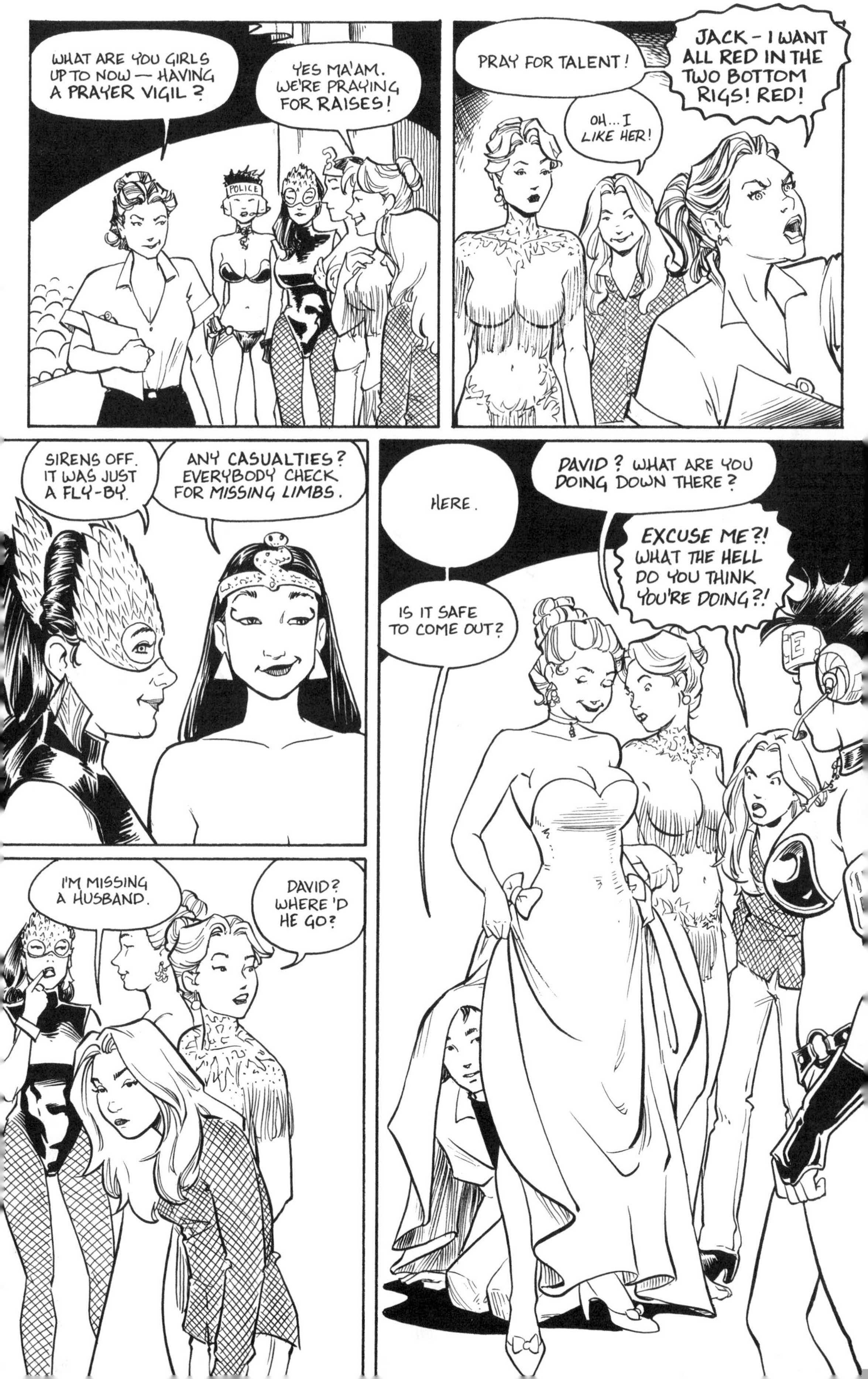
WHAT ARE YOU GIRLS UP TO NOW — HAVING A PRAYER VIGIL?
YES MA'AM. WE'RE PRAYING FOR RAISES!
POLICE
PRAY FOR TALENT!
OH... I LIKE HER!
JACK - I WANT ALL RED IN THE TWO BOTTOM RIGS! RED!
SIRENS OFF. IT WAS JUST A FLY-BY.
ANY CASUALTIES? EVERYBODY CHECK FOR MISSING LIMBS.
I'M MISSING A HUSBAND.
DAVID? WHERE'D HE GO?
HERE.
IS IT SAFE TO COME OUT?
DAVID? WHAT ARE YOU DOING DOWN THERE?
EXCUSE ME?! WHAT THE HELL DO YOU THINK YOU'RE DOING?!

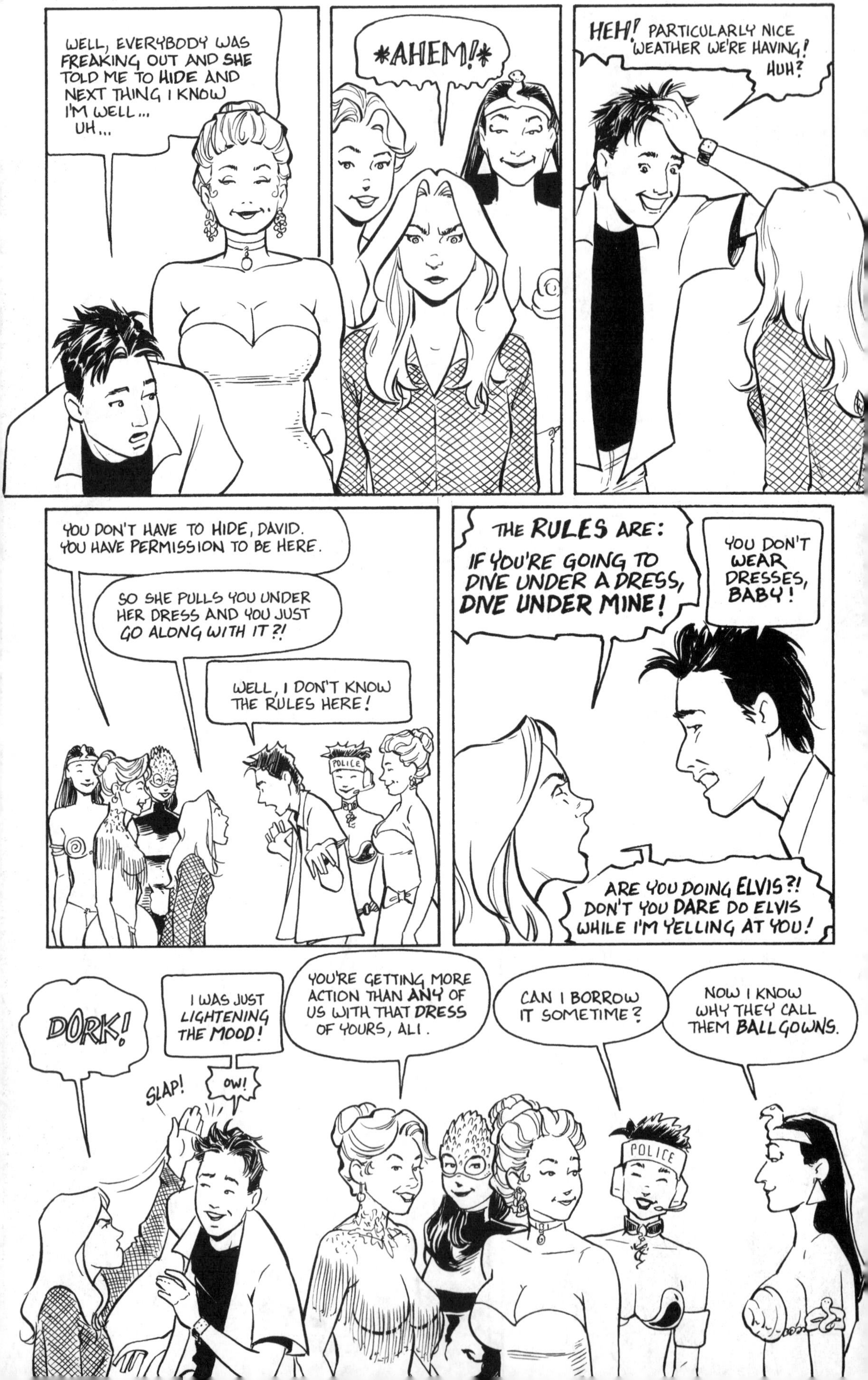
WELL, EVERYBODY WAS FREAKING OUT AND SHE TOLD ME TO HIDE AND NEXT THING I KNOW I'M WELL... UH...
AHEM!
HEH! PARTICULARLY NICE WEATHER WE'RE HAVING! HUH?
YOU DON'T HAVE TO HIDE, DAVID. YOU HAVE PERMISSION TO BE HERE.
SO SHE PULLS YOU UNDER HER DRESS AND YOU JUST GO ALONG WITH IT?!
WELL, I DON'T KNOW THE RULES HERE!
POLICE
THE RULES ARE: IF YOU'RE GOING TO DIVE UNDER A DRESS, DIVE UNDER MINE!
YOU DON'T WEAR DRESSES, BABY!
ARE YOU DOING ELVIS?! DON'T YOU DARE DO ELVIS WHILE I'M YELLING AT YOU!
DORK!
I WAS JUST LIGHTENING THE MOOD!
SLAP!
OW!
YOU'RE GETTING MORE ACTION THAN ANY OF US WITH THAT DRESS OF YOURS, ALI.
CAN I BORROW IT SOMETIME?
NOW I KNOW WHY THEY CALL THEM BALLGOWNS.
POLICE

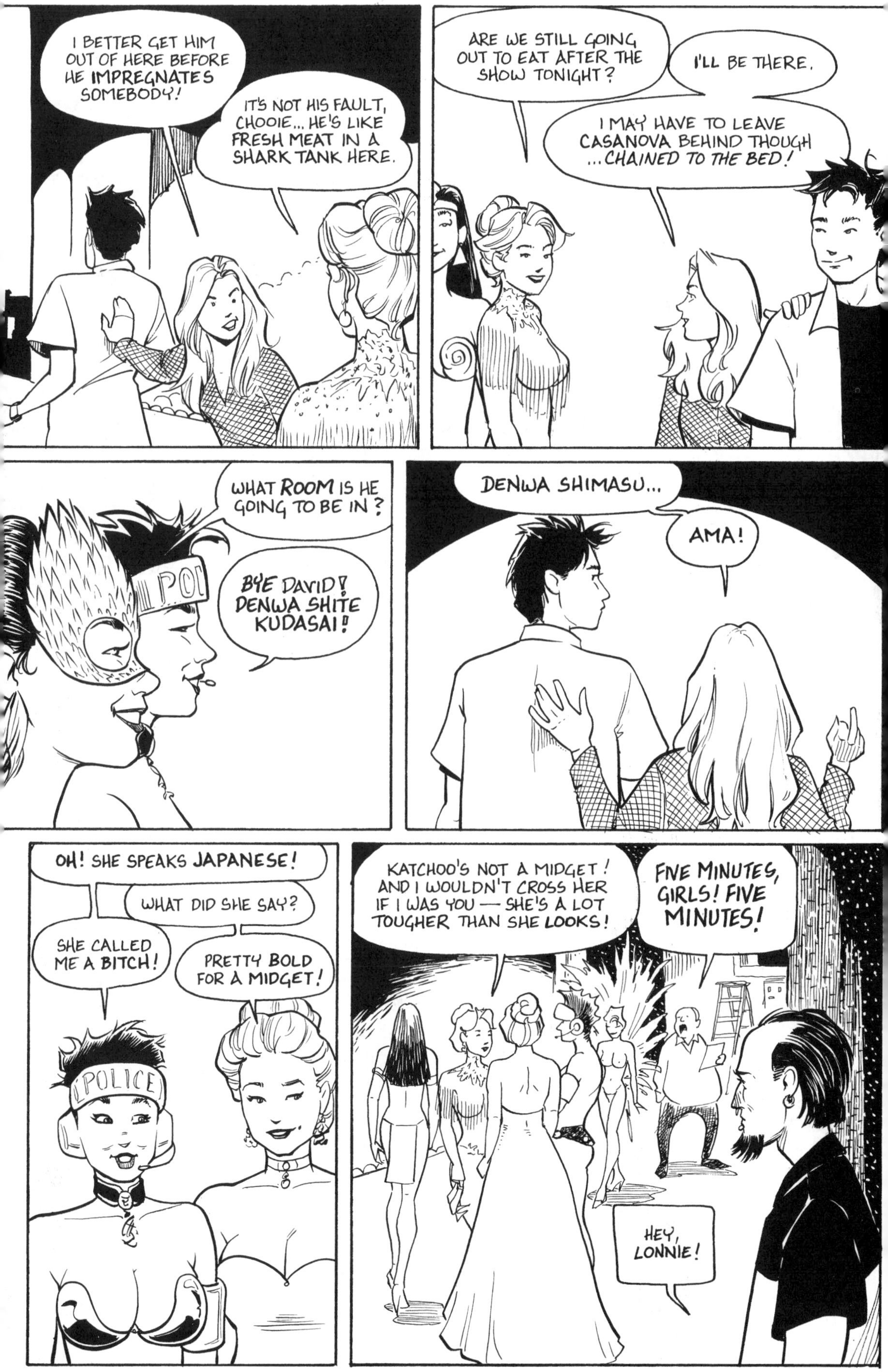
I BETTER GET HIM OUT OF HERE BEFORE HE IMPREGNATES SOMEBODY!
IT'S NOT HIS FAULT, CHOOIE... HE'S LIKE FRESH MEAT IN A SHARK TANK HERE.
ARE WE STILL GOING OUT TO EAT AFTER THE SHOW TONIGHT?
I'LL BE THERE.
I MAY HAVE TO LEAVE CASANOVA BEHIND THOUGH ...CHAINED TO THE BED!
WHAT ROOM IS HE GOING TO BE IN?
BYE DAVID! DENWA SHITE KUDASAI!
POLICE
DENWA SHIMASU...
AMA!
OH! SHE SPEAKS JAPANESE!
WHAT DID SHE SAY?
SHE CALLED ME A BITCH!
PRETTY BOLD FOR A MIDGET!
KATCHOO'S NOT A MIDGET! AND I WOULDN'T CROSS HER IF I WAS YOU — SHE'S A LOT TOUGHER THAN SHE LOOKS!
FIVE MINUTES, GIRLS! FIVE MINUTES!
HEY, LONNIE!

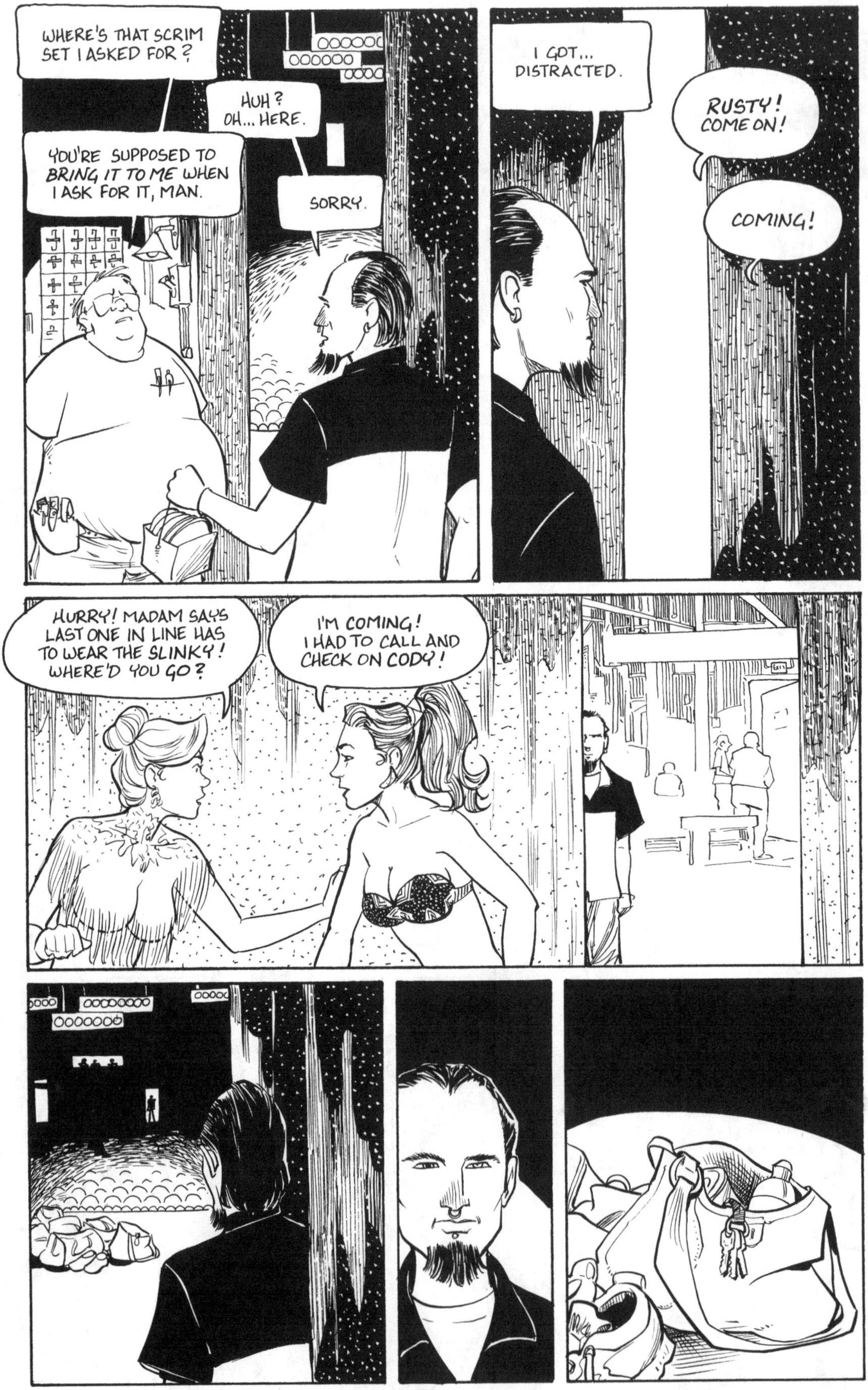
WHERE'S THAT SCRIM SET I ASKED FOR?
YOU'RE SUPPOSED TO BRING IT TO ME WHEN I ASK FOR IT, MAN.
HUH? OH... HERE.
SORRY.
I GOT... DISTRACTED.
RUSTY! COME ON!
COMING!
HURRY! MADAM SAYS LAST ONE IN LINE HAS TO WEAR THE SLINKY! WHERE'D YOU GO?
I'M COMING! I HAD TO CALL AND CHECK ON CODY!

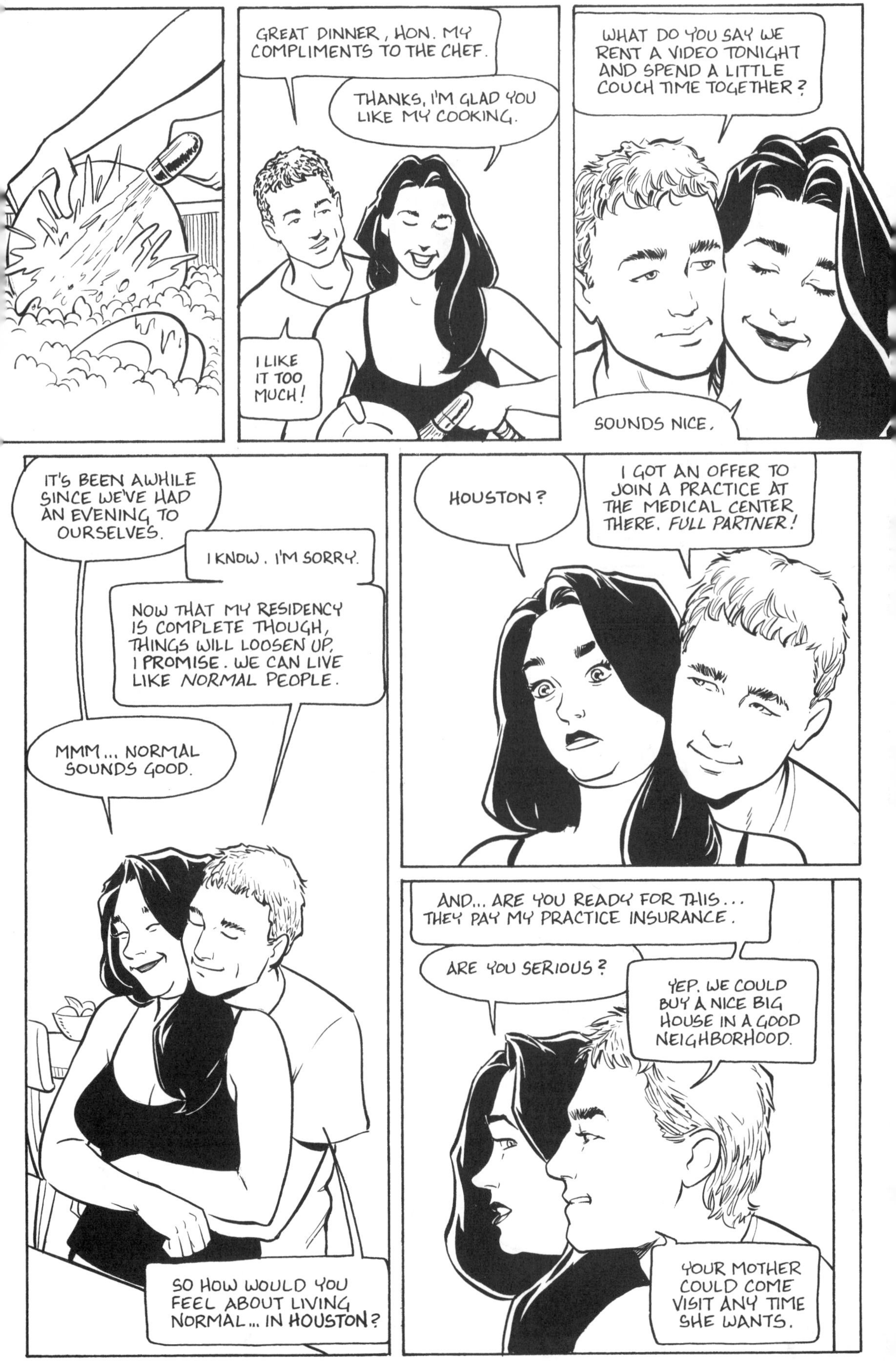
GREAT DINNER, HON. MY COMPLIMENTS TO THE CHEF.
THANKS, I'M GLAD YOU LIKE MY COOKING.
I LIKE IT TOO MUCH!
WHAT DO YOU SAY WE RENT A VIDEO TONIGHT AND SPEND A LITTLE COUCH TIME TOGETHER?
SOUNDS NICE.
IT'S BEEN AWHILE SINCE WE'VE HAD AN EVENING TO OURSELVES.
I KNOW. I'M SORRY.
NOW THAT MY RESIDENCY IS COMPLETE THOUGH, THINGS WILL LOOSEN UP, I PROMISE. WE CAN LIVE LIKE *NORMAL* PEOPLE.
MMM... NORMAL SOUNDS GOOD.
SO HOW WOULD YOU FEEL ABOUT LIVING NORMAL... IN HOUSTON?
HOUSTON?
I GOT AN OFFER TO JOIN A PRACTICE AT THE MEDICAL CENTER THERE. *FULL PARTNER!*
AND... ARE YOU READY FOR THIS... THEY PAY MY PRACTICE INSURANCE.
ARE YOU SERIOUS?
YEP. WE COULD BUY A NICE BIG HOUSE IN A GOOD NEIGHBORHOOD.
YOUR MOTHER COULD COME VISIT ANY TIME SHE WANTS.

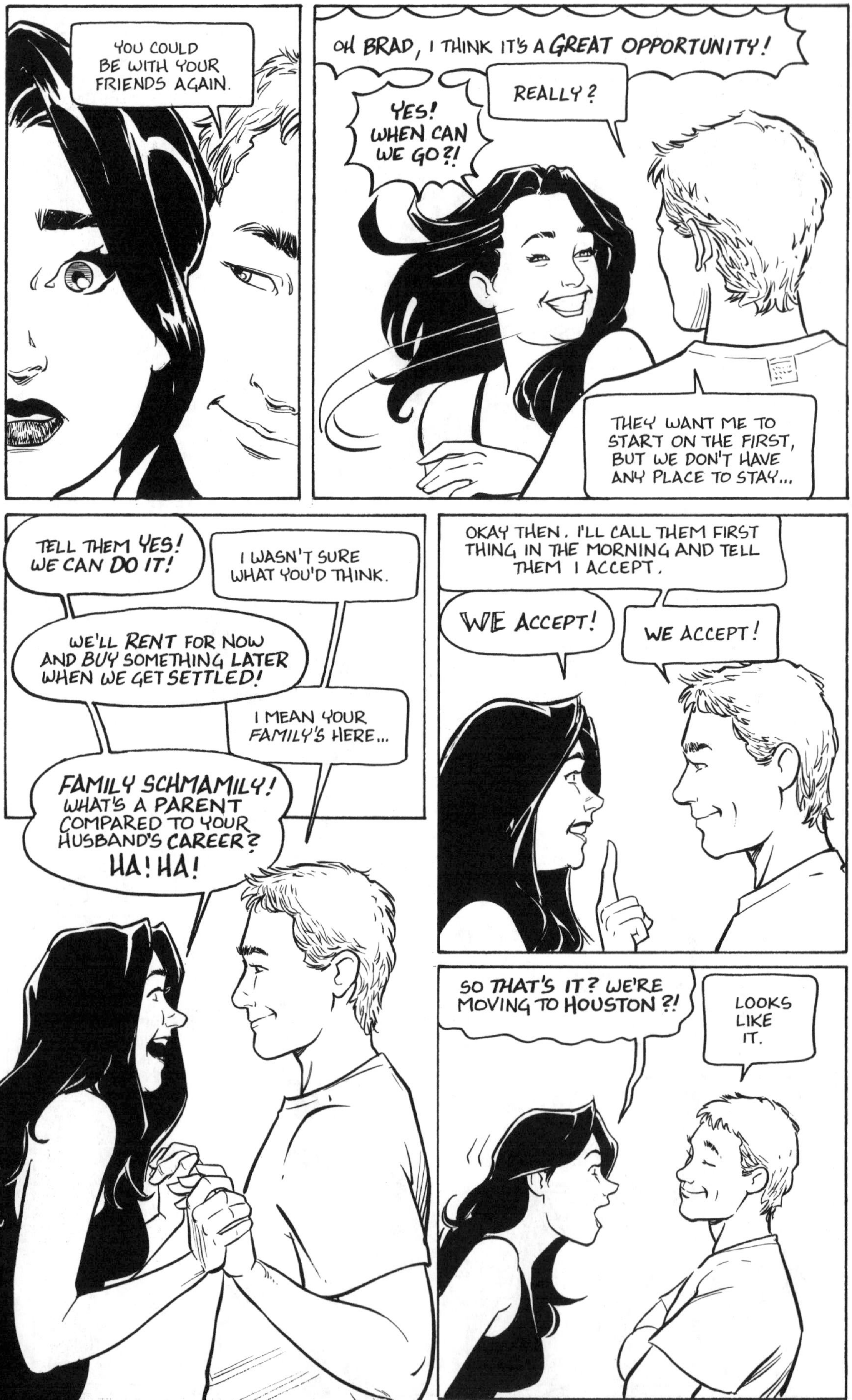
YOU COULD BE WITH YOUR FRIENDS AGAIN.
OH BRAD, I THINK IT'S A GREAT OPPORTUNITY!
REALLY?
YES! WHEN CAN WE GO?!
THEY WANT ME TO START ON THE FIRST, BUT WE DON'T HAVE ANY PLACE TO STAY...
TELL THEM YES! WE CAN DO IT!
I WASN'T SURE WHAT YOU'D THINK.
WE'LL RENT FOR NOW AND BUY SOMETHING LATER WHEN WE GET SETTLED!
I MEAN YOUR FAMILY'S HERE...
FAMILY SCHMAMILY! WHAT'S A PARENT COMPARED TO YOUR HUSBAND'S CAREER? HA! HA!
OKAY THEN. I'LL CALL THEM FIRST THING IN THE MORNING AND TELL THEM I ACCEPT.
WE ACCEPT!
WE ACCEPT!
SO THAT'S IT? WE'RE MOVING TO HOUSTON?!
LOOKS LIKE IT.

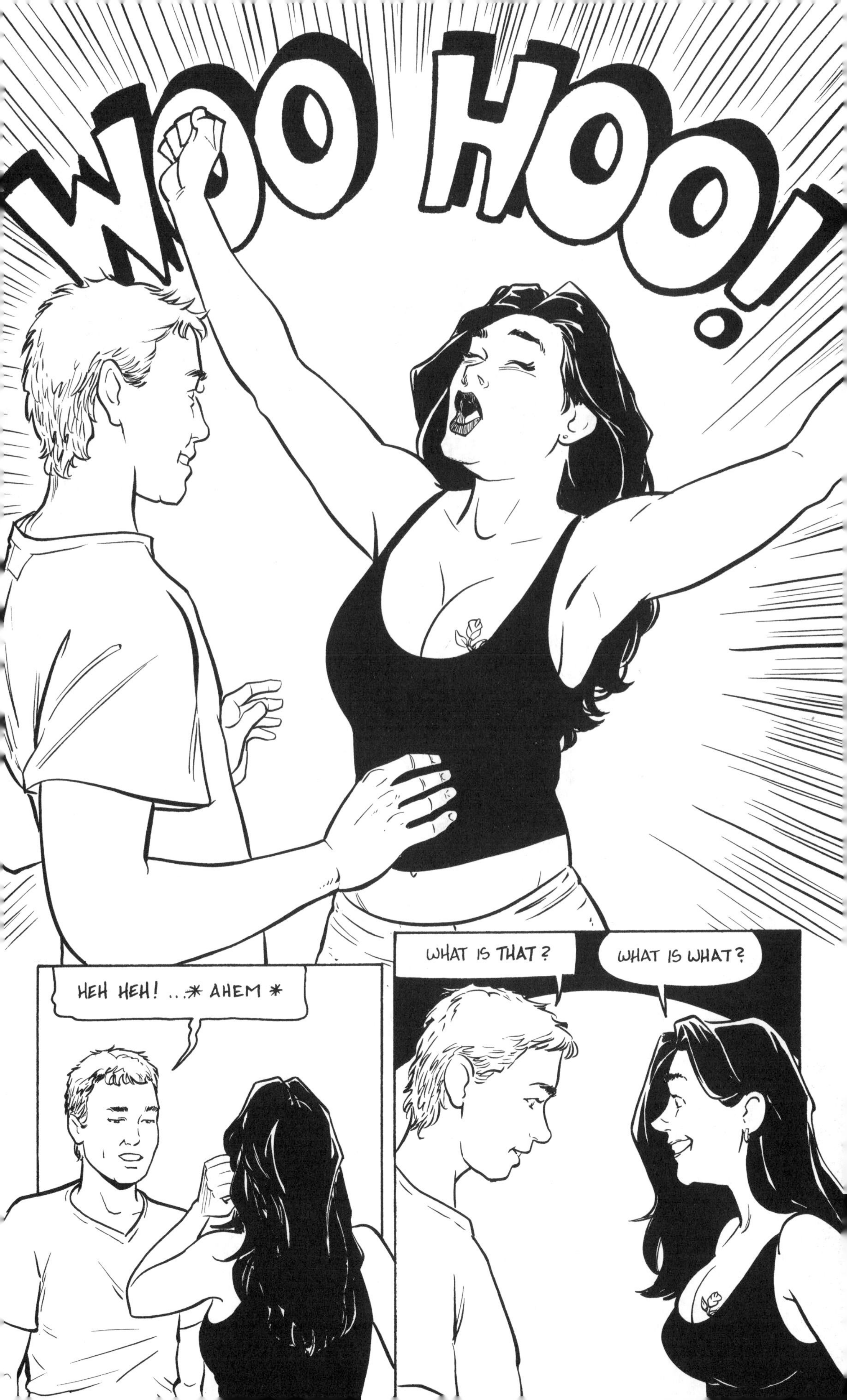
WOO HOO!
HEH HEH! ...* AHEM *
WHAT IS THAT?
WHAT IS WHAT?

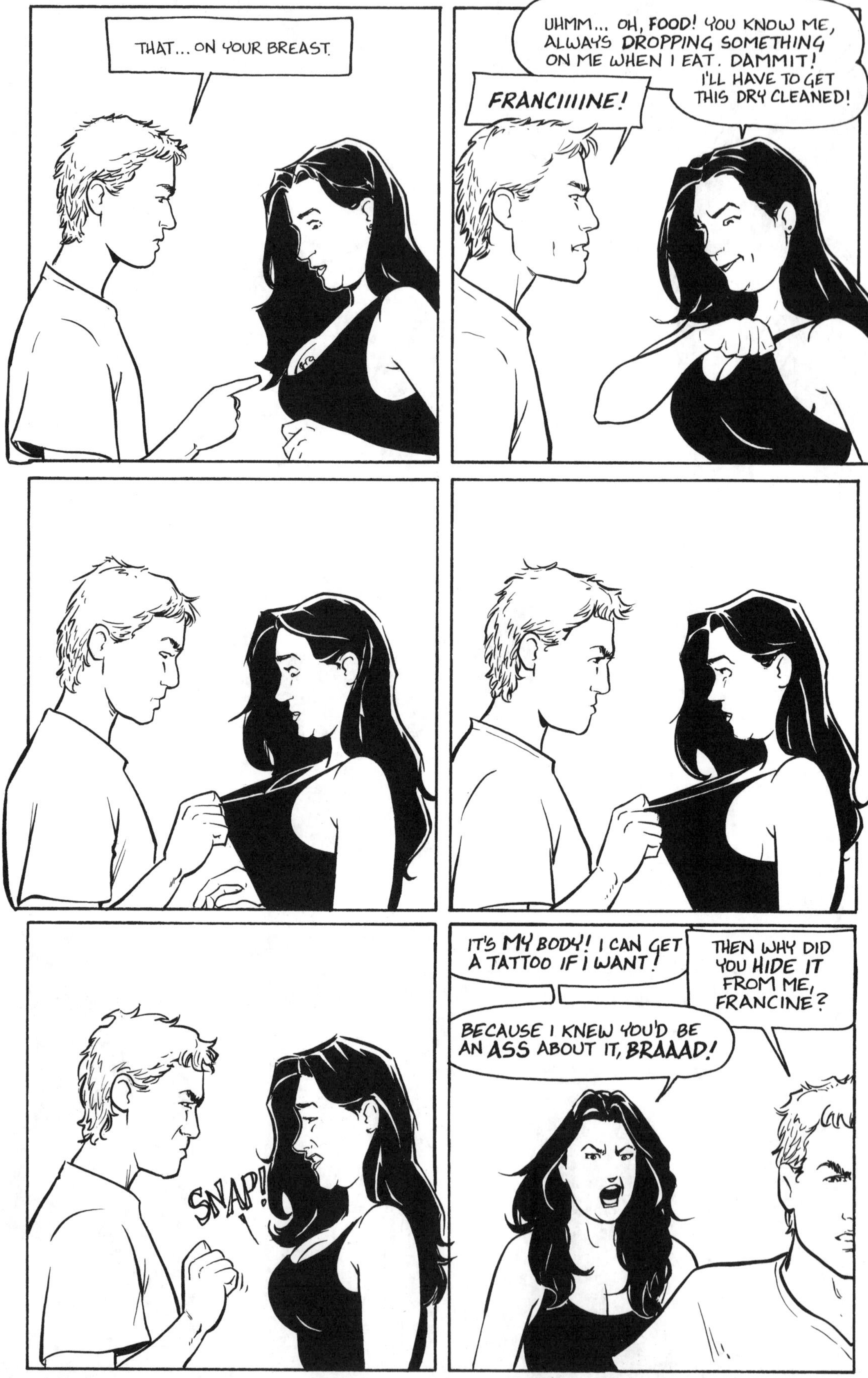
THAT... ON YOUR BREAST.
UHMM... OH, FOOD! YOU KNOW ME, ALWAYS DROPPING SOMETHING ON ME WHEN I EAT. DAMMIT! I'LL HAVE TO GET THIS DRY CLEANED!
FRANCIIIINE!
SNAP!
IT'S MY BODY! I CAN GET A TATTOO IF I WANT!
THEN WHY DID YOU HIDE IT FROM ME, FRANCINE?
BECAUSE I KNEW YOU'D BE AN ASS ABOUT IT, BRAAAD!

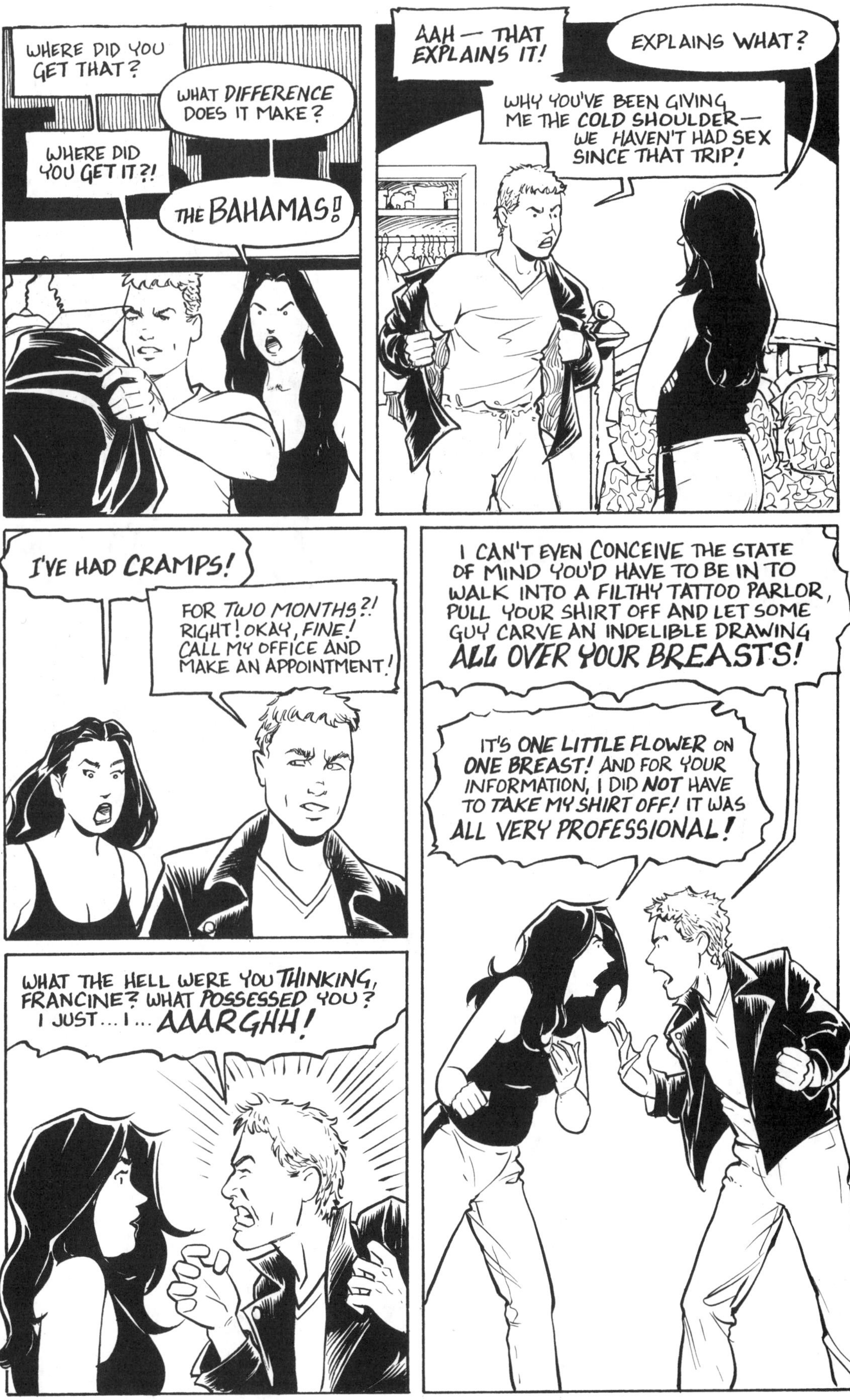
WHERE DID YOU GET THAT?
WHAT DIFFERENCE DOES IT MAKE?
WHERE DID YOU GET IT?!
THE BAHAMAS!
AAH — THAT EXPLAINS IT!
EXPLAINS WHAT?
WHY YOU'VE BEEN GIVING ME THE COLD SHOULDER— WE HAVEN'T HAD SEX SINCE THAT TRIP!
I'VE HAD CRAMPS!
FOR TWO MONTHS?! RIGHT! OKAY, FINE! CALL MY OFFICE AND MAKE AN APPOINTMENT!
I CAN'T EVEN CONCEIVE THE STATE OF MIND YOU'D HAVE TO BE IN TO WALK INTO A FILTHY TATTOO PARLOR, PULL YOUR SHIRT OFF AND LET SOME GUY CARVE AN INDELIBLE DRAWING ALL OVER YOUR BREASTS!
IT'S ONE LITTLE FLOWER ON ONE BREAST! AND FOR YOUR INFORMATION, I DID NOT HAVE TO TAKE MY SHIRT OFF! IT WAS ALL VERY PROFESSIONAL!
WHAT THE HELL WERE YOU THINKING, FRANCINE? WHAT POSSESSED YOU? I JUST... I... AAARGHH!

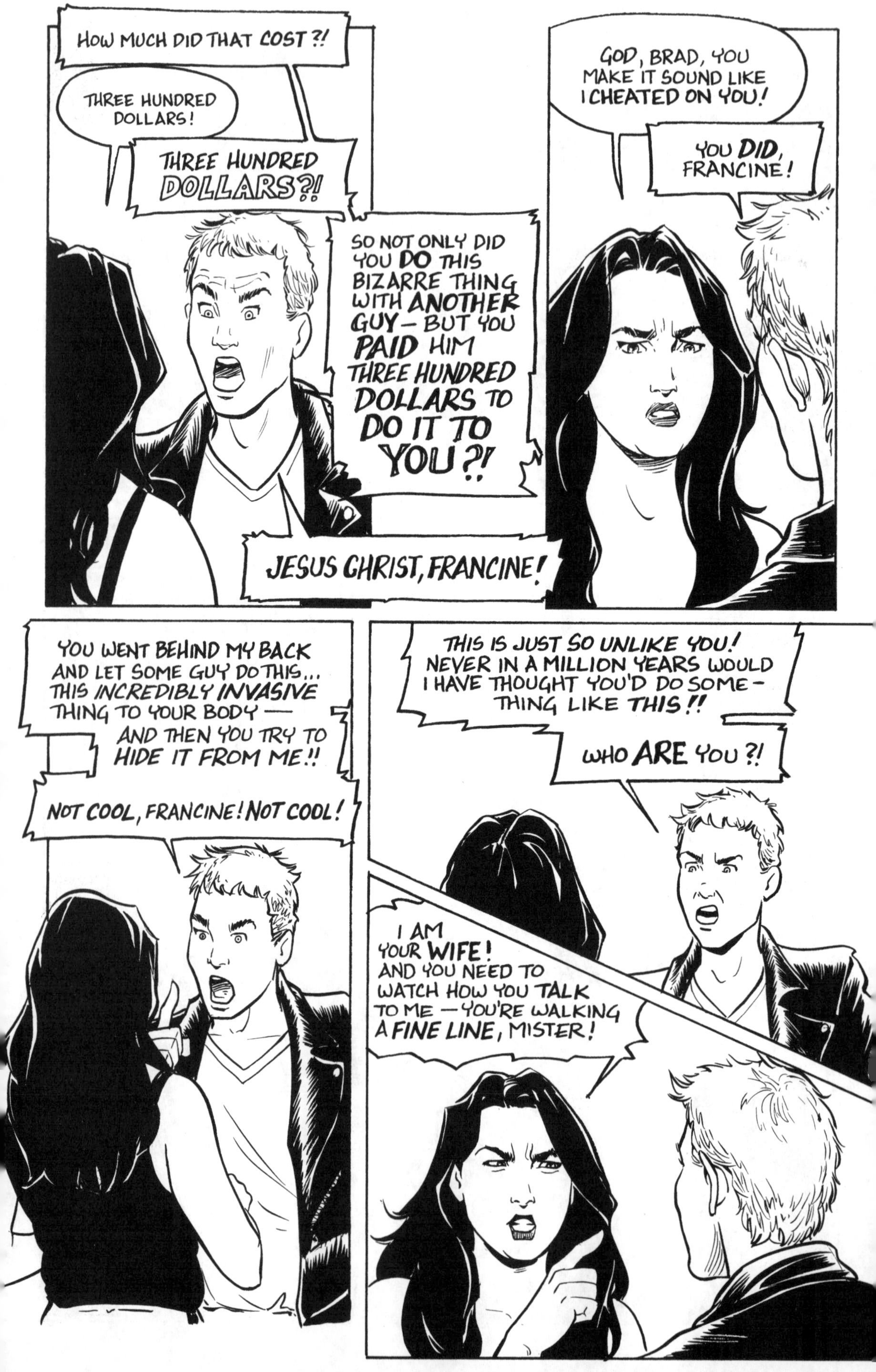

HOW MUCH DID THAT COST?!
THREE HUNDRED DOLLARS!
THREE HUNDRED DOLLARS?!
SO NOT ONLY DID YOU DO THIS BIZARRE THING WITH ANOTHER GUY – BUT YOU PAID HIM THREE HUNDRED DOLLARS TO DO IT TO YOU?!
JESUS CHRIST, FRANCINE!
GOD, BRAD, YOU MAKE IT SOUND LIKE I CHEATED ON YOU!
YOU DID, FRANCINE!
YOU WENT BEHIND MY BACK AND LET SOME GUY DO THIS... THIS INCREDIBLY INVASIVE THING TO YOUR BODY —
AND THEN YOU TRY TO HIDE IT FROM ME!!
NOT COOL, FRANCINE! NOT COOL!
THIS IS JUST SO UNLIKE YOU! NEVER IN A MILLION YEARS WOULD I HAVE THOUGHT YOU'D DO SOME-THING LIKE THIS!!
WHO ARE YOU?!
I AM YOUR WIFE! AND YOU NEED TO WATCH HOW YOU TALK TO ME — YOU'RE WALKING A FINE LINE, MISTER!

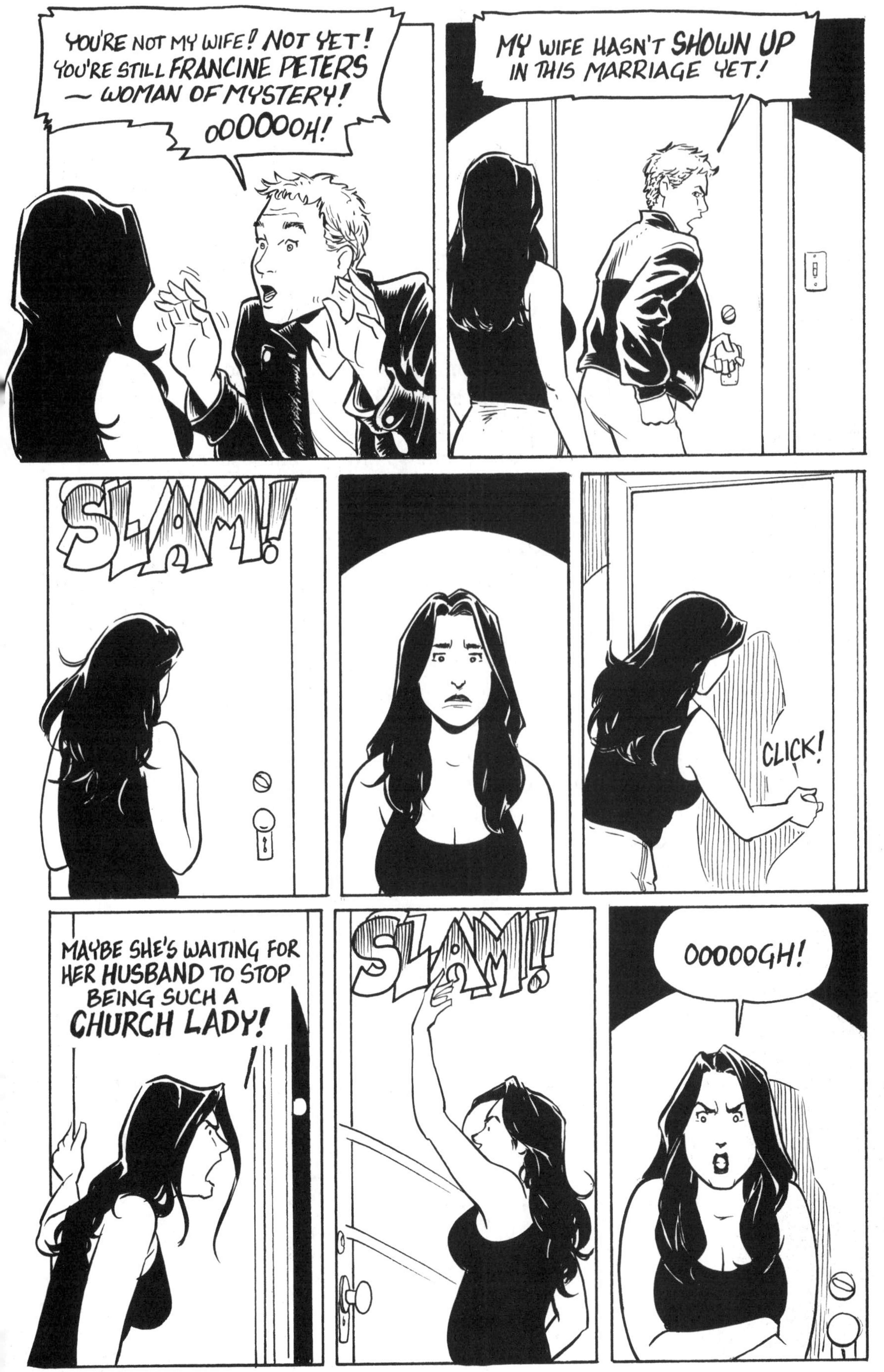
YOU'RE NOT MY WIFE! NOT YET! YOU'RE STILL FRANCINE PETERS — WOMAN OF MYSTERY! OOOOOOH!
MY WIFE HASN'T SHOWN UP IN THIS MARRIAGE YET!
SLAM!
CLICK!
MAYBE SHE'S WAITING FOR HER HUSBAND TO STOP BEING SUCH A CHURCH LADY!
SLAM!
OOOOOGH!

Katchoo tore open a packet of sugar and poured half the contents into her coffee. "Wedding rings are just antiquated symbols of slavery." she said. "It's like wearing a brand. You're saying, some guy owns you and here's the shackle to prove it."

"I don't know," Rusty said, fingering the simple gold band on her left hand, "sometimes my wedding ring is the only symbol of hope I have. It reminds me that Beau loves me…wherever he is."

The group fell silent. The remains of a 3 A.M. breakfast sat on the table before them at the Kibitz Grill, a popular late night stop for the working class of Las Vegas. Casey touched Rusty's arm in sympathy as David and Katchoo exchanged looks.

"I'm sorry, Rusty. I wasn't thinking."

"It's okay. You don't have to walk on eggshells around me, Katchoo. My husband has been missing for two years. It's a fact, there's no use pretending otherwise. Honestly though, there was never a day with Beau when I resented wearing the ring he gave me. Now it's my most valued possession."

David put his arm around Katchoo. "So," he said with a smile, "what's the verdict? Wedding rings, yes or no?"

Katchoo looked up at him. "We'll talk about it."

The couple kissed and Casey giggled. "You two are SO CUTE! Look at you! God, I'm so happy for you guys. We need to have a party or something to celebrate."

"Celebrate what?" said Katchoo with a deadpan expression.

"You're MARRIED!"

"We are?" Katchoo looked at David and frowned. "Do you know anything about this?"

"I've heard rumors."

"Oh c'mon you guys!" exclaimed Casey. "You're perfect for each other and now it's official! We should celebrate!"

Katchoo sipped her coffee. "We have an application for a license and some guy in an Elvis suit said we were married in the eyes of Graceland, but I doubt any of that makes it legal."

"It's legal if we send in the application," David said.

"So where is it?" Katchoo replied.

"You have it. Don't you?"

"Uh oh." Casey frowned. "Are you guys married or not? Come on, be honest."

Katchoo and David replied in unison:

> David: "We're married."

> Katchoo: "We're not married."

"I give up." Casey tossed her napkin in the air in disgust. "Rusty, see what you can do with them."

Rusty laughed. "Hey, this is Vegas, y'know? Anything goes." She poked Casey in the arm to let her out. "If you'll excuse me, I just drank two cups of coffee."

Casey stood up and let Rusty out of the booth. "Do you want me to go with you?"

"I'll just be a minute," Rusty replied over her shoulder. She made her way through the tables and walked to the back of the restaurant. A wood paneled alcove harbored matching doors with hand painted signs that read Hot Dogs and Pussy Cats. Rusty pushed open the door labeled Pussy Cats. The door squeeked loudly all the way open and all the way closed.

Inside, a middle-aged woman with beauty parlor hair wearing an Oklahoma Sooners sweatshirt was drying her hands at the sink. Rusty stepped into the middle of three stalls and closed the door. As she sat down she heard the sound of the woman's tennis shoes walking away. The door opened and closed with matching squeeks, then silence.

Moments later, the door squeeked open again and swung to a close. Rusty heard the slow tap of footsteps ringing sharply in the tile room. Her first thought was tap shoes. Why would somebody be wearing tap shoes at a diner?

The shoes stopped in the middle of the room. Rusty remained perfectly still. She heard the sound of labored breathing. The smell of cigarettes and cheap aftershave filled the room.

For several long moments there was no sound but the breathing. Rusty leaned forward and cocked her head to peek under the door. A deep, rasping cough startled her upright.

It was a man!

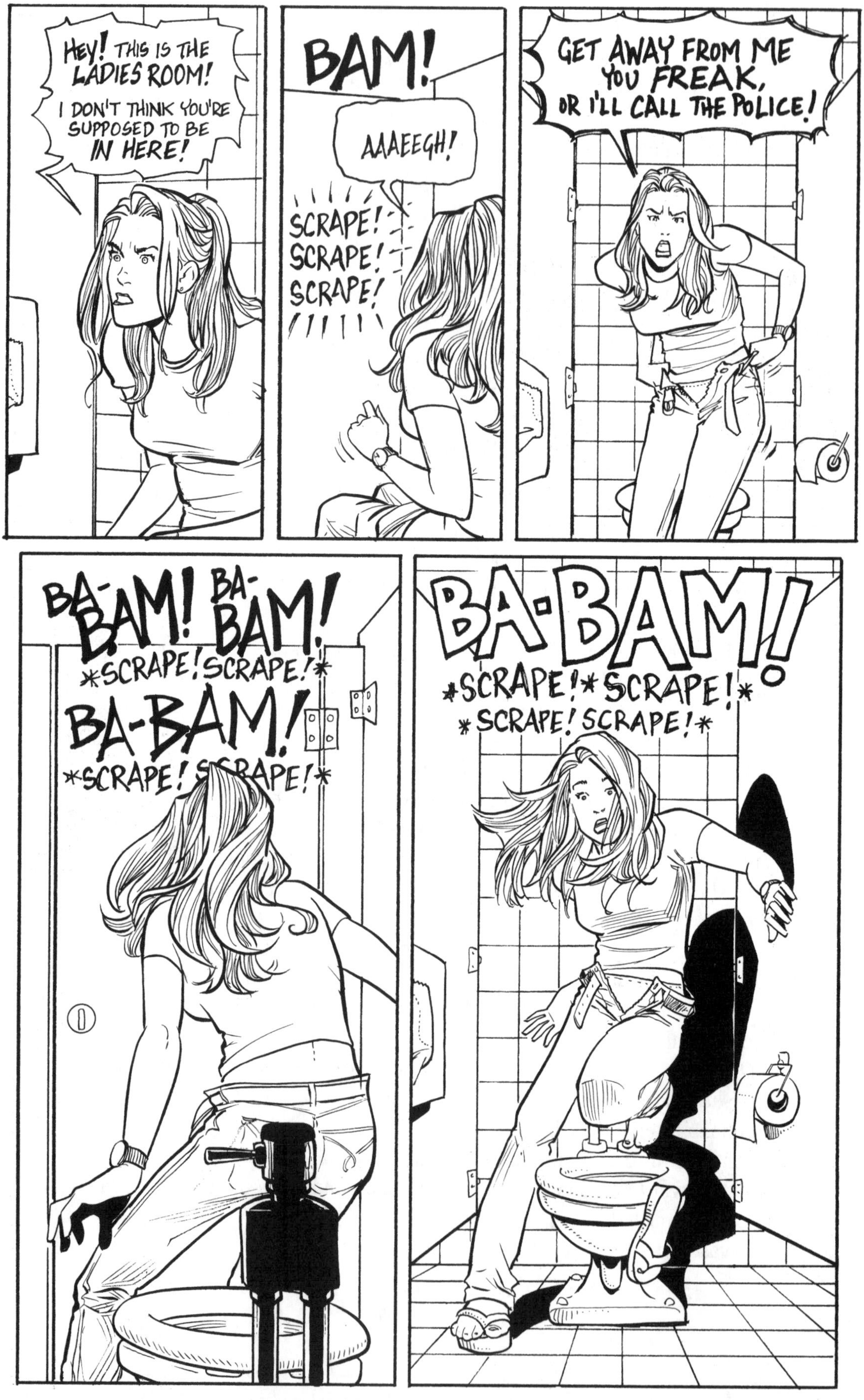
HEY! THIS IS THE LADIES ROOM!
I DON'T THINK YOU'RE SUPPOSED TO BE IN HERE!
BAM!
AAAEEGH!
SCRAPE! SCRAPE! SCRAPE!
GET AWAY FROM ME YOU FREAK, OR I'LL CALL THE POLICE!
BA-BAM! BA-BAM!
SCRAPE! SCRAPE!
BA-BAM!
BA-BAM!
SCRAPE! SCRAPE!*
SCRAPE! SCRAPE!

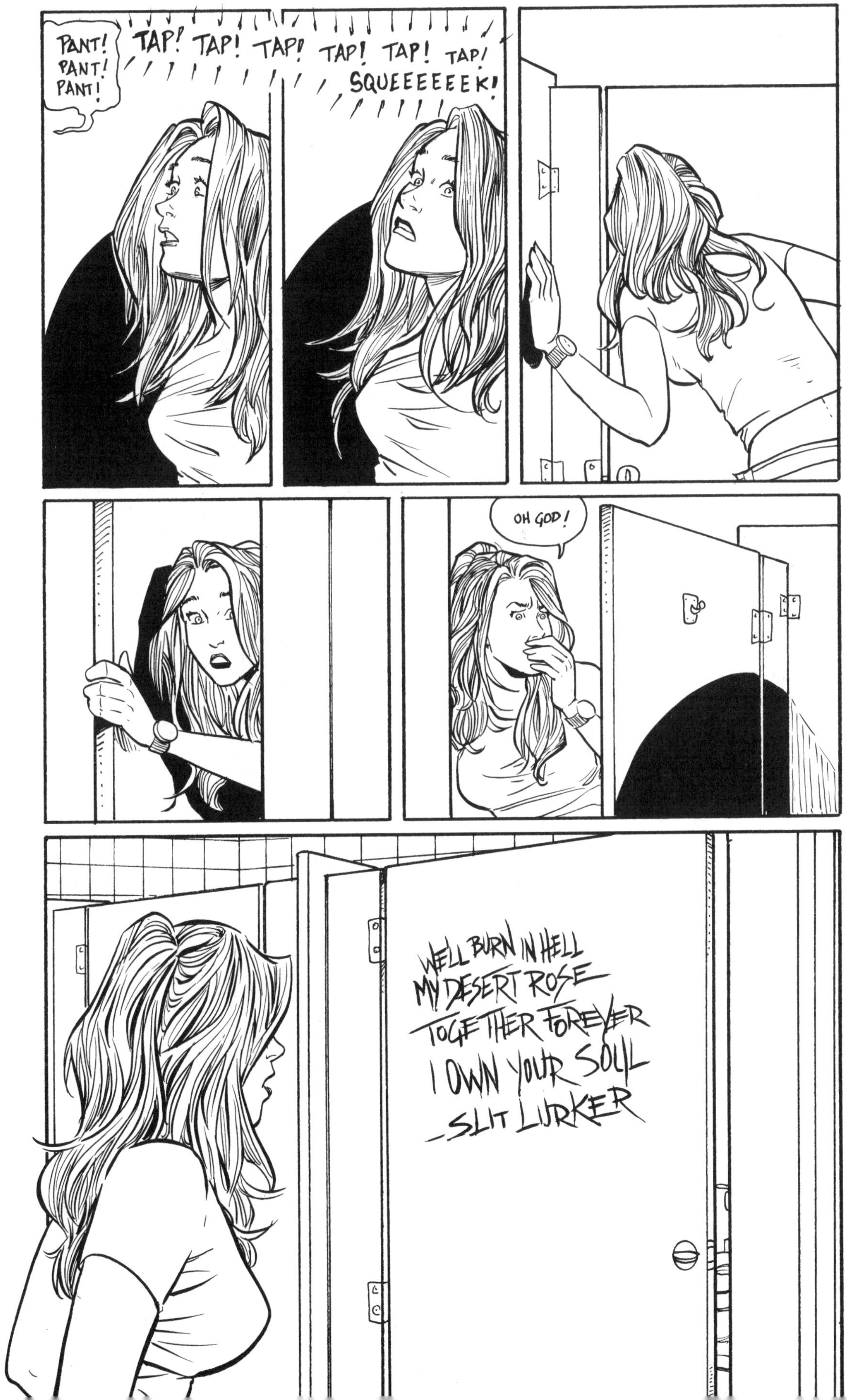
PANT! PANT! PANT!
TAP! TAP! TAP! TAP! TAP! TAP!
SQUEEEEEEK!
OH GOD!
WELL BURN IN HELL
MY DESERT ROSE
TOGETHER FOREVER
I OWN YOUR SOUL
_SLIT LURKER

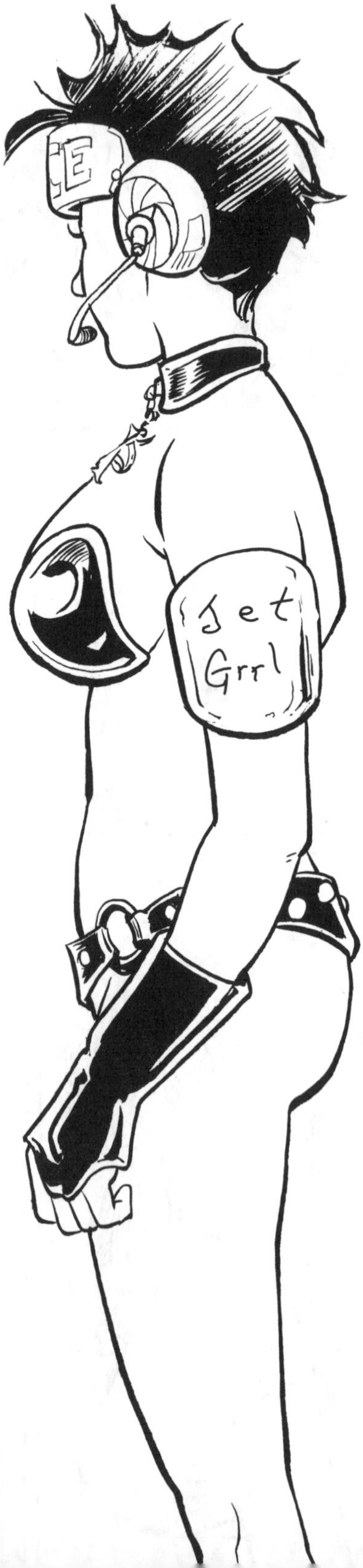
Jet Grrl

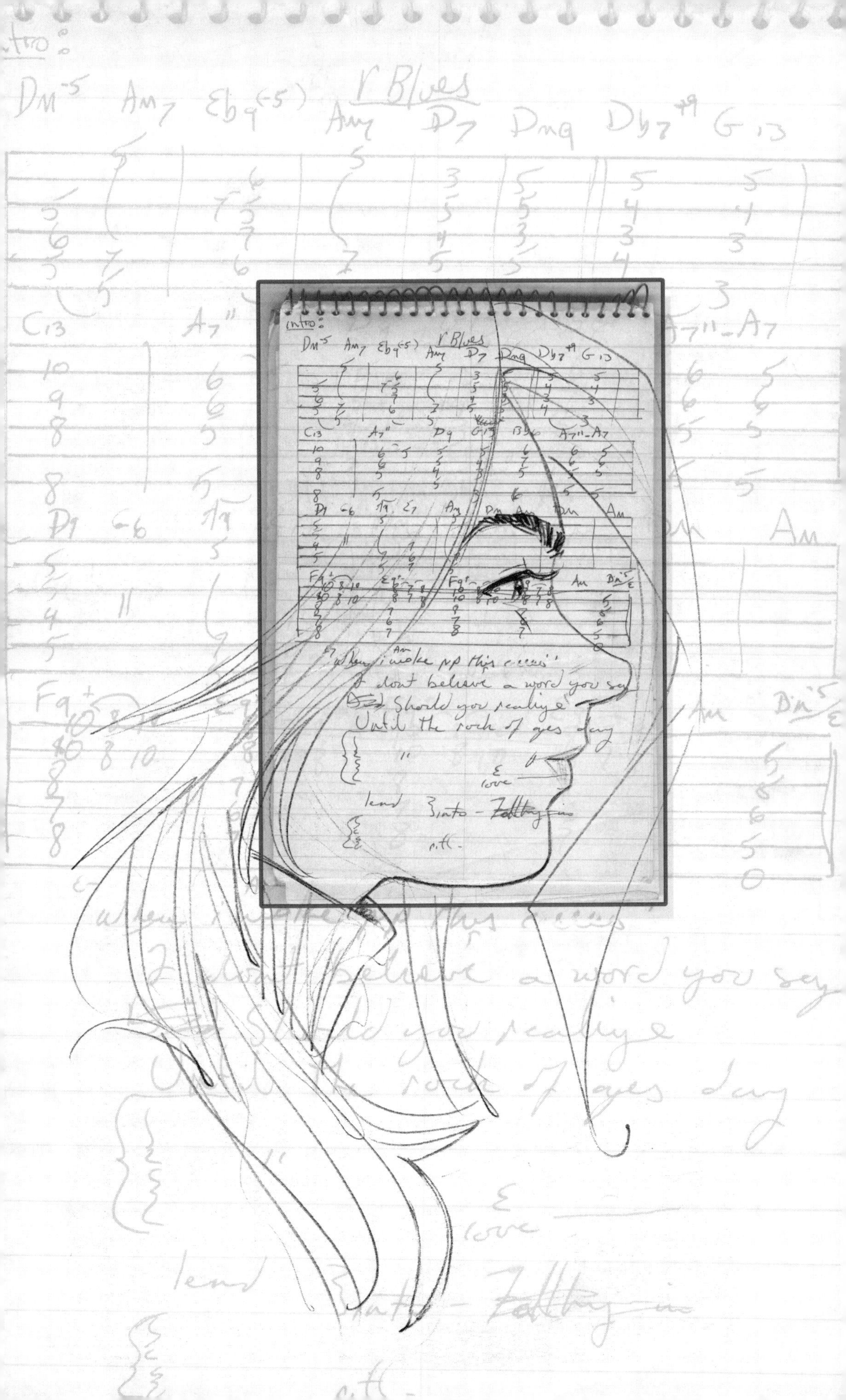
Intro:
V Blues
I don't believe a word you say
Until the rock of ages day

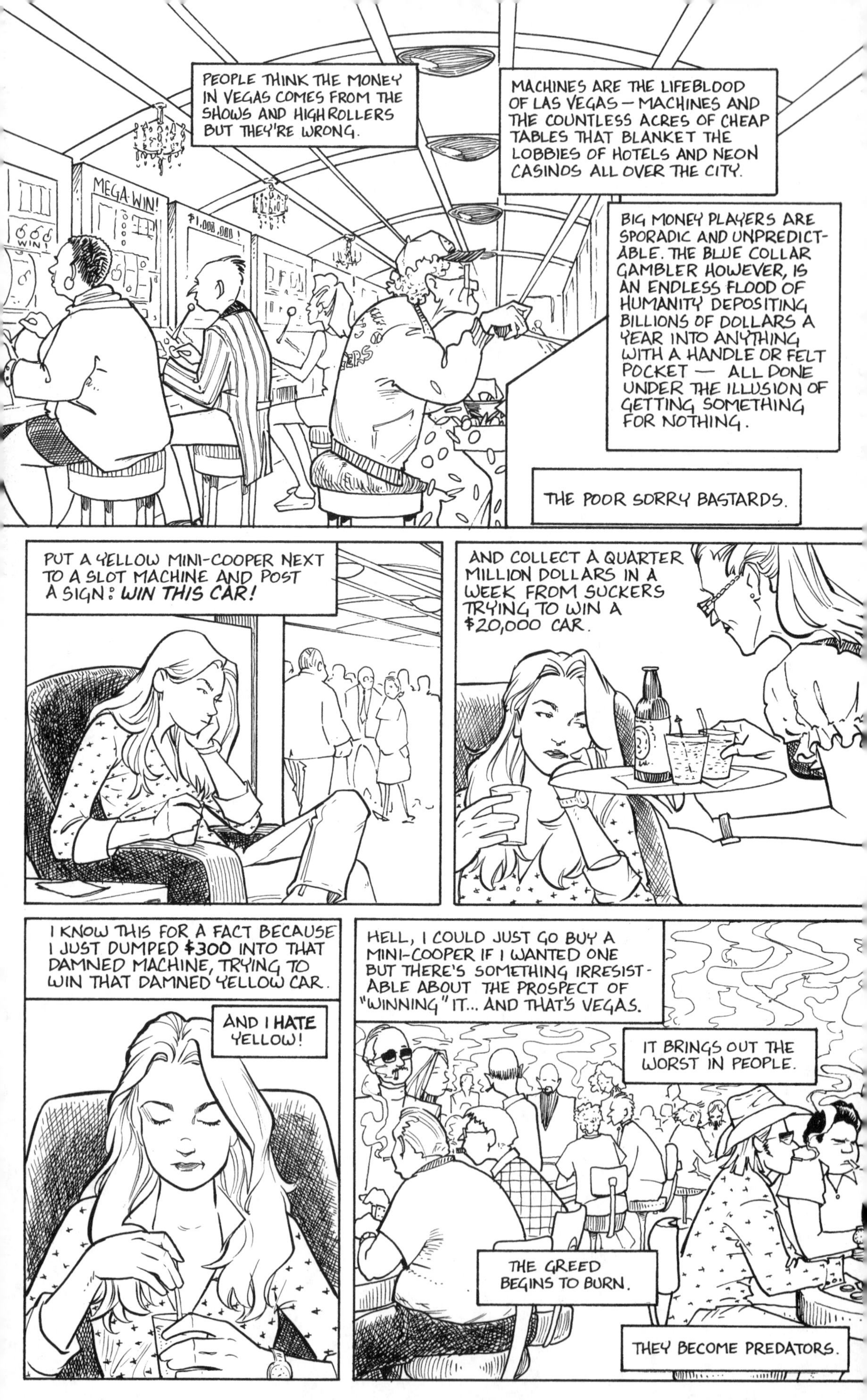
PEOPLE THINK THE MONEY IN VEGAS COMES FROM THE SHOWS AND HIGHROLLERS BUT THEY'RE WRONG.
MACHINES ARE THE LIFEBLOOD OF LAS VEGAS — MACHINES AND THE COUNTLESS ACRES OF CHEAP TABLES THAT BLANKET THE LOBBIES OF HOTELS AND NEON CASINOS ALL OVER THE CITY.
MEGA-WIN!
666
WIN!
$1,000,000!
BIG MONEY PLAYERS ARE SPORADIC AND UNPREDICTABLE. THE BLUE COLLAR GAMBLER HOWEVER, IS AN ENDLESS FLOOD OF HUMANITY DEPOSITING BILLIONS OF DOLLARS A YEAR INTO ANYTHING WITH A HANDLE OR FELT POCKET — ALL DONE UNDER THE ILLUSION OF GETTING SOMETHING FOR NOTHING.
THE POOR SORRY BASTARDS.
PUT A YELLOW MINI-COOPER NEXT TO A SLOT MACHINE AND POST A SIGN: WIN THIS CAR!
AND COLLECT A QUARTER MILLION DOLLARS IN A WEEK FROM SUCKERS TRYING TO WIN A $20,000 CAR.
I KNOW THIS FOR A FACT BECAUSE I JUST DUMPED $300 INTO THAT DAMNED MACHINE, TRYING TO WIN THAT DAMNED YELLOW CAR.
AND I HATE YELLOW!
HELL, I COULD JUST GO BUY A MINI-COOPER IF I WANTED ONE BUT THERE'S SOMETHING IRRESISTABLE ABOUT THE PROSPECT OF "WINNING" IT... AND THAT'S VEGAS.
IT BRINGS OUT THE WORST IN PEOPLE.
THE GREED BEGINS TO BURN.
THEY BECOME PREDATORS.

I KNOW ALL ABOUT GREED — I USED TO LIVE IN L.A. AND I KNOW A LOT ABOUT PREDATORS — I USED TO LIVE WITH ONE. BUT LAST NIGHT MY FRIENDS GOT A NASTY LESSON IN HOW DISGUSTING A HUMAN BEING CAN GET.

RUSTY HAS A STALKER. HE'S BEEN MAKING HER LIFE A CREEPY HELL FOR WEEKS NOW BUT LAST NIGHT HE SLUNK HIS HYENA ASS OUT OF THE SHADOWS AND PAID HER A VISIT WHILE SHE WAS TRAPPED IN THE CAN AT THE KIBITZ GRILL.

SHE NEVER SAW HIS FACE, BUT SHE SAID HE SMELLED LIKE DISCO MUSK. GAG.

AFTER RATTLING THE DOOR AND ACTING LIKE THE BOOGIE MAN, THE SLIMEBALL SCRAWLED A MESSAGE ON THE DOOR AND LEFT. THE POLICE CAME AND TOOK A REPORT BUT YOU KNOW HOW THAT GOES... THIS IS JUST ONE OF HUNDREDS FOR THEM.

I DIDN'T TELL RUSTY THAT TO ME THE STALKER'S REPUGNANT SIGNATURE READ LIKE AN ANAGRAM —

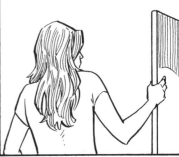

RUST KILLER!

NOW RUSTY AND HER LITTLE BOY CODY ARE SHACKED UP IN MY HOTEL ROOM UNTIL THIS HYENA IS CAUGHT OR I CAN KILL HIM — WHICHEVER COMES FIRST, I DON'T CARE.

ALL OF WHICH DOES NOTHING TO EXPLAIN WHY I'M HIDING OUT IN THE KENO PARLOR OF OUR HOTEL NURSING A DRINK I SHOULDN'T EVEN TOUCH.

TO EXPLAIN THAT WE'D HAVE TO TURN BACK THE CLOCK A COUPLE OF HOURS.

THIS AFTERNOON... IN THE COFFEE SHOP...

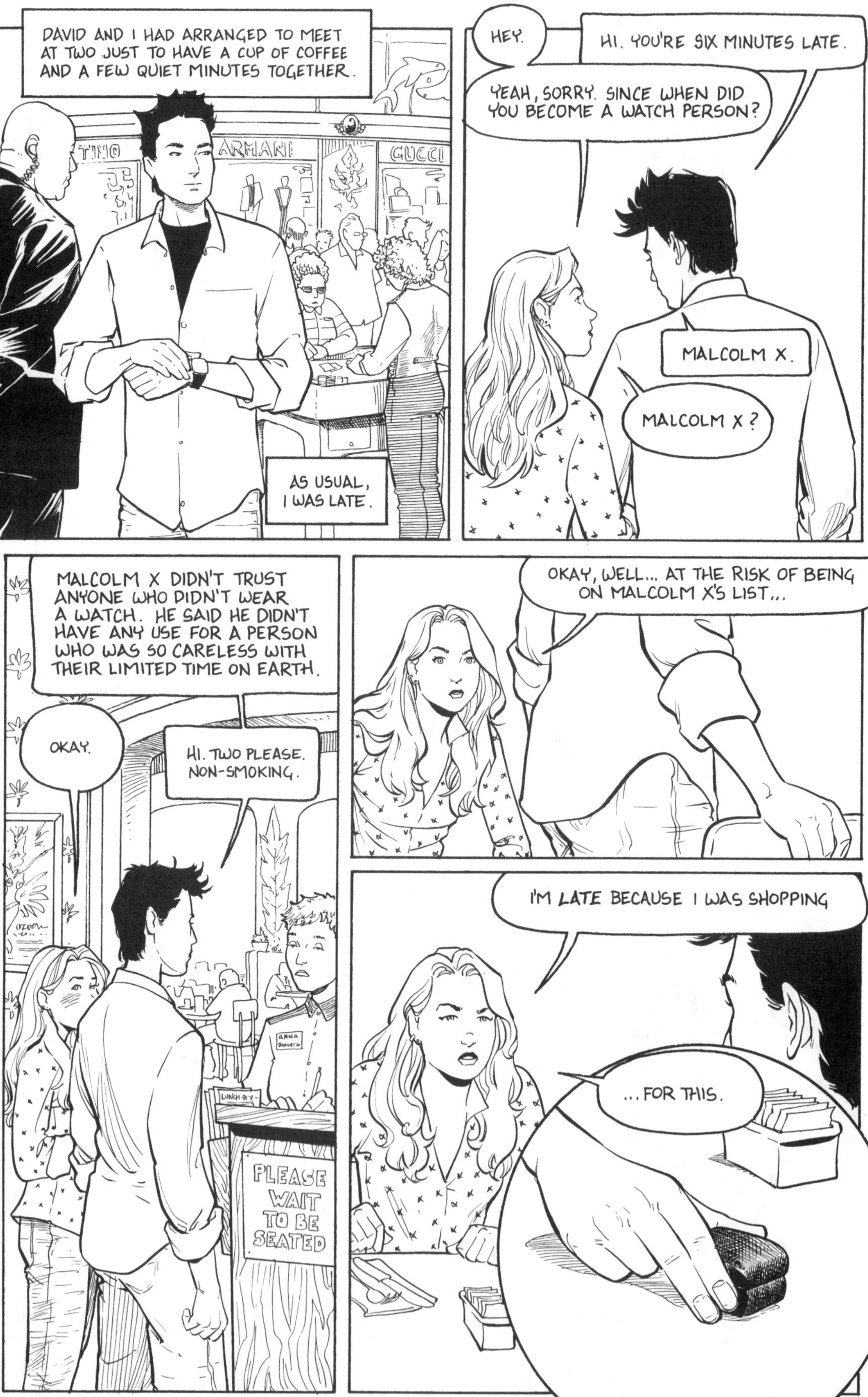
DAVID AND I HAD ARRANGED TO MEET AT TWO JUST TO HAVE A CUP OF COFFEE AND A FEW QUIET MINUTES TOGETHER.
TINO
ARMANI
GUCCI
AS USUAL, I WAS LATE.
HEY.
HI. YOU'RE SIX MINUTES LATE.
YEAH, SORRY. SINCE WHEN DID YOU BECOME A WATCH PERSON?
MALCOLM X.
MALCOLM X?
MALCOLM X DIDN'T TRUST ANYONE WHO DIDN'T WEAR A WATCH. HE SAID HE DIDN'T HAVE ANY USE FOR A PERSON WHO WAS SO CARELESS WITH THEIR LIMITED TIME ON EARTH.
OKAY.
HI. TWO PLEASE. NON-SMOKING.
PLEASE WAIT TO BE SEATED
OKAY, WELL... AT THE RISK OF BEING ON MALCOLM X'S LIST...
I'M LATE BECAUSE I WAS SHOPPING
...FOR THIS.

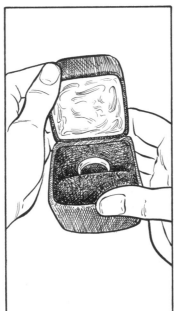

ABOUT THE QUESTION OF RINGS... YES OR NO...

I VOTE YES.

KATCHOO, I...

THEY HAD ONE WITH RUBIES BUT I THOUGHT, Y'KNOW... LIBERACE.

SNAP!

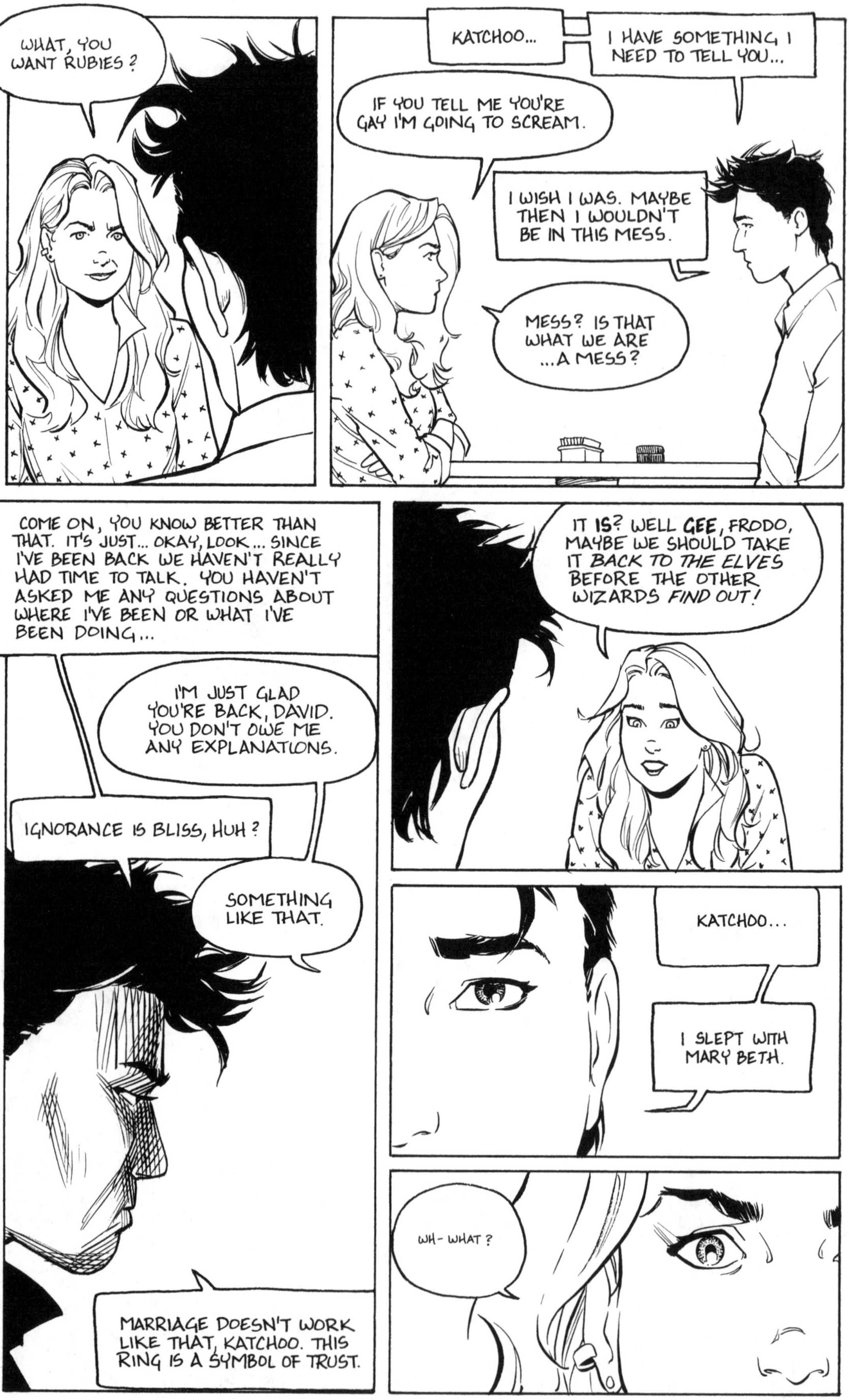
WHAT, YOU WANT RUBIES?
KATCHOO...
I HAVE SOMETHING I NEED TO TELL YOU...
IF YOU TELL ME YOU'RE GAY I'M GOING TO SCREAM.
I WISH I WAS. MAYBE THEN I WOULDN'T BE IN THIS MESS.
MESS? IS THAT WHAT WE ARE ...A MESS?
COME ON, YOU KNOW BETTER THAN THAT. IT'S JUST... OKAY, LOOK... SINCE I'VE BEEN BACK WE HAVEN'T REALLY HAD TIME TO TALK. YOU HAVEN'T ASKED ME ANY QUESTIONS ABOUT WHERE I'VE BEEN OR WHAT I'VE BEEN DOING...
I'M JUST GLAD YOU'RE BACK, DAVID. YOU DON'T OWE ME ANY EXPLANATIONS.
IGNORANCE IS BLISS, HUH?
SOMETHING LIKE THAT.
MARRIAGE DOESN'T WORK LIKE THAT, KATCHOO. THIS RING IS A SYMBOL OF TRUST.
IT **IS**? WELL **GEE**, FRODO, MAYBE WE SHOULD TAKE IT *BACK TO THE ELVES* BEFORE THE OTHER WIZARDS *FIND OUT!*
KATCHOO...
I SLEPT WITH MARY BETH.
WH- WHAT?

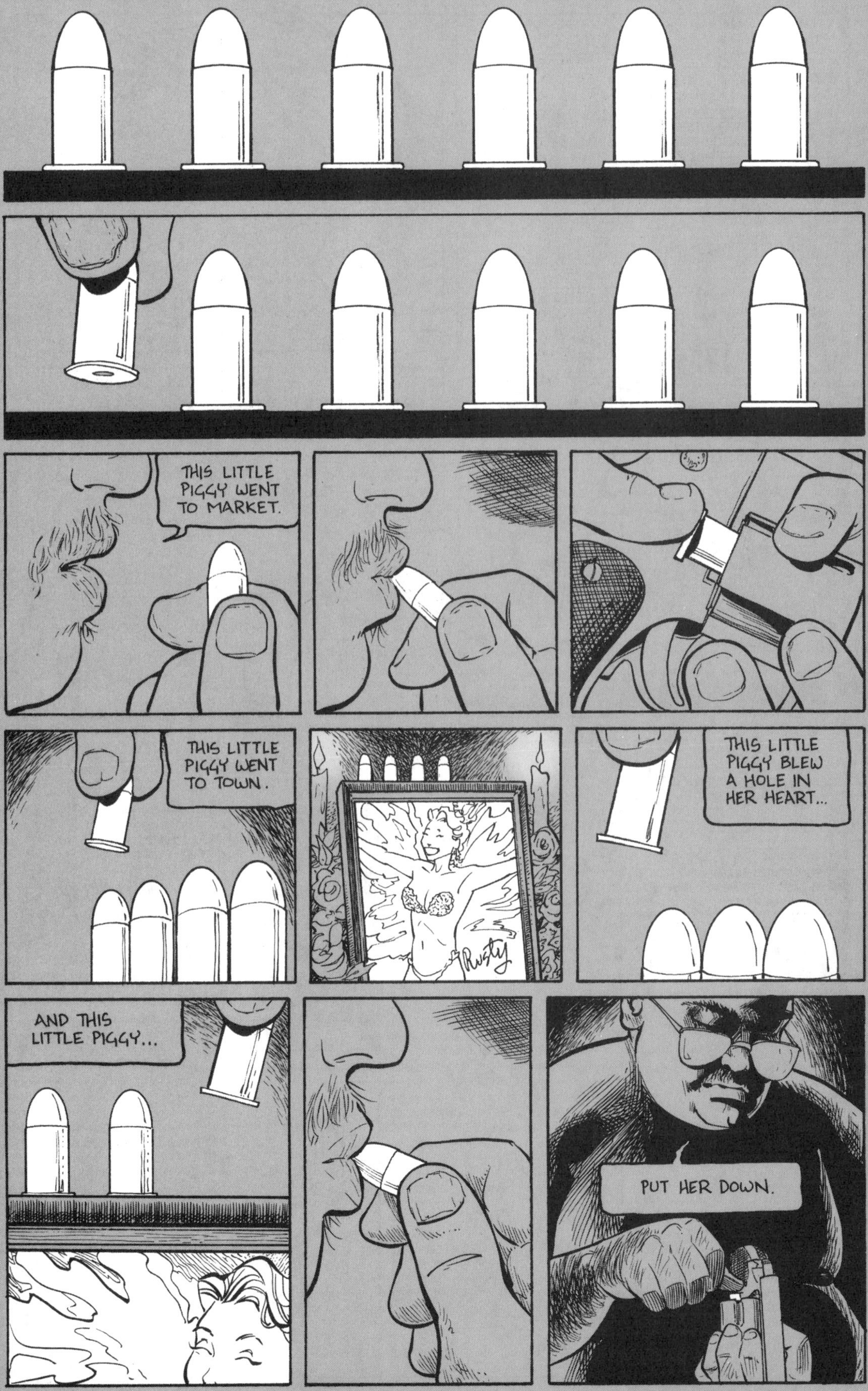
THIS LITTLE PIGGY WENT TO MARKET.
THIS LITTLE PIGGY WENT TO TOWN.
Rusty
THIS LITTLE PIGGY BLEW A HOLE IN HER HEART...
AND THIS LITTLE PIGGY...
PUT HER DOWN.

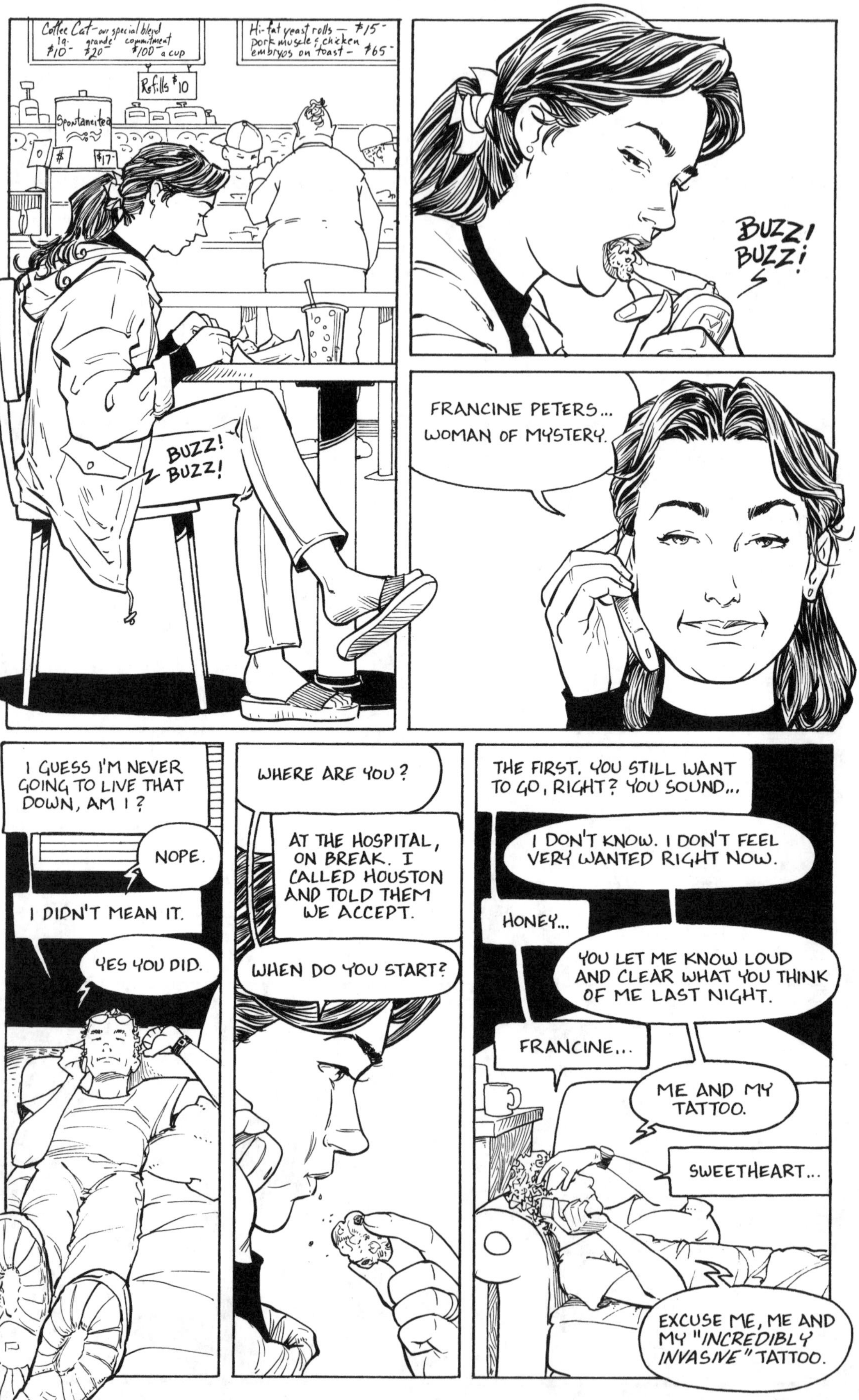
Coffee Cat - our special blend
lg. grande commitment
$10 $20 $100 a cup
Hi-fat yeast rolls — $15
pork muscle & chicken embryos on toast — $65
Refills $10
Spontaneitea
BUZZ! BUZZ!
BUZZ! BUZZ!
FRANCINE PETERS... WOMAN OF MYSTERY.
I GUESS I'M NEVER GOING TO LIVE THAT DOWN, AM I?
NOPE.
I DIDN'T MEAN IT.
YES YOU DID.
WHERE ARE YOU?
AT THE HOSPITAL, ON BREAK. I CALLED HOUSTON AND TOLD THEM WE ACCEPT.
WHEN DO YOU START?
THE FIRST. YOU STILL WANT TO GO, RIGHT? YOU SOUND...
I DON'T KNOW. I DON'T FEEL VERY WANTED RIGHT NOW.
HONEY...
YOU LET ME KNOW LOUD AND CLEAR WHAT YOU THINK OF ME LAST NIGHT.
FRANCINE...
ME AND MY TATTOO.
SWEETHEART...
EXCUSE ME, ME AND MY "INCREDIBLY INVASIVE" TATTOO.

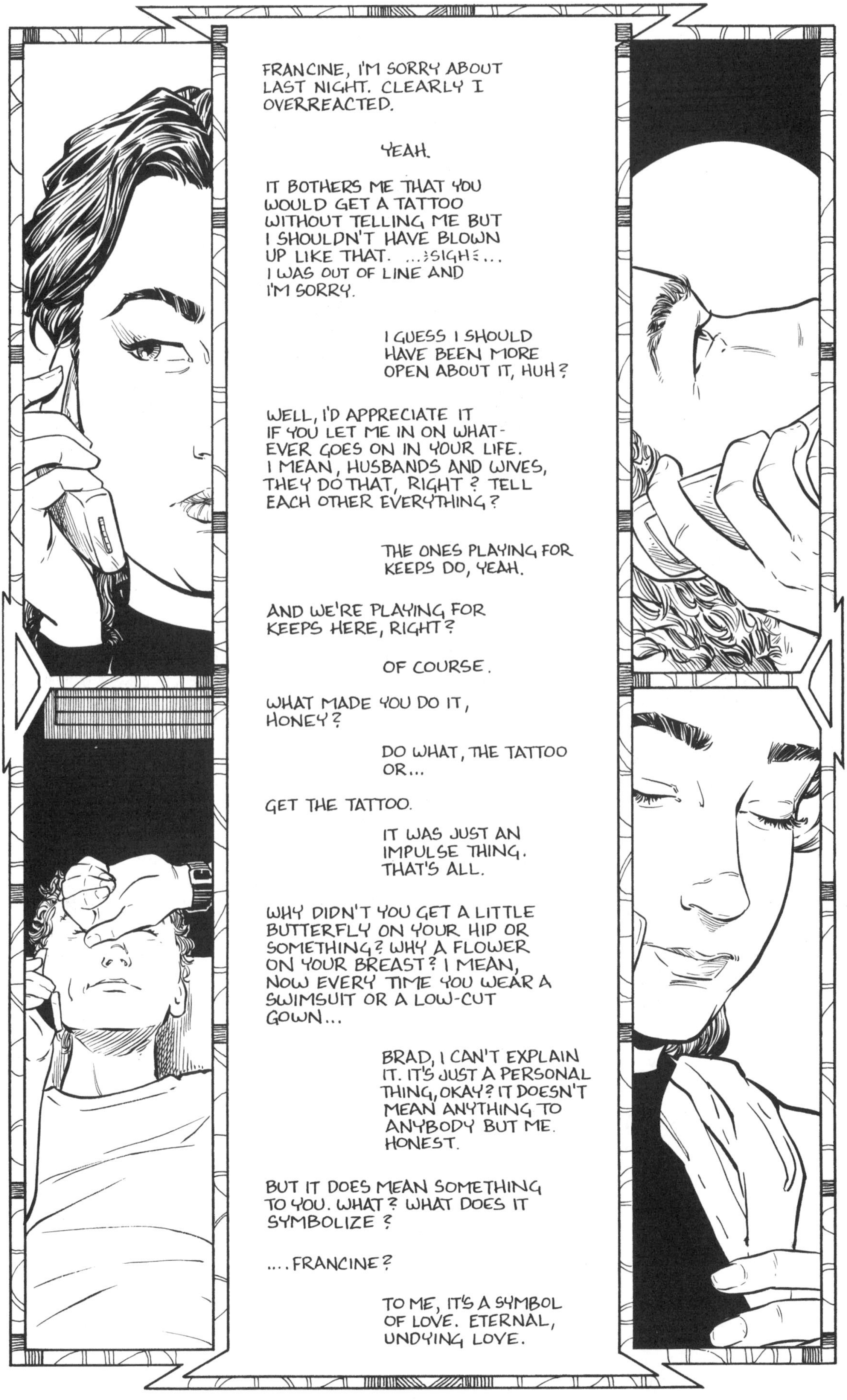

FRANCINE, I'M SORRY ABOUT LAST NIGHT. CLEARLY I OVERREACTED.
YEAH.
IT BOTHERS ME THAT YOU WOULD GET A TATTOO WITHOUT TELLING ME BUT I SHOULDN'T HAVE BLOWN UP LIKE THAT. ...SIGH... I WAS OUT OF LINE AND I'M SORRY.
I GUESS I SHOULD HAVE BEEN MORE OPEN ABOUT IT, HUH?
WELL, I'D APPRECIATE IT IF YOU LET ME IN ON WHATEVER GOES ON IN YOUR LIFE. I MEAN, HUSBANDS AND WIVES, THEY DO THAT, RIGHT? TELL EACH OTHER EVERYTHING?
THE ONES PLAYING FOR KEEPS DO, YEAH.
AND WE'RE PLAYING FOR KEEPS HERE, RIGHT?
OF COURSE.
WHAT MADE YOU DO IT, HONEY?
DO WHAT, THE TATTOO OR...
GET THE TATTOO.
IT WAS JUST AN IMPULSE THING. THAT'S ALL.
WHY DIDN'T YOU GET A LITTLE BUTTERFLY ON YOUR HIP OR SOMETHING? WHY A FLOWER ON YOUR BREAST? I MEAN, NOW EVERY TIME YOU WEAR A SWIMSUIT OR A LOW-CUT GOWN...
BRAD, I CAN'T EXPLAIN IT. IT'S JUST A PERSONAL THING, OKAY? IT DOESN'T MEAN ANYTHING TO ANYBODY BUT ME. HONEST.
BUT IT DOES MEAN SOMETHING TO YOU. WHAT? WHAT DOES IT SYMBOLIZE?
....FRANCINE?
TO ME, IT'S A SYMBOL OF LOVE. ETERNAL, UNDYING LOVE.

"I don't believe you."

"I'm sorry. It's the the truth."

"Why are you saying this to me, David?"

"If I don't tell you about this now, our relationship will always be a lie. I want you to know you can trust me, Katchoo."

"You've lost your frikkin' mind," I said. "First of all, the idea of Tambi having sex with you is ridiculous. And second, you want me to trust you for doing it? You're psychotic."

"I did it for you," he said, in all seriousness.

I laughed. "Oh you have lost it, my friend. Seriously, I think you're having a stroke."

"She came to me in Japan," David said, ignoring my protest. "She was very upset. Angry. She wanted us to have a child together, you and me; an heir to the family business who would bring the Takahashi and Choovanski families together. But I had left you and gone to Japan. I told her I wasn't going back because you didn't want me. She was very angry about it. She threatened to kill me. I didn't know what she might do to you, pull you back into the business or something. You'd been through so much already and I knew you didn't want any part of all that. I begged her to leave you alone, leave you out of the whole crime family thing. I offered to give her the child. At first she said no, but then..."

I could feel the tears welling up in my eyes as he spoke. Although Tambi and I had never talked about an heir to the family business, it sounded like her. It sounded like something she would think was important. But, Tambi and David? No way. Not unless...

"We got very drunk on sake," David said.

"Mary Beth... drunk?"

David's expression was grim. "We were both stoned out of our minds. I think she needed it more than I did."

I shook my head, trying to clear the cobwebs. This was unreal. It couldn't be happening. David's next words hit me like a crosstown bus.

"You called while she was with me, Katchoo."

"What?"

"When we were...together, you called Tambi on her cell phone. You said something about a cherry hammer and it made her laugh. Do you remember that?"

I could feel the blood run from my face and my stomach began to tighten into a knot. I recalled the night I met Cherry Hammer in a bar and called Tambi to check on her. I was shocked to find Tambi stoned and giddy on the phone, it was so unlike her. When I asked her if she was drunk, she replied "I'm so screwed!"

"I don't know what a cherry hammer is," David continued, "but I remember being afraid she might do it to me." Then he added, under his breath, "She did everything else."

"Oh my god."

David saw the realization sweep over my face. "You do remember, don't you?" He leaned towards me and spoke softly, urgently, as if what he said next would make it all better. "Katchoo, I love you. I don't love Tambi. I let her use my body, that's all. What I did, at the time I felt I had no choice. I never thought I'd see you again."

"Did it work?" I asked. My voice sounded small and far away. "Did she get pregnant?"

"I don't know. She left and I haven't talked to her since." David reached his hand across the table. "Katchoo, I…"

"Don't touch me!" I stood abruptly, shoving my chair backwards on the tile floor with a loud scrape. People stared.

"Just…don't, Okay?" I held my hand out to him to stop and fought to keep it together. "Stop. Enough. You win." I turned and walked out before I melted into a pool of betrayed goo.

I'd been a fool. I knew better and still I had been a fool and taken him back like a naïve teenager. Tears of anger burned my eyes and blurred the lobby of the hotel into a rain-soaked watercolor. I made my way through the casino to the dark solace of the keno parlor and found a plush chair in the corner. Immediately a waitress was there to take my order. I ordered a bourbon on the rocks. When she brought it to me I downed it, put the empty glass back on her tray and ordered another. Images of Tambi and David wrecking the bed and each other shot through my brain like seizures. Not love...mutual rape. Brutal. Complete.

I downed three drinks before I realized I had left the ring on the table.

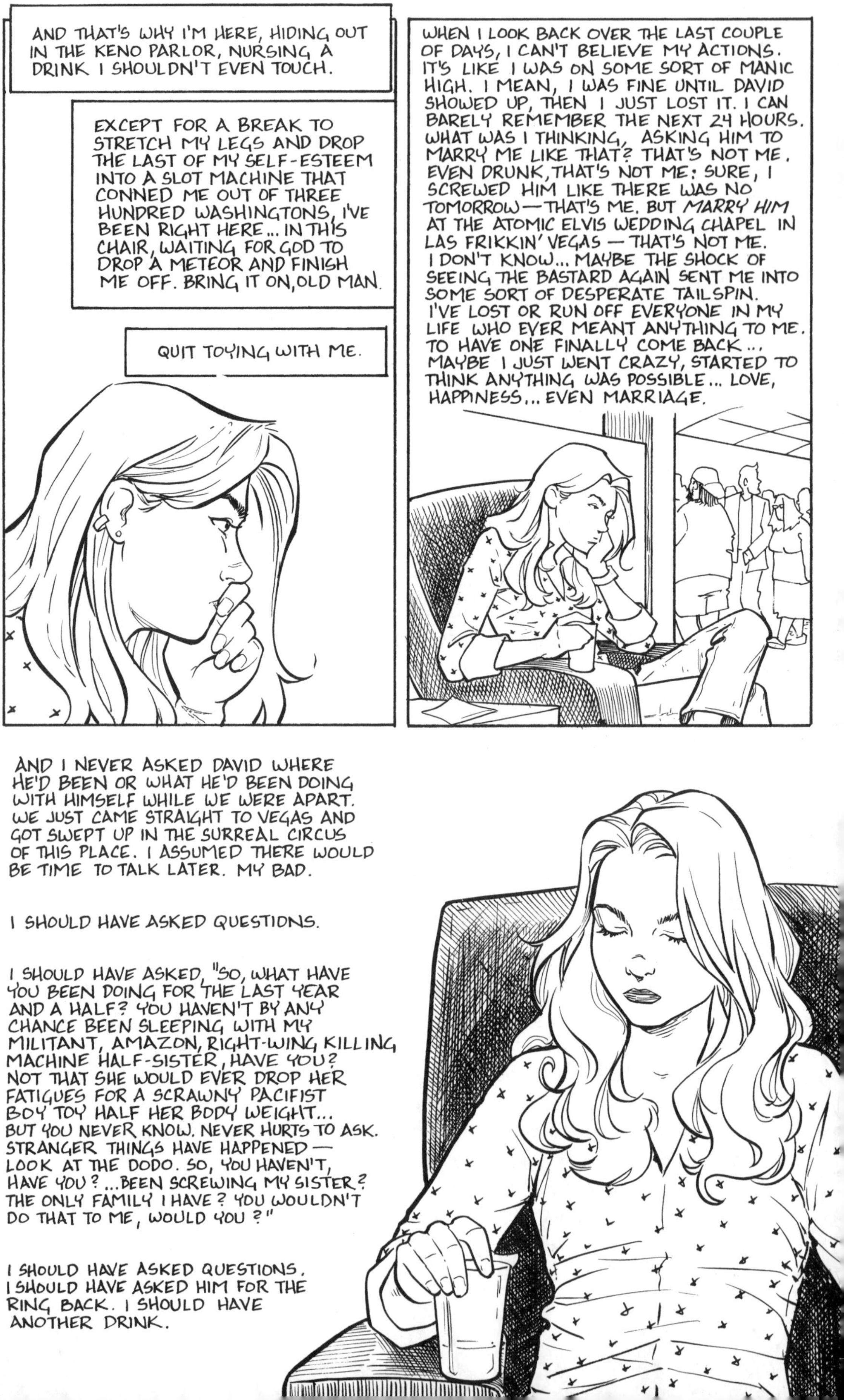
AND THAT'S WHY I'M HERE, HIDING OUT IN THE KENO PARLOR, NURSING A DRINK I SHOULDN'T EVEN TOUCH.
EXCEPT FOR A BREAK TO STRETCH MY LEGS AND DROP THE LAST OF MY SELF-ESTEEM INTO A SLOT MACHINE THAT CONNED ME OUT OF THREE HUNDRED WASHINGTONS, I'VE BEEN RIGHT HERE... IN THIS CHAIR, WAITING FOR GOD TO DROP A METEOR AND FINISH ME OFF. BRING IT ON, OLD MAN.
QUIT TOYING WITH ME.
WHEN I LOOK BACK OVER THE LAST COUPLE OF DAYS, I CAN'T BELIEVE MY ACTIONS. IT'S LIKE I WAS ON SOME SORT OF MANIC HIGH. I MEAN, I WAS FINE UNTIL DAVID SHOWED UP, THEN I JUST LOST IT. I CAN BARELY REMEMBER THE NEXT 24 HOURS. WHAT WAS I THINKING, ASKING HIM TO MARRY ME LIKE THAT? THAT'S NOT ME. EVEN DRUNK, THAT'S NOT ME: SURE, I SCREWED HIM LIKE THERE WAS NO TOMORROW—THAT'S ME. BUT *MARRY HIM* AT THE ATOMIC ELVIS WEDDING CHAPEL IN LAS FRIKKIN' VEGAS — THAT'S NOT ME. I DON'T KNOW... MAYBE THE SHOCK OF SEEING THE BASTARD AGAIN SENT ME INTO SOME SORT OF DESPERATE TAILSPIN. I'VE LOST OR RUN OFF EVERYONE IN MY LIFE WHO EVER MEANT ANYTHING TO ME. TO HAVE ONE FINALLY COME BACK... MAYBE I JUST WENT CRAZY, STARTED TO THINK ANYTHING WAS POSSIBLE... LOVE, HAPPINESS... EVEN MARRIAGE.
AND I NEVER ASKED DAVID WHERE HE'D BEEN OR WHAT HE'D BEEN DOING WITH HIMSELF WHILE WE WERE APART. WE JUST CAME STRAIGHT TO VEGAS AND GOT SWEPT UP IN THE SURREAL CIRCUS OF THIS PLACE. I ASSUMED THERE WOULD BE TIME TO TALK LATER. MY BAD.
I SHOULD HAVE ASKED QUESTIONS.
I SHOULD HAVE ASKED, "SO, WHAT HAVE YOU BEEN DOING FOR THE LAST YEAR AND A HALF? YOU HAVEN'T BY ANY CHANCE BEEN SLEEPING WITH MY MILITANT, AMAZON, RIGHT-WING KILLING MACHINE HALF-SISTER, HAVE YOU? NOT THAT SHE WOULD EVER DROP HER FATIGUES FOR A SCRAWNY PACIFIST BOY TOY HALF HER BODY WEIGHT... BUT YOU NEVER KNOW. NEVER HURTS TO ASK. STRANGER THINGS HAVE HAPPENED — LOOK AT THE DODO. SO, YOU HAVEN'T, HAVE YOU? ...BEEN SCREWING MY SISTER? THE ONLY FAMILY I HAVE? YOU WOULDN'T DO THAT TO ME, WOULD YOU?"
I SHOULD HAVE ASKED QUESTIONS. I SHOULD HAVE ASKED HIM FOR THE RING BACK. I SHOULD HAVE ANOTHER DRINK.

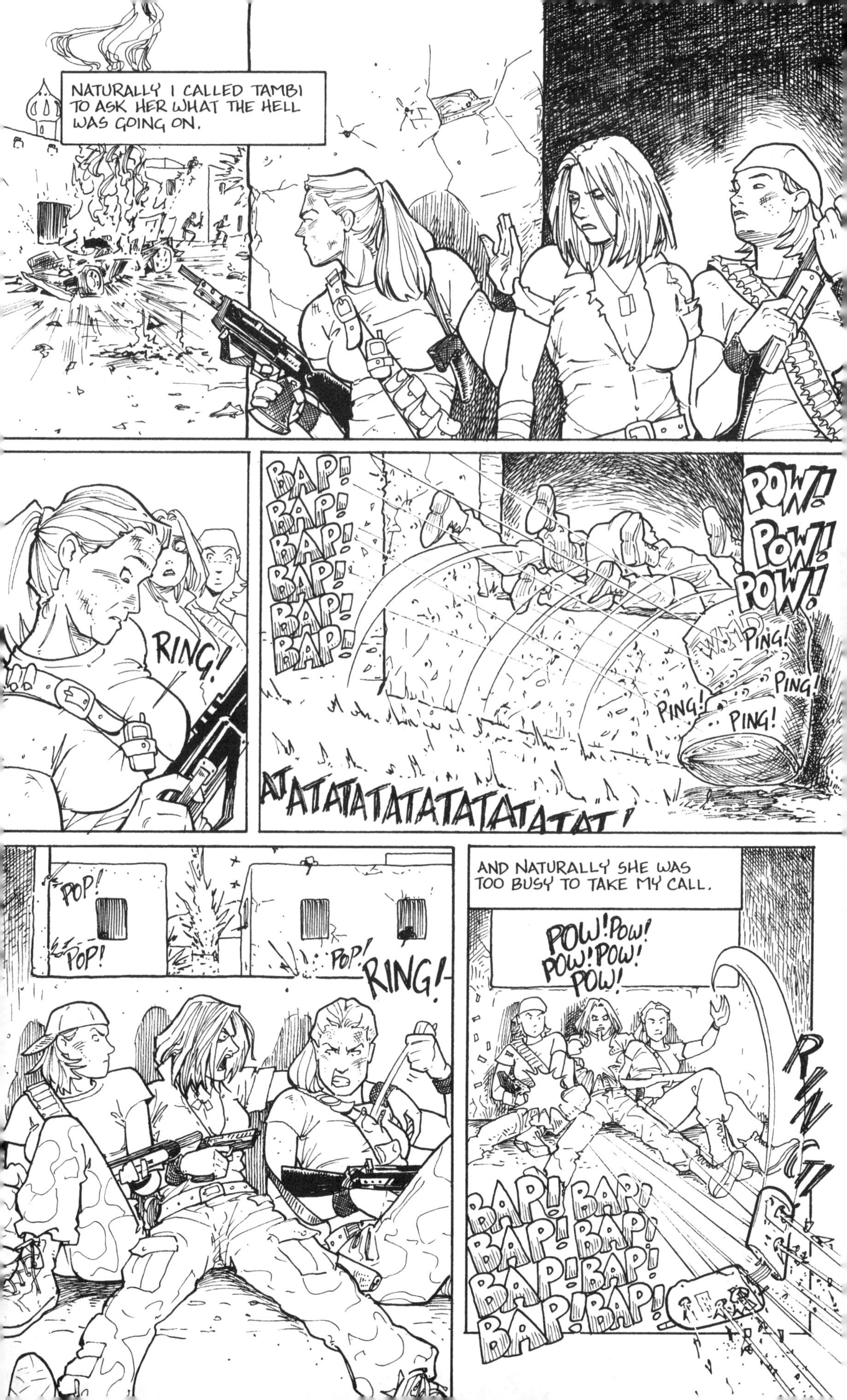
NATURALLY I CALLED TAMBI TO ASK HER WHAT THE HELL WAS GOING ON.
RING!
BAP! BAP! BAP! BAP! BAP! BAP!
POW! POW! POW!
PING! PING! PING! PING!
ATATATATATATATATATATAT!
POP! POP! POP!
RING!
AND NATURALLY SHE WAS TOO BUSY TO TAKE MY CALL.
POW! POW! POW! POW! POW!
RINNG!
BAP! BAP! BAP! BAP! BAP! BAP! BAP! BAP!

AND THERE YOU HAVE IT. THAT WAS MY DAY, HOW THE HELL WAS YOURS?

WHAT SHOULD I DO?

I PROBABLY WOULD HAVE STAYED IN THE KENO PARLOR DRINKING ALL NIGHT IF CASEY HADN'T CALLED — RUSTY WAS ON THE MOVE. SHE INSISTED ON GOING TO WORK.

WE TOLD HER IT WAS DANGEROUS, SHE WOULDN'T LISTEN. SHE SAID SHE NEEDED THE MONEY.

I WAS WAITING FOR THEM IN THE EMPLOYEE PARKING LOT WHEN THEY ARRIVED.

I SMELLED HIM BEFORE I SAW HIM. THE WARM DESERT BREEZE TURNED RIGHT AND CARRIED THE SCENT OF CHEAP COLOGNE ACROSS THE TAR AND ASPHALT. THE CLICK OF BOOTS WITH TAP HEELS CAUGHT MY EAR. *THE STALKER!*

CASEY AND RUSTY WERE OBLIVIOUS, GETTING THEIR BAGS OUT OF THE TRUNK OF RUSTY'S VINTAGE OLDSMOBILE. THEY WERE TALKING, OF ALL THINGS, ABOUT KNEE SURGERY.

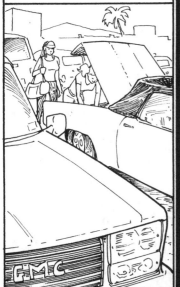

THE STALKER WAS ONE ROW OVER, CLOSING IN FAST...THE TAP OF HIS STEP GROWING QUICKER. I COULDN'T SEE HIS FACE, ONLY A SHADOW SWIMMING BEHIND STEEL AND GLASS.

RUSTY?

RUSTY SMITH?

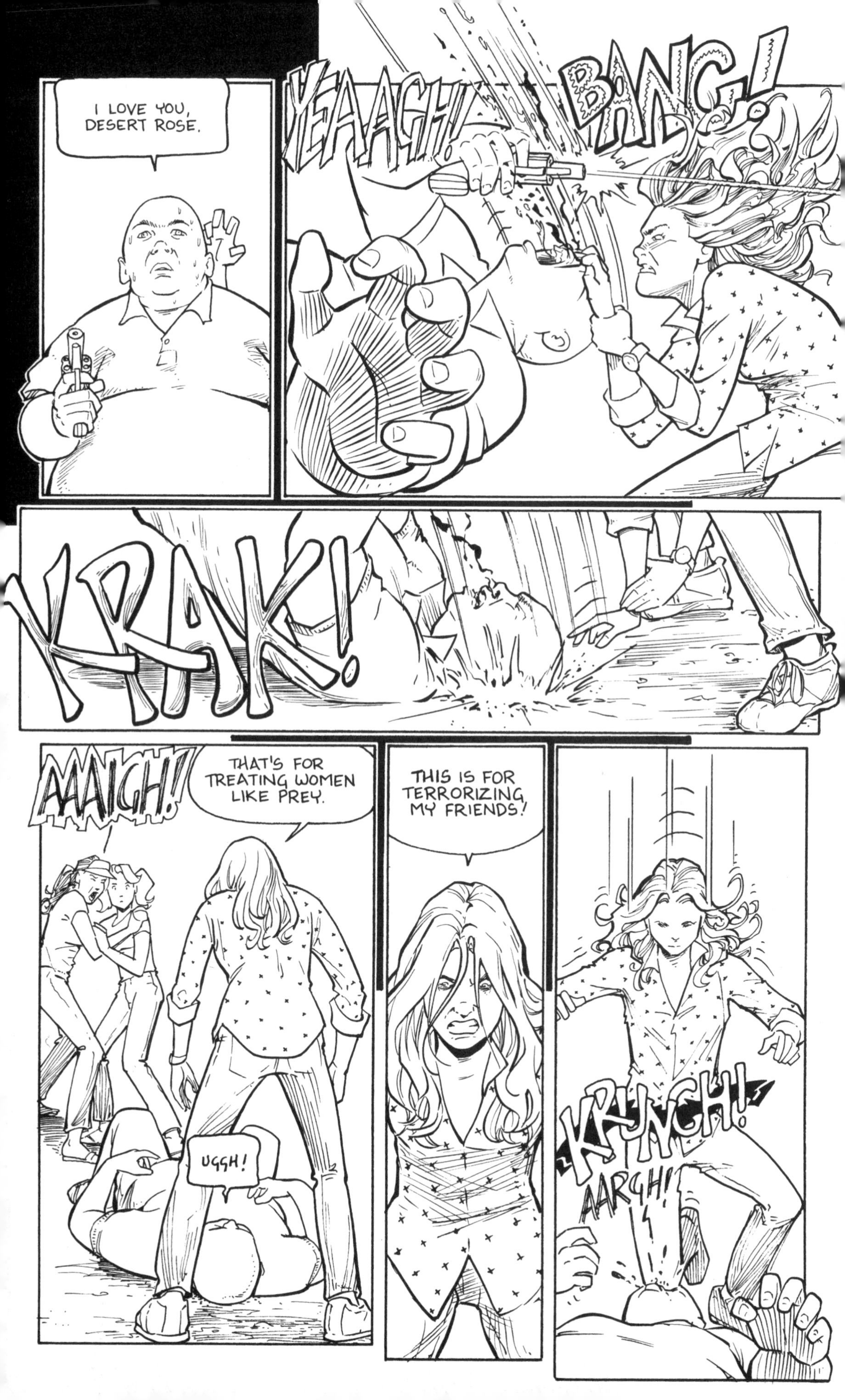
I LOVE YOU, DESERT ROSE.
YEAAGH!
BANG!
KRAK!
AAAIGH!
THAT'S FOR TREATING WOMEN LIKE PREY.
UGGH!
THIS IS FOR TERRORIZING MY FRIENDS!
KRUNCH!
AARGH!

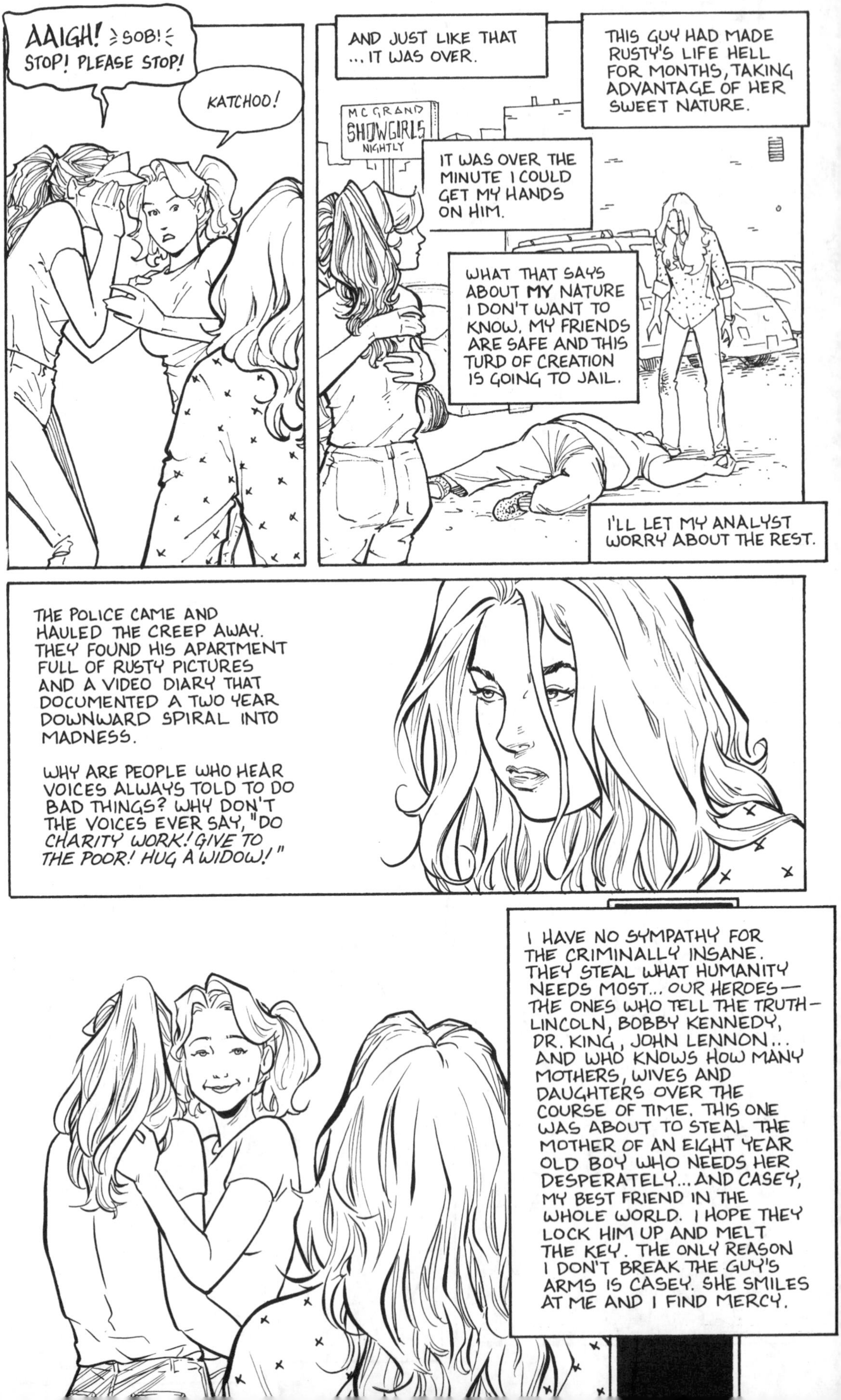
AAIGH! SOB! STOP! PLEASE STOP!
KATCHOO!
AND JUST LIKE THAT ... IT WAS OVER.
THIS GUY HAD MADE RUSTY'S LIFE HELL FOR MONTHS, TAKING ADVANTAGE OF HER SWEET NATURE.
MC GRAND SHOWGIRLS NIGHTLY
IT WAS OVER THE MINUTE I COULD GET MY HANDS ON HIM.
WHAT THAT SAYS ABOUT **MY** NATURE I DON'T WANT TO KNOW. MY FRIENDS ARE SAFE AND THIS TURD OF CREATION IS GOING TO JAIL.
I'LL LET MY ANALYST WORRY ABOUT THE REST.
THE POLICE CAME AND HAULED THE CREEP AWAY. THEY FOUND HIS APARTMENT FULL OF RUSTY PICTURES AND A VIDEO DIARY THAT DOCUMENTED A TWO YEAR DOWNWARD SPIRAL INTO MADNESS.
WHY ARE PEOPLE WHO HEAR VOICES ALWAYS TOLD TO DO BAD THINGS? WHY DON'T THE VOICES EVER SAY, "DO *CHARITY WORK! GIVE TO THE POOR! HUG A WIDOW!*"
I HAVE NO SYMPATHY FOR THE CRIMINALLY INSANE. THEY STEAL WHAT HUMANITY NEEDS MOST... OUR HEROES— THE ONES WHO TELL THE TRUTH— LINCOLN, BOBBY KENNEDY, DR. KING, JOHN LENNON... AND WHO KNOWS HOW MANY MOTHERS, WIVES AND DAUGHTERS OVER THE COURSE OF TIME. THIS ONE WAS ABOUT TO STEAL THE MOTHER OF AN EIGHT YEAR OLD BOY WHO NEEDS HER DESPERATELY... AND CASEY, MY BEST FRIEND IN THE WHOLE WORLD. I HOPE THEY LOCK HIM UP AND MELT THE KEY. THE ONLY REASON I DON'T BREAK THE GUY'S ARMS IS CASEY. SHE SMILES AT ME AND I FIND MERCY.

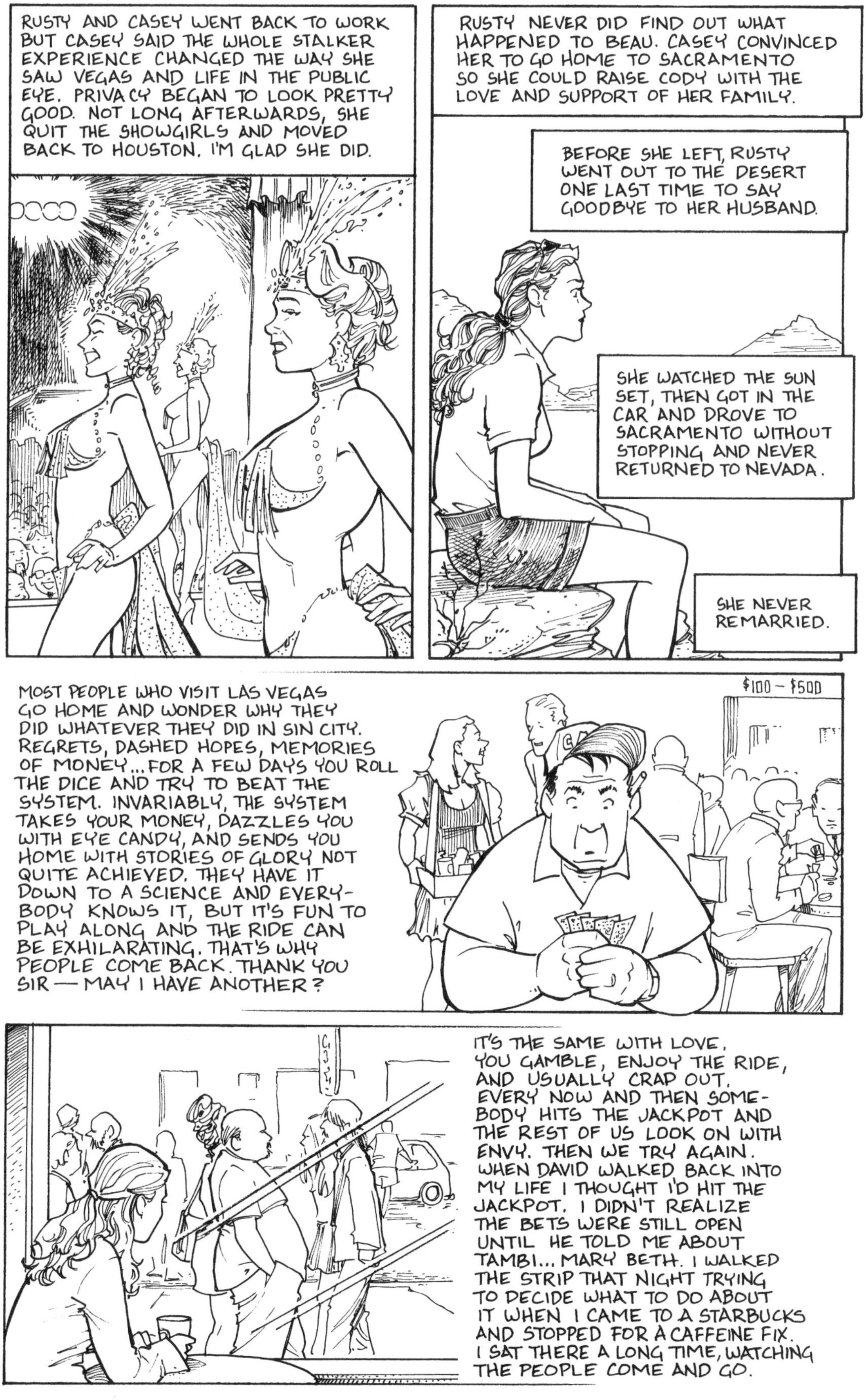
RUSTY AND CASEY WENT BACK TO WORK BUT CASEY SAID THE WHOLE STALKER EXPERIENCE CHANGED THE WAY SHE SAW VEGAS AND LIFE IN THE PUBLIC EYE. PRIVACY BEGAN TO LOOK PRETTY GOOD. NOT LONG AFTERWARDS, SHE QUIT THE SHOWGIRLS AND MOVED BACK TO HOUSTON. I'M GLAD SHE DID.
RUSTY NEVER DID FIND OUT WHAT HAPPENED TO BEAU. CASEY CONVINCED HER TO GO HOME TO SACRAMENTO SO SHE COULD RAISE CODY WITH THE LOVE AND SUPPORT OF HER FAMILY.
BEFORE SHE LEFT, RUSTY WENT OUT TO THE DESERT ONE LAST TIME TO SAY GOODBYE TO HER HUSBAND.
SHE WATCHED THE SUN SET, THEN GOT IN THE CAR AND DROVE TO SACRAMENTO WITHOUT STOPPING AND NEVER RETURNED TO NEVADA.
SHE NEVER REMARRIED.
MOST PEOPLE WHO VISIT LAS VEGAS GO HOME AND WONDER WHY THEY DID WHATEVER THEY DID IN SIN CITY. REGRETS, DASHED HOPES, MEMORIES OF MONEY... FOR A FEW DAYS YOU ROLL THE DICE AND TRY TO BEAT THE SYSTEM. INVARIABLY, THE SYSTEM TAKES YOUR MONEY, DAZZLES YOU WITH EYE CANDY, AND SENDS YOU HOME WITH STORIES OF GLORY NOT QUITE ACHIEVED. THEY HAVE IT DOWN TO A SCIENCE AND EVERYBODY KNOWS IT, BUT IT'S FUN TO PLAY ALONG AND THE RIDE CAN BE EXHILARATING. THAT'S WHY PEOPLE COME BACK. THANK YOU SIR — MAY I HAVE ANOTHER?
$100 – $500
IT'S THE SAME WITH LOVE. YOU GAMBLE, ENJOY THE RIDE, AND USUALLY CRAP OUT. EVERY NOW AND THEN SOMEBODY HITS THE JACKPOT AND THE REST OF US LOOK ON WITH ENVY. THEN WE TRY AGAIN. WHEN DAVID WALKED BACK INTO MY LIFE I THOUGHT I'D HIT THE JACKPOT. I DIDN'T REALIZE THE BETS WERE STILL OPEN UNTIL HE TOLD ME ABOUT TAMBI... MARY BETH. I WALKED THE STRIP THAT NIGHT TRYING TO DECIDE WHAT TO DO ABOUT IT WHEN I CAME TO A STARBUCKS AND STOPPED FOR A CAFFEINE FIX. I SAT THERE A LONG TIME, WATCHING THE PEOPLE COME AND GO.

DAVID HOLDS A SPECIAL PLACE IN MY HEART. HE ALWAYS WILL. I KNOW WHERE HE COMES FROM AND WHAT HE'S BEEN THROUGH. I KNOW HOW HARD IT'S BEEN FOR HIM. I KNOW HOW HARD HE TRIES TO DO THE RIGHT THING. AS MUCH AS THE CREEPY STALKER REPULSES ME, DAVID'S GOOD HEART AND STRONG SENSE OF HONOR ATTRACT ME.

I LOVE HIM.

BUT DO I LOVE HIM THE WAY RUSTY LOVES BEAU? DO I NEED HIM TO COMPLETE ME LIKE RENEE ZELLWEGER? I COULD GET PAST DAVID SLEEPING WITH MY SISTER... AFTER ALL, I'D SLEPT WITH HIS.

THEN THE TRUTH HIT ME LIKE A TON OF BRICKS: *SEX WITH DARCY HAD BEEN BETTER THAN SEX WITH DAVID! LIKE, NO COMPARISON BETTER!*

WHEN I REALIZED WHAT THIS MEANT MY HEART SKIPPED A BEAT. OR MAYBE IT WAS JUST THE CAFFEINE, WHATEVER. IT BEGAN TO DAWN ON ME THAT WHILE I'D BEEN SITTING THERE PEOPLE WATCHING I'D TAKEN INVENTORY OF EVERY WOMAN WHO WALKED BY WHILE THE MEN HAD BEEN INVISIBLE. NOT ONE MAN HAD CAUGHT MY EYE, BUT I COULD RECALL DOZENS OF WOMEN FROM THE PAST HOUR, WHAT THEY WORE, AND WHAT I THOUGHT OF THEM IN RELATION TO ME. AT LEAST SIX HAD STRUCK ME AS WOMEN I'D LIKE TO KNOW AND TWO OF THOSE COULD HAVE ASKED ME TO "DANCE" AND I'D HAVE DONE IT RIGHT THEN AND THERE.

MY CUP WAS EMPTY AND MY SPIRIT RELAXED... AT PEACE. I FELT LIKE A GREAT WEIGHT HAD BEEN LIFTED FROM ME. I FELT... FREE.

ON IMPULSE I WALKED ACROSS THE STREET TO A TATTOO PARLOR AND SELECTED A SYMBOL OF MY NEWLY REALIZED IDENTITY.... PILGRIM. EACH OF THE TWO TATTOOS I ALREADY HAD REPRESENTED A DISTINCT PERIOD IN MY LIFE — ONE FOR *PASSION*, THE OTHER *POSSESSION*. THE THIRD TATTOO WOULD BE MY LAST... *PILGRIMAGE*.
I'D WEAR IT LIKE A WAR MEDAL. IT WOULD REMIND ME TO FIND MY OWN WAY IN THIS WORLD, TO LISTEN TO MY HEART AND GO WHERE IT LEADS ME, EVEN IF IT'S TO PLACES WHERE OTHERS WON'T GO.

BY THE TIME I GOT BACK TO THE HOTEL IT WAS ALMOST FOUR IN THE MORNING. I SLEPT LATE AND WOKE UP SORE. MY JEANS WERE TOO PAINFUL TO ZIP UP SO I WAS FORCED TO HOBBLE DOWNSTAIRS AND PROWL THE SHOPS FOR A DRESS.

I ENDED UP WITH A YELLOW SUN DRESS (I KNOW, I HATE YELLOW, BUT THE ALTERNATIVE WAS *PINK!*) AND A PAIR OF FLIP FLOPS. I LOOKED LIKE A TEEN PRINCESS BUT I WAS COMFY. THE COOL BREEZE ON MY LEGS MADE ME WONDER WHY I ALWAYS WEAR JEANS, EVEN DURING THE SUMMER. MAYBE IT WAS TIME TO RETHINK THAT.

MY BAG WAS PACKED AND I HAD ABOUT AN HOUR BEFORE I NEEDED TO CHECK OUT AND HEAD FOR THE AIRPORT. I CALLED DAVID'S ROOM, THE ONE HE GOT WHEN RUSTY AND CODY CAME TO STAY IN OUR ROOM. DAVID ANSWERED ON THE FIRST RING. I ASKED HIM TO MEET ME ON THE SUN DECK IN FIFTEEN MINUTES, THEN I WENT INTO THE BATHROOM TO REMOVE MY BANDAGE. I SHOULD HAVE REMOVED IT EARLIER THAT MORNING, BUT THEN I WOULD HAVE HAD TO GO DOWNSTAIRS NAKED BECAUSE I'M TELLING YOU, THERE'S *NO WAY* THOSE JEANS WERE GOING ANYWHERE NEAR THIS THING. I RINSED MY BACKSIDE WITH COLD WATER AND GENTLY BLOTTED IT DRY BEFORE APPLYING A THIN LAYER OF BACITRACIN TO THE ENTIRE AREA. I WOULD HAVE TO REPEAT THIS PRO- CEDURE FOUR TIMES A DAY FOR A WEEK, KEEPING THE TAT SLIGHTLY MOIST WITH BACITRACIN AND OPEN TO THE AIR — NO BANDAGE FROM HERE ON. I DREADED THE FLIGHT HOME — THREE HOURS IN A BURLAP CHAIR WITH A SEATBELT FOR ADDED PAIN.

WHEN I GOT TO THE SUN DECK, DAVID WAS WAITING FOR ME. AS I STROLLED OVER TO HIM I FELT TRANQUIL AND CALM, AT PEACE WITH THE WORLD, WHILE EVERY STEP PRODUCED A STINGING REMINDER OF MY OVER- NIGHT DECLARATION OF INDEPENDENCE.

DAVID TOOK ONE LOOK AT MY FACE AND KNEW WHAT I WAS GOING TO SAY. I SAW HIS SMILE FADE.

"IT'S OVER, ISN'T IT?"

"I'M SORRY."

"NO, IT'S OKAY. IT'S TOO MUCH. TOO MUCH HISTORY."

"NOT REALLY. I THINK IF IT'S A CHOICE BETWEEN LOVE AND HISTORY YOU CAN THROW HISTORY OUT THE WINDOW. I'M NOT GOING TO HOLD THE PAST AGAINST YOU, DAVID. YOU'VE NEVER HELD IT AGAINST ME AND GOD KNOWS YOU HAVE PLENTY TO WORK WITH."

"I LOVE YOU, KATCHOO."

"I KNOW. I LOVE YOU, TOO."

"DO YOU STILL HAVE THE LICENSE APPLICATION?"

"YEAH. I THINK I'LL KEEP IT...SOUVENIR. MAYBE SEE WHAT IT'LL BRING ON EBAY."

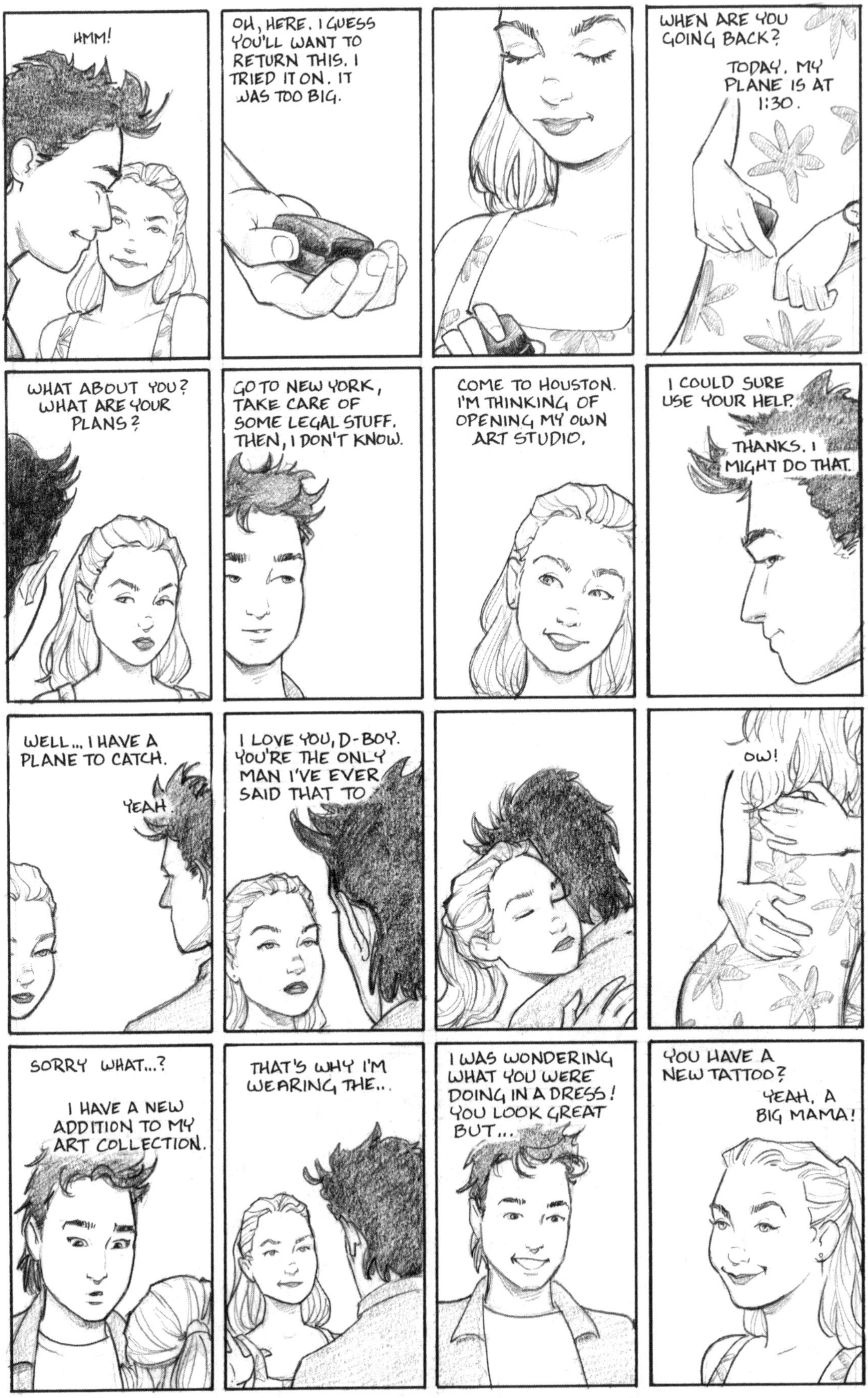
HMM!
OH, HERE. I GUESS YOU'LL WANT TO RETURN THIS. I TRIED IT ON. IT WAS TOO BIG.
WHEN ARE YOU GOING BACK?
TODAY. MY PLANE IS AT 1:30.
WHAT ABOUT YOU? WHAT ARE YOUR PLANS?
GO TO NEW YORK, TAKE CARE OF SOME LEGAL STUFF. THEN, I DON'T KNOW.
COME TO HOUSTON. I'M THINKING OF OPENING MY OWN ART STUDIO.
I COULD SURE USE YOUR HELP.
THANKS. I MIGHT DO THAT.
WELL... I HAVE A PLANE TO CATCH.
YEAH.
I LOVE YOU, D-BOY. YOU'RE THE ONLY MAN I'VE EVER SAID THAT TO.
OW!
SORRY WHAT...?
I HAVE A NEW ADDITION TO MY ART COLLECTION.
THAT'S WHY I'M WEARING THE..
I WAS WONDERING WHAT YOU WERE DOING IN A DRESS! YOU LOOK GREAT BUT...
YOU HAVE A NEW TATTOO?
YEAH. A BIG MAMA!

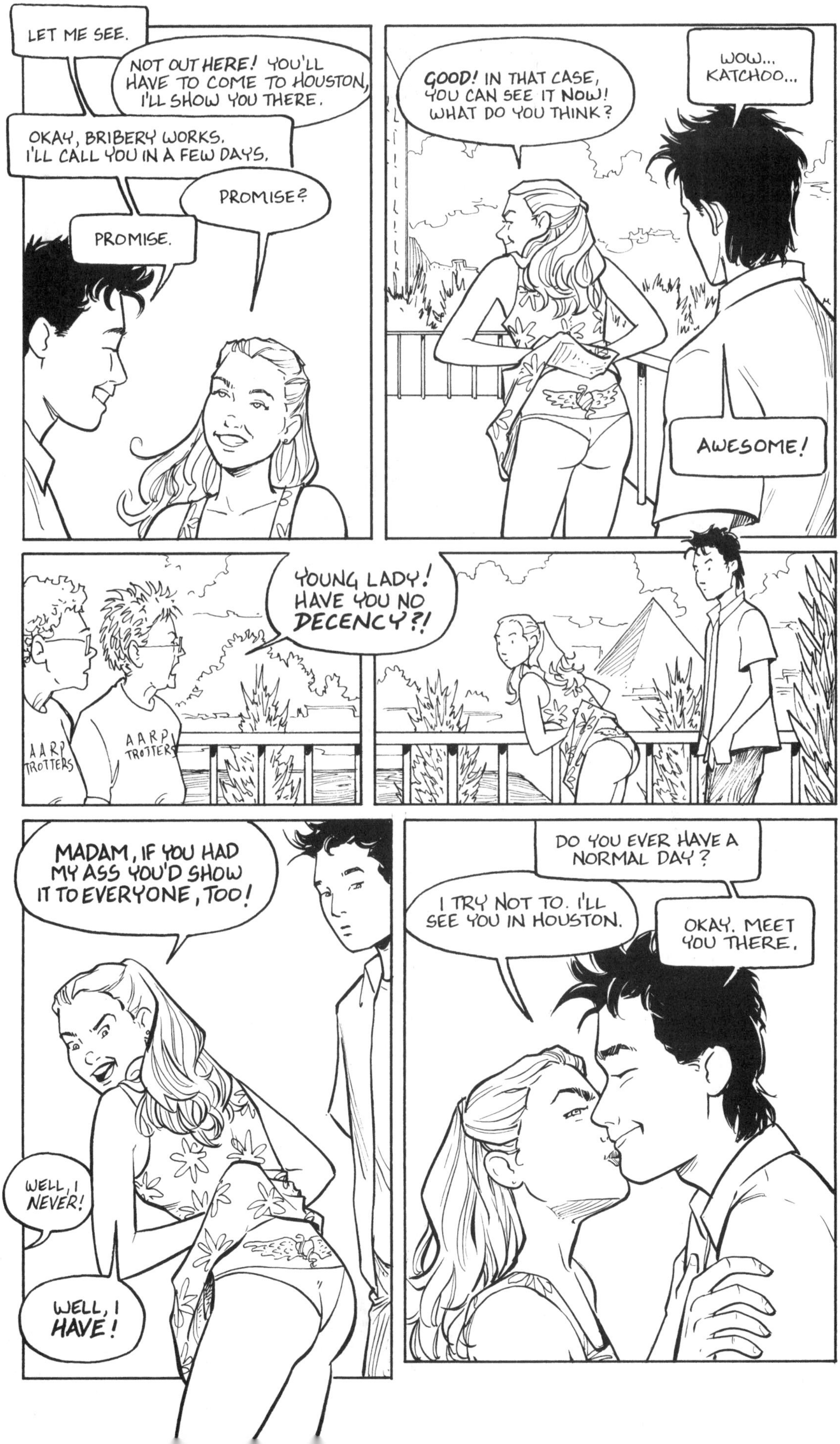
LET ME SEE.
NOT OUT HERE! YOU'LL HAVE TO COME TO HOUSTON, I'LL SHOW YOU THERE.
OKAY, BRIBERY WORKS. I'LL CALL YOU IN A FEW DAYS.
PROMISE?
PROMISE.
GOOD! IN THAT CASE, YOU CAN SEE IT NOW! WHAT DO YOU THINK?
WOW... KATCHOO...
AWESOME!
YOUNG LADY! HAVE YOU NO DECENCY?!
AARP TROTTERS
AARP TROTTERS
MADAM, IF YOU HAD MY ASS YOU'D SHOW IT TO EVERYONE, TOO!
WELL, I NEVER!
WELL, I HAVE!
DO YOU EVER HAVE A NORMAL DAY?
I TRY NOT TO. I'LL SEE YOU IN HOUSTON.
OKAY. MEET YOU THERE.

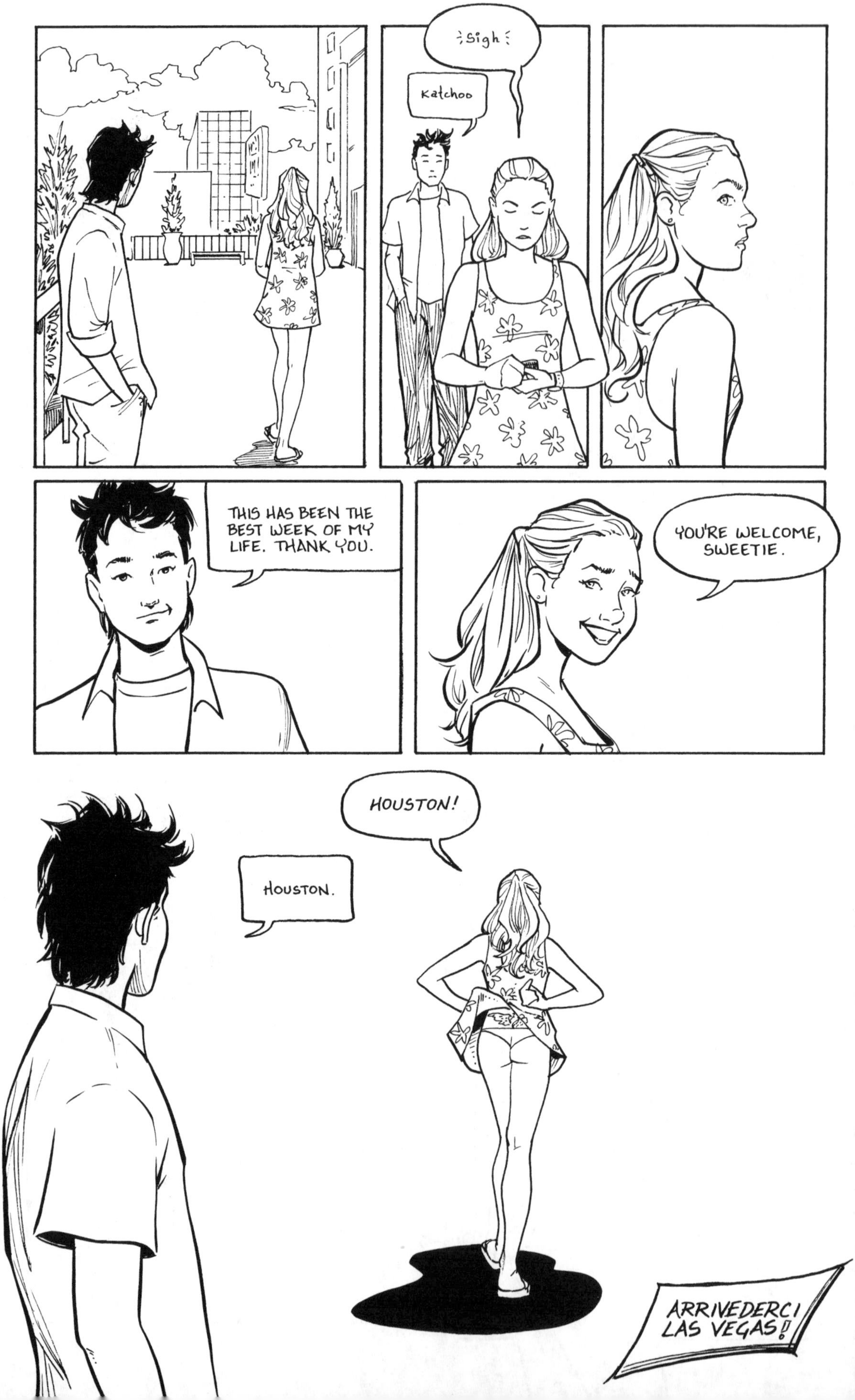
Katchoo
Sigh
THIS HAS BEEN THE BEST WEEK OF MY LIFE. THANK YOU.
YOU'RE WELCOME, SWEETIE.
HOUSTON!
HOUSTON.
ARRIVEDERCI LAS VEGAS!

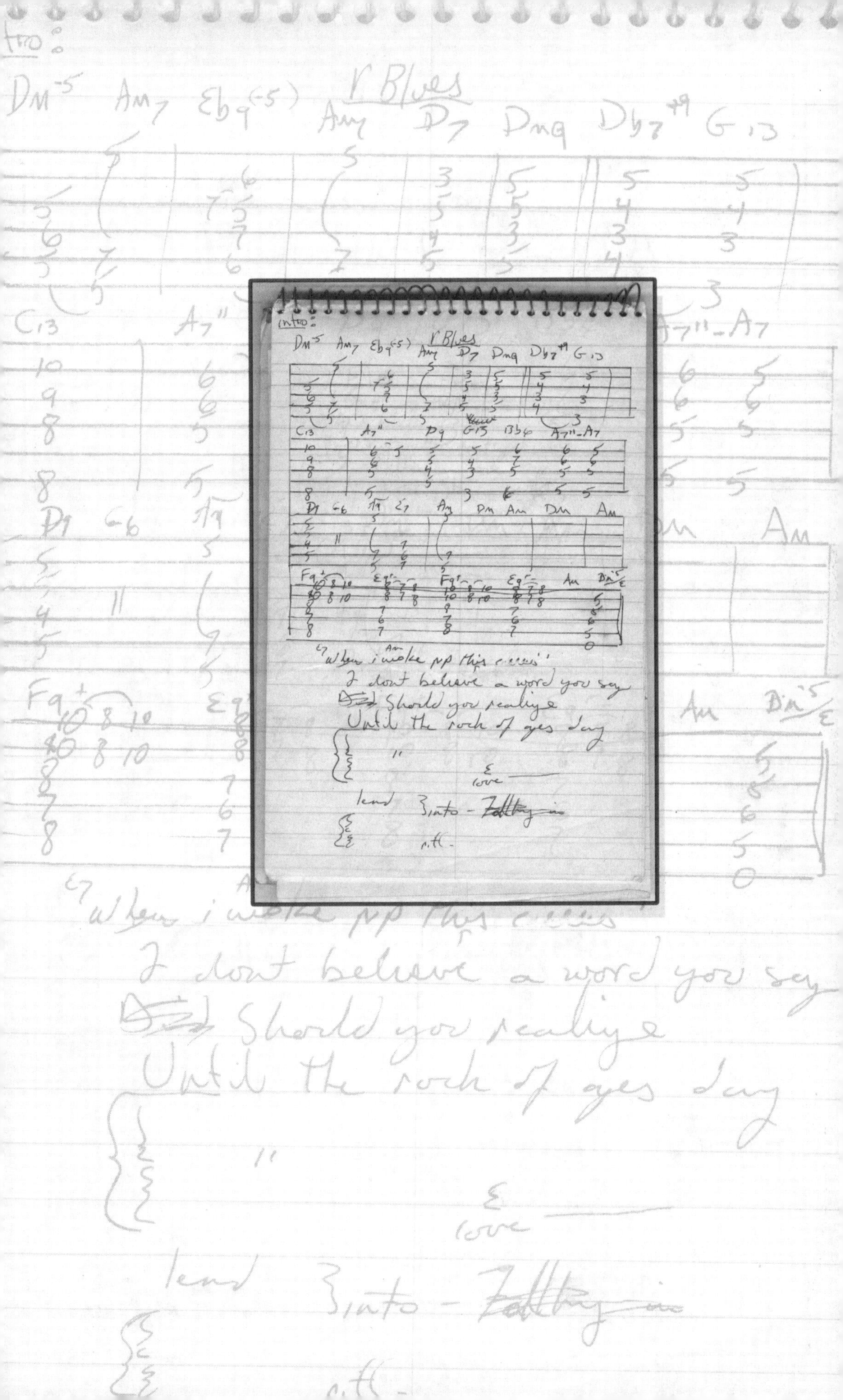

Dm^{-5} Am$_7$ Eb$_9$$^{(-5)}$ V Blues

Am$_7$ D$_7$ Dm$_9$ Db$_7$$^{+9}$ G$_{13}$

C$_{13}$ A$_7$^{11} ... A$_7$^{11} – A$_7$

D$_7$ G$_6$ ... Dm   Am

Fe$_9$$^+$ E$_9$ ...   Am   Dm^{-5}

"When i woke up this morning"
I don't believe a word you say
Should you realize
Until the rock of yes day

love ———

lead   3 into –

r.h. –

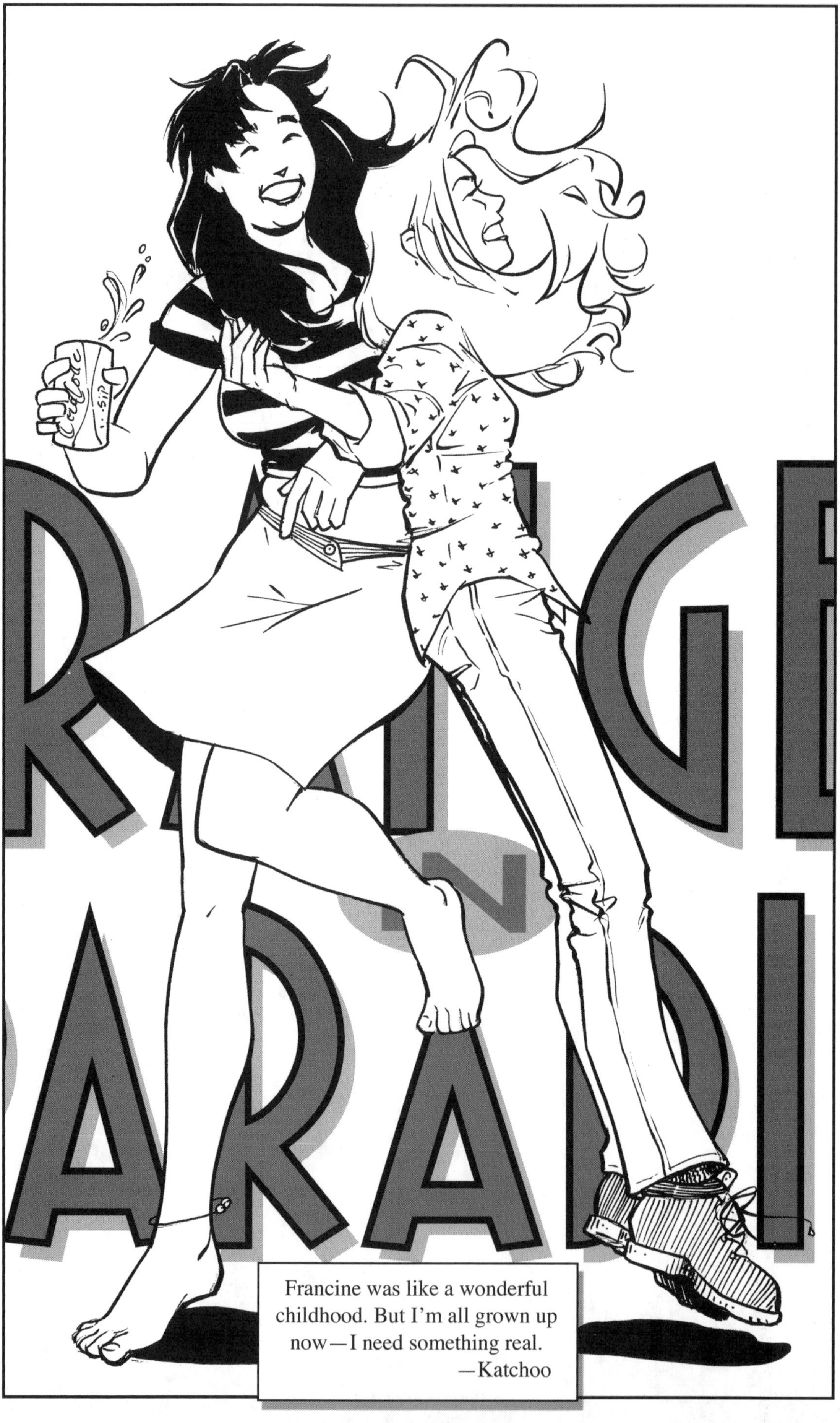
Francine was like a wonderful childhood. But I'm all grown up now—I need something real.
—Katchoo

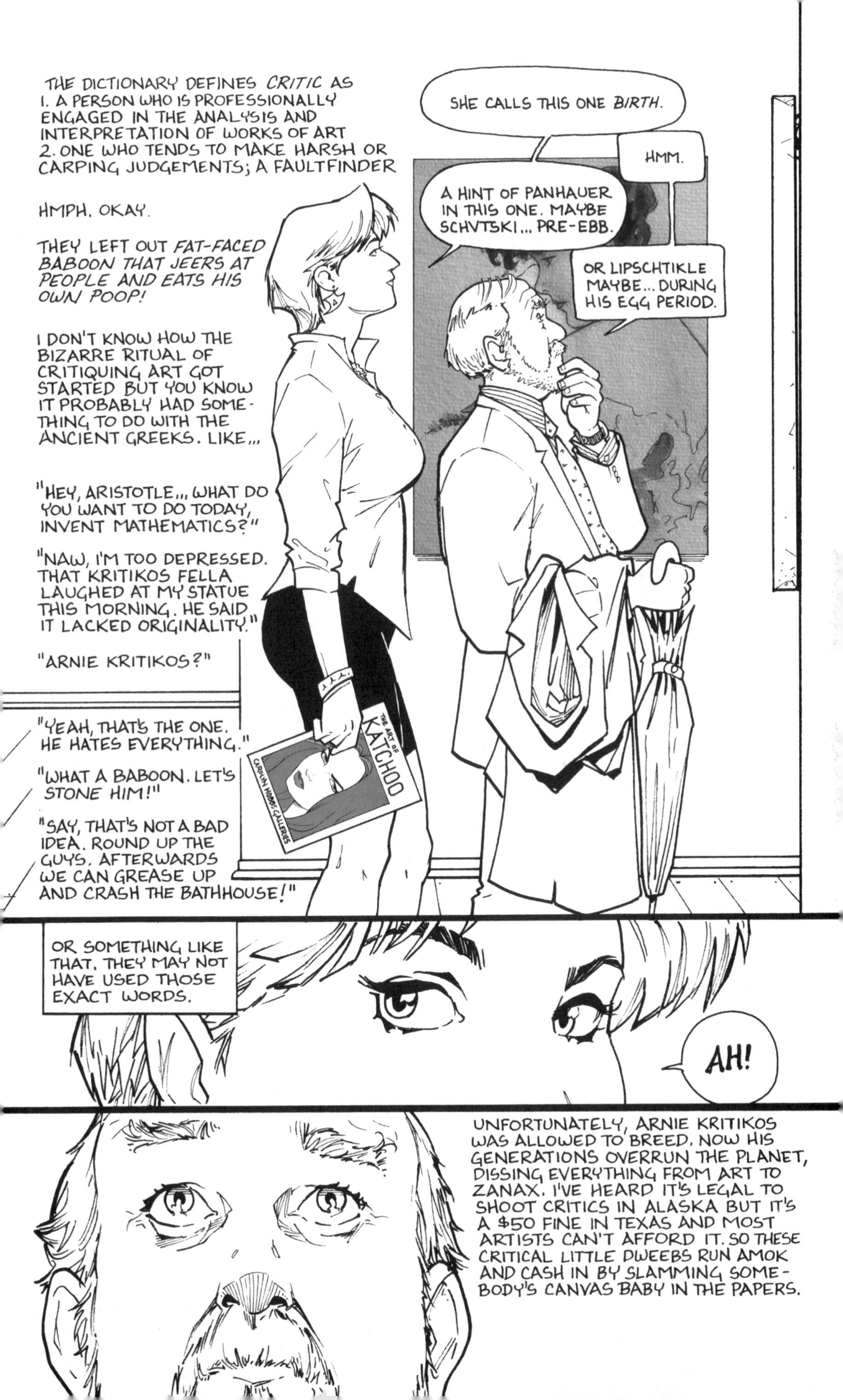
THE DICTIONARY DEFINES CRITIC AS 1. A PERSON WHO IS PROFESSIONALLY ENGAGED IN THE ANALYSIS AND INTERPRETATION OF WORKS OF ART 2. ONE WHO TENDS TO MAKE HARSH OR CARPING JUDGEMENTS; A FAULTFINDER
HMPH. OKAY.
THEY LEFT OUT FAT-FACED BABOON THAT JEERS AT PEOPLE AND EATS HIS OWN POOP!
I DON'T KNOW HOW THE BIZARRE RITUAL OF CRITIQUING ART GOT STARTED BUT YOU KNOW IT PROBABLY HAD SOMETHING TO DO WITH THE ANCIENT GREEKS. LIKE...
"HEY, ARISTOTLE... WHAT DO YOU WANT TO DO TODAY, INVENT MATHEMATICS?"
"NAW, I'M TOO DEPRESSED. THAT KRITIKOS FELLA LAUGHED AT MY STATUE THIS MORNING. HE SAID IT LACKED ORIGINALITY."
"ARNIE KRITIKOS?"
"YEAH, THAT'S THE ONE. HE HATES EVERYTHING."
"WHAT A BABOON. LET'S STONE HIM!"
"SAY, THAT'S NOT A BAD IDEA. ROUND UP THE GUYS. AFTERWARDS WE CAN GREASE UP AND CRASH THE BATHHOUSE!"
SHE CALLS THIS ONE BIRTH.
HMM.
A HINT OF PANHAUER IN THIS ONE. MAYBE SCHVTSKI... PRE-EBB.
OR LIPSCHTIKLE MAYBE... DURING HIS EGG PERIOD.
THE ART OF KATCHOO
CAROLYN HOBBS GALLERIES
OR SOMETHING LIKE THAT. THEY MAY NOT HAVE USED THOSE EXACT WORDS.
AH!
UNFORTUNATELY, ARNIE KRITIKOS WAS ALLOWED TO BREED. NOW HIS GENERATIONS OVERRUN THE PLANET, DISSING EVERYTHING FROM ART TO ZANAX. I'VE HEARD IT'S LEGAL TO SHOOT CRITICS IN ALASKA BUT IT'S A $50 FINE IN TEXAS AND MOST ARTISTS CAN'T AFFORD IT. SO THESE CRITICAL LITTLE DWEEBS RUN AMOK AND CASH IN BY SLAMMING SOMEBODY'S CANVAS BABY IN THE PAPERS.

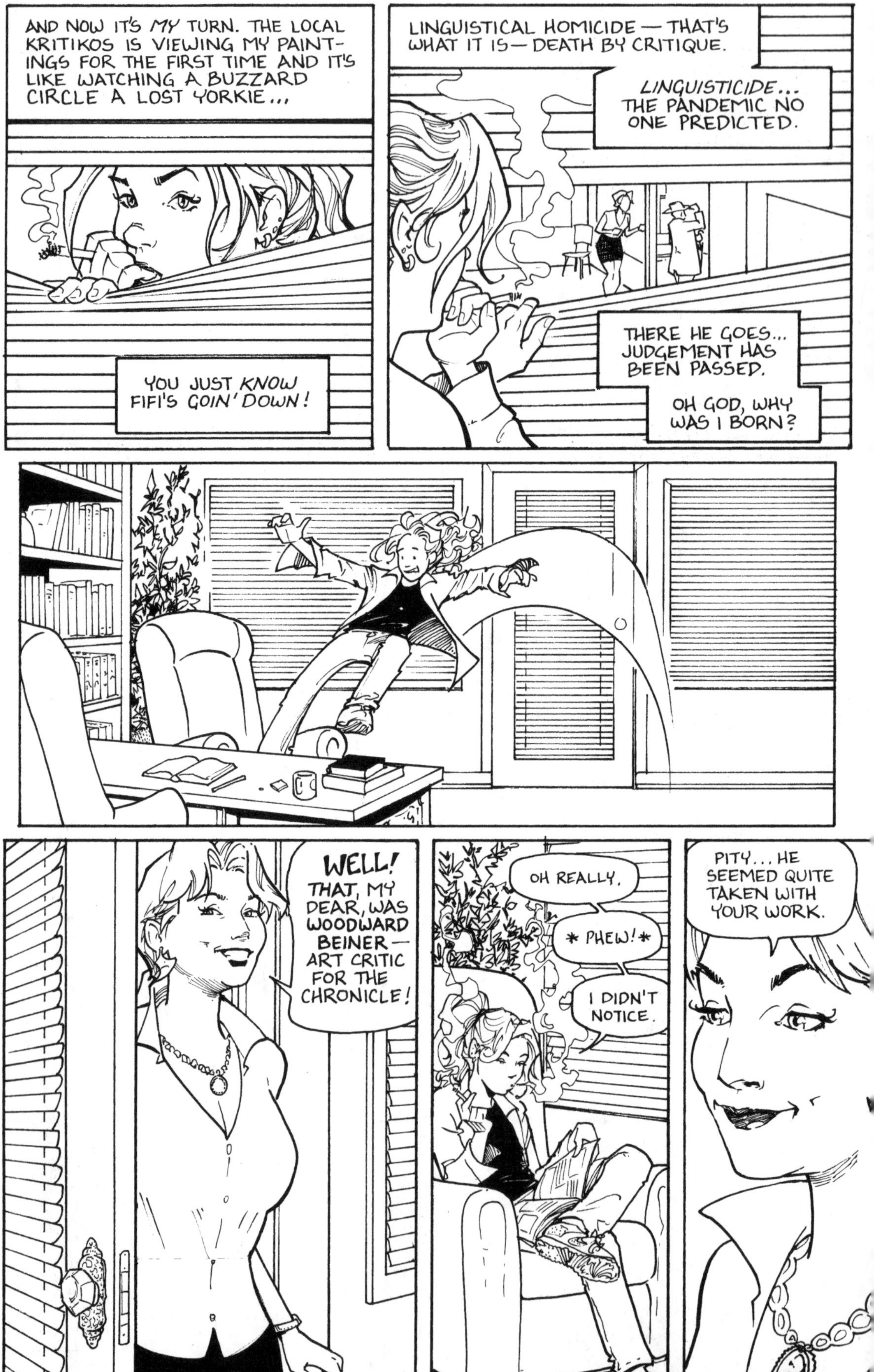
AND NOW IT'S MY TURN. THE LOCAL KRITIKOS IS VIEWING MY PAINTINGS FOR THE FIRST TIME AND IT'S LIKE WATCHING A BUZZARD CIRCLE A LOST YORKIE...
YOU JUST KNOW FIFI'S GOIN' DOWN!
LINGUISTICAL HOMICIDE — THAT'S WHAT IT IS — DEATH BY CRITIQUE.
LINGUISTICIDE... THE PANDEMIC NO ONE PREDICTED.
THERE HE GOES... JUDGEMENT HAS BEEN PASSED.
OH GOD, WHY WAS I BORN?
WELL! THAT, MY DEAR, WAS WOODWARD BEINER — ART CRITIC FOR THE CHRONICLE!
OH REALLY.
* PHEW! *
I DIDN'T NOTICE.
PITY... HE SEEMED QUITE TAKEN WITH YOUR WORK.

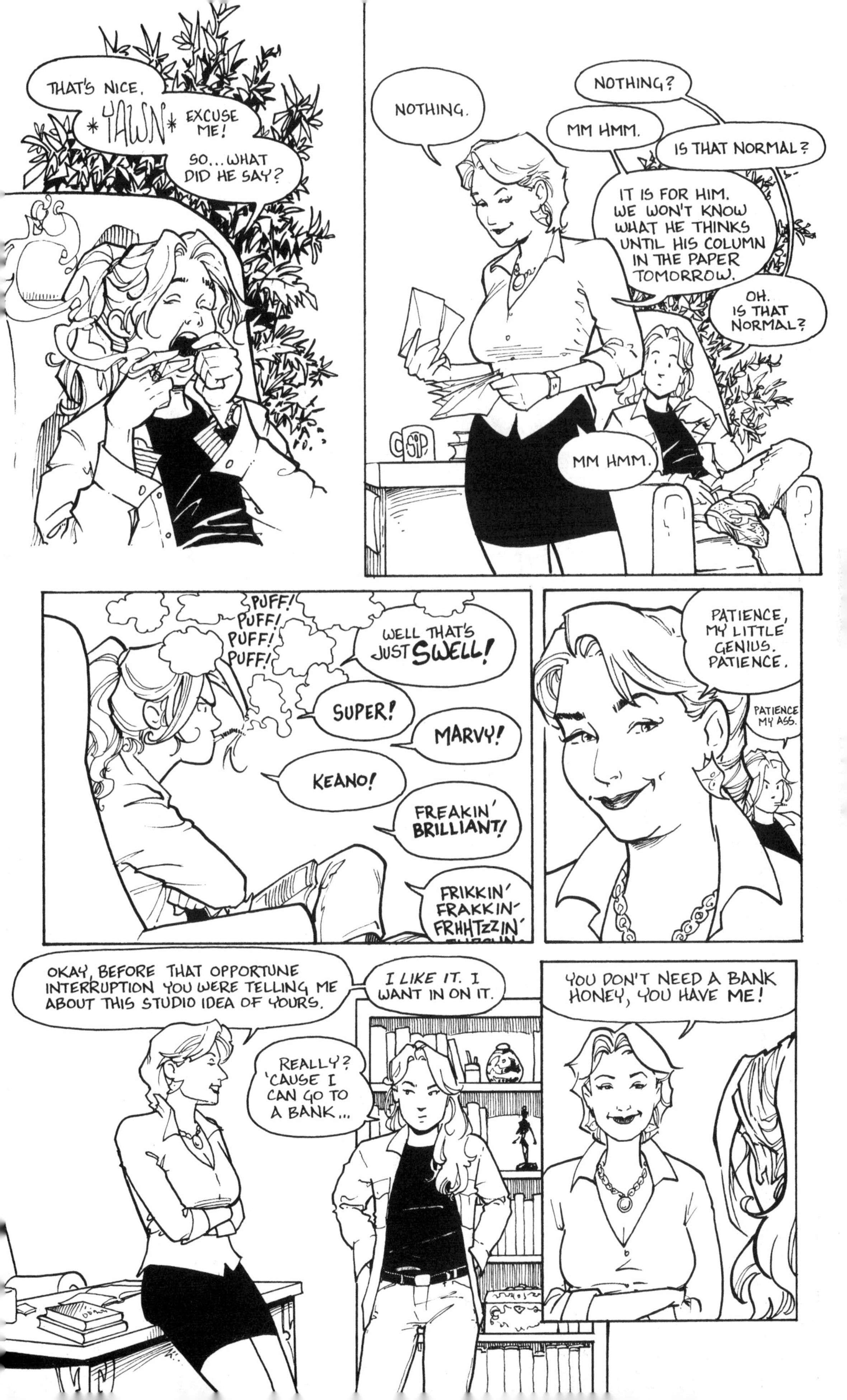
THAT'S NICE.
YAWN
EXCUSE ME!
SO...WHAT DID HE SAY?
NOTHING.
NOTHING?
MM HMM.
IS THAT NORMAL?
IT IS FOR HIM. WE WON'T KNOW WHAT HE THINKS UNTIL HIS COLUMN IN THE PAPER TOMORROW.
OH. IS THAT NORMAL?
MM HMM.
PUFF! PUFF! PUFF! PUFF!
WELL THAT'S JUST SWELL!
SUPER!
MARVY!
KEANO!
FREAKIN' BRILLIANT!
FRIKKIN' FRAKKIN' FRHHTZZIN'
PATIENCE, MY LITTLE GENIUS. PATIENCE.
PATIENCE MY ASS.
OKAY, BEFORE THAT OPPORTUNE INTERRUPTION YOU WERE TELLING ME ABOUT THIS STUDIO IDEA OF YOURS.
I LIKE IT. I WANT IN ON IT.
REALLY? 'CAUSE I CAN GO TO A BANK...
YOU DON'T NEED A BANK HONEY, YOU HAVE ME!

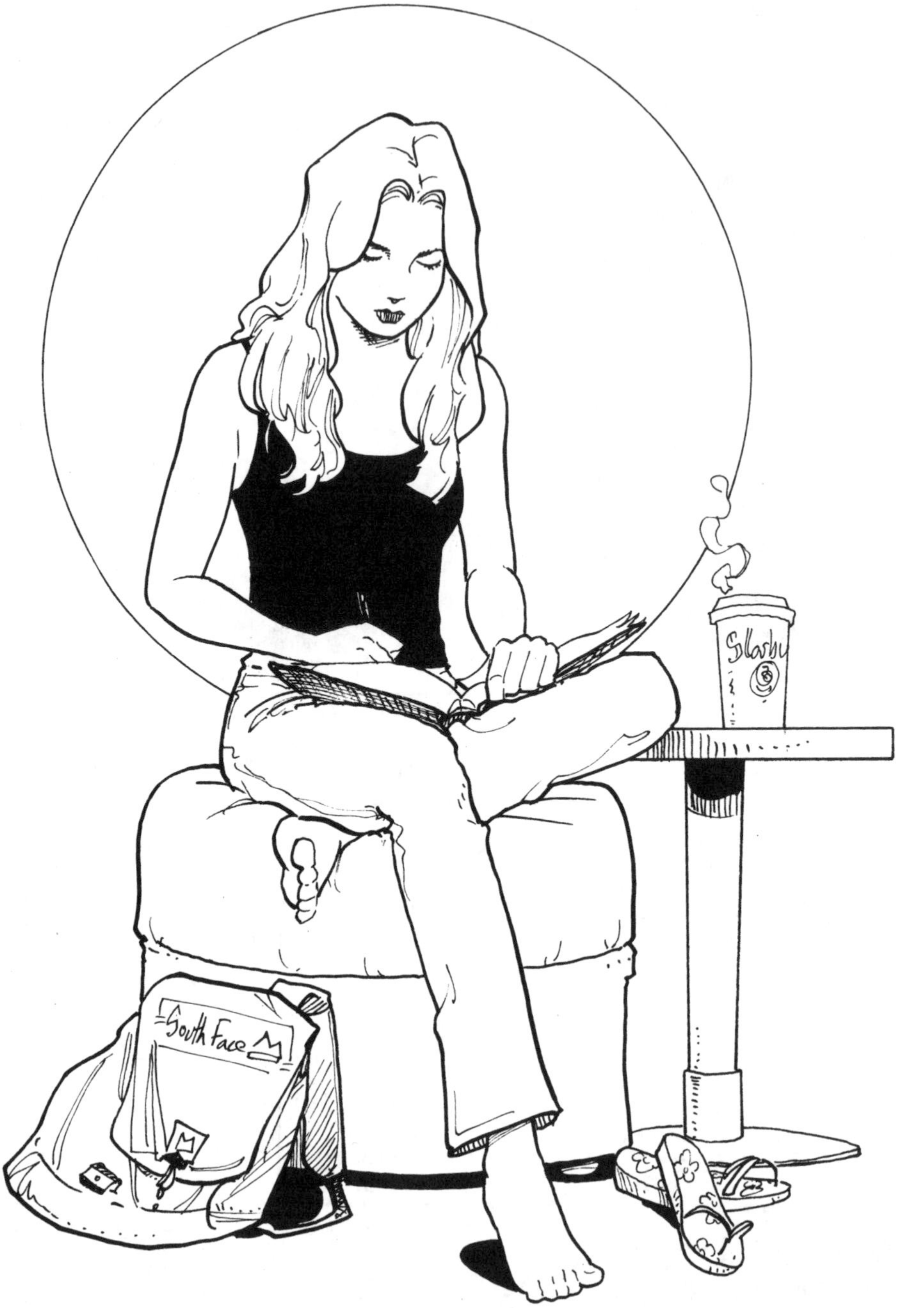
South Face

Actually, I did need a bank, I was bluffing about that, but I had no intentions of milking Carolyn to fund my ambitions. Carolyn had been nothing but kind to me from the day we met. She was a smart businesswoman who worked hard and had a lot on the ball. True, she seemed to have a fondness for patting me on the butt a little too often, but I guess I could live with that. We all have our eccentricities.

The fact is, I was starting over and Carolyn's galleries played an important part in all that. I was determined to make something of my art and I wasn't getting any younger. When I think about all the time I wasted running around doing everything except art...making a mess of my life and Francine's...maybe David's...God, I can't think about it. It's too much.

Anyway, back to the bank thing. I needed one because I was broke. How did that happen, you ask? It's a long story but I'll give you the Reader's Digest version.

WHEN I GOT BACK FROM VEGAS I HAD NO PROSPECTS AND ONE WEEK LEFT ON THE TWO BEDROOM APARTMENT I SHARED WITH CASEY. OR I SHOULD SAY *USED TO SHARE* UNTIL SHE MOVED TO LAS VEGAS TO BECOME A SHOWGIRL.
I ALSO HAD A NEW TATTOO AND AN IDEA I CALLED STUDIO KATCHOO.
AUSTIN CITY LIM
GRIFFIN SILVER (PBS)
STUDIO KATCHOO. I PICTURED IT AS A WORKING AND TEACHING STUDIO. LOTS OF ROOMS FOR DIFFERENT GROUPS AND PROJECTS. CLASSES FOR THE ASPIRING ARTISTS, STUDIO SPACE FOR WORKING ARTISTS. SOMETHING FOR EVERYONE.
EVERYONE INTERESTED IN ART, THAT IS.
I WROTE UP MY IDEA AND DECIDED TO WITHDRAW SOME OF MY "FAMILY MONEY" TO MAKE IT HAPPEN.
FIRST THING MONDAY MORNING I WENT TO THE BANK AND DISCOVERED THAT THE COMPANY I'D SET UP WITH TAMBI NO LONGER EXISTED — AND NEITHER DID ITS CONSIDERABLE ASSETS.
AFTER THE INITIAL SHOCK, I REALIZED THE FEDS HAD TAKEN IT AS PART OF THE DEAL TAMBI MADE TO KEEP ME OUT OF PRISON. SO... HERE I WAS... FREE. BROKE, BUT FREE. WHOOPEE.
IT SURE DIDN'T TAKE THEM LONG TO CLEAN HOUSE. TAMBI MADE THAT DEAL NOT EVEN TWO WEEKS AGO. I'D BEEN SO DISTRACTED WITH DAVID AND CASEY AND ALL THAT STUFF IN VEGAS, I DIDN'T TAKE THE TIME TO PREPARE FOR THE FEDERAL TORNADO THAT CAME THROUGH AND WIPED ME OUT. NADA. ZIP. ZERO. NOTHING.
I COULD HAVE TAKEN SOME OF THAT MONEY AND MOVED IT TO A SAFE PLACE — BUT NOOO — I HAD TO GO TO SIN CITY WITH DAVID AND HAVE MY VERY OWN *"LOST WEEKEND"*!
IDIOT.
L
BANG
PRESIDENT LOSERS CLUB

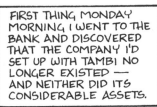

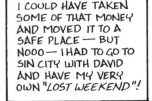

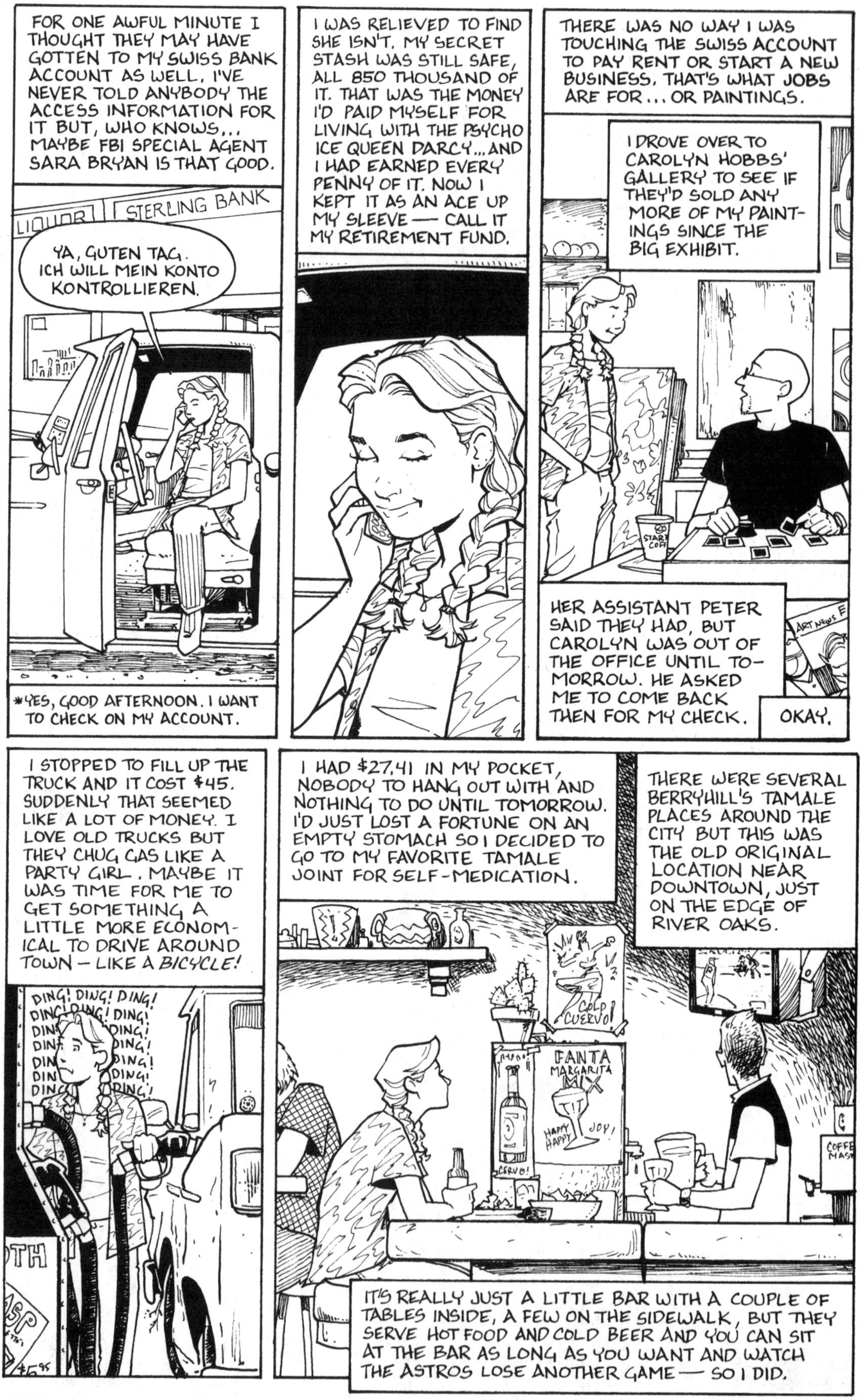
FOR ONE AWFUL MINUTE I THOUGHT THEY MAY HAVE GOTTEN TO MY SWISS BANK ACCOUNT AS WELL. I'VE NEVER TOLD ANYBODY THE ACCESS INFORMATION FOR IT BUT, WHO KNOWS... MAYBE FBI SPECIAL AGENT SARA BRYAN IS THAT GOOD.
LIQUOR
STERLING BANK
YA, GUTEN TAG. ICH WILL MEIN KONTO KONTROLLIEREN.
*YES, GOOD AFTERNOON. I WANT TO CHECK ON MY ACCOUNT.
I WAS RELIEVED TO FIND SHE ISN'T. MY SECRET STASH WAS STILL SAFE, ALL 850 THOUSAND OF IT. THAT WAS THE MONEY I'D PAID MYSELF FOR LIVING WITH THE PSYCHO ICE QUEEN DARCY... AND I HAD EARNED EVERY PENNY OF IT. NOW I KEPT IT AS AN ACE UP MY SLEEVE — CALL IT MY RETIREMENT FUND.
THERE WAS NO WAY I WAS TOUCHING THE SWISS ACCOUNT TO PAY RENT OR START A NEW BUSINESS. THAT'S WHAT JOBS ARE FOR... OR PAINTINGS.
I DROVE OVER TO CAROLYN HOBBS' GALLERY TO SEE IF THEY'D SOLD ANY MORE OF MY PAINTINGS SINCE THE BIG EXHIBIT.
HER ASSISTANT PETER SAID THEY HAD, BUT CAROLYN WAS OUT OF THE OFFICE UNTIL TOMORROW. HE ASKED ME TO COME BACK THEN FOR MY CHECK.
OKAY.
ART NEWS
I STOPPED TO FILL UP THE TRUCK AND IT COST $45. SUDDENLY THAT SEEMED LIKE A LOT OF MONEY. I LOVE OLD TRUCKS BUT THEY CHUG GAS LIKE A PARTY GIRL. MAYBE IT WAS TIME FOR ME TO GET SOMETHING A LITTLE MORE ECONOMICAL TO DRIVE AROUND TOWN — LIKE A *BICYCLE*!
DING! DING! DING!
DING! DING! DING!
I HAD $27.41 IN MY POCKET, NOBODY TO HANG OUT WITH AND NOTHING TO DO UNTIL TOMORROW. I'D JUST LOST A FORTUNE ON AN EMPTY STOMACH SO I DECIDED TO GO TO MY FAVORITE TAMALE JOINT FOR SELF-MEDICATION.
THERE WERE SEVERAL BERRYHILL'S TAMALE PLACES AROUND THE CITY BUT THIS WAS THE OLD ORIGINAL LOCATION NEAR DOWNTOWN, JUST ON THE EDGE OF RIVER OAKS.
COLD CUERVO!
FANTA MARGARITA MIX
HAPPY HAPPY JOY!
CUERVO!
IT'S REALLY JUST A LITTLE BAR WITH A COUPLE OF TABLES INSIDE, A FEW ON THE SIDEWALK, BUT THEY SERVE HOT FOOD AND COLD BEER AND YOU CAN SIT AT THE BAR AS LONG AS YOU WANT AND WATCH THE ASTROS LOSE ANOTHER GAME — SO I DID.

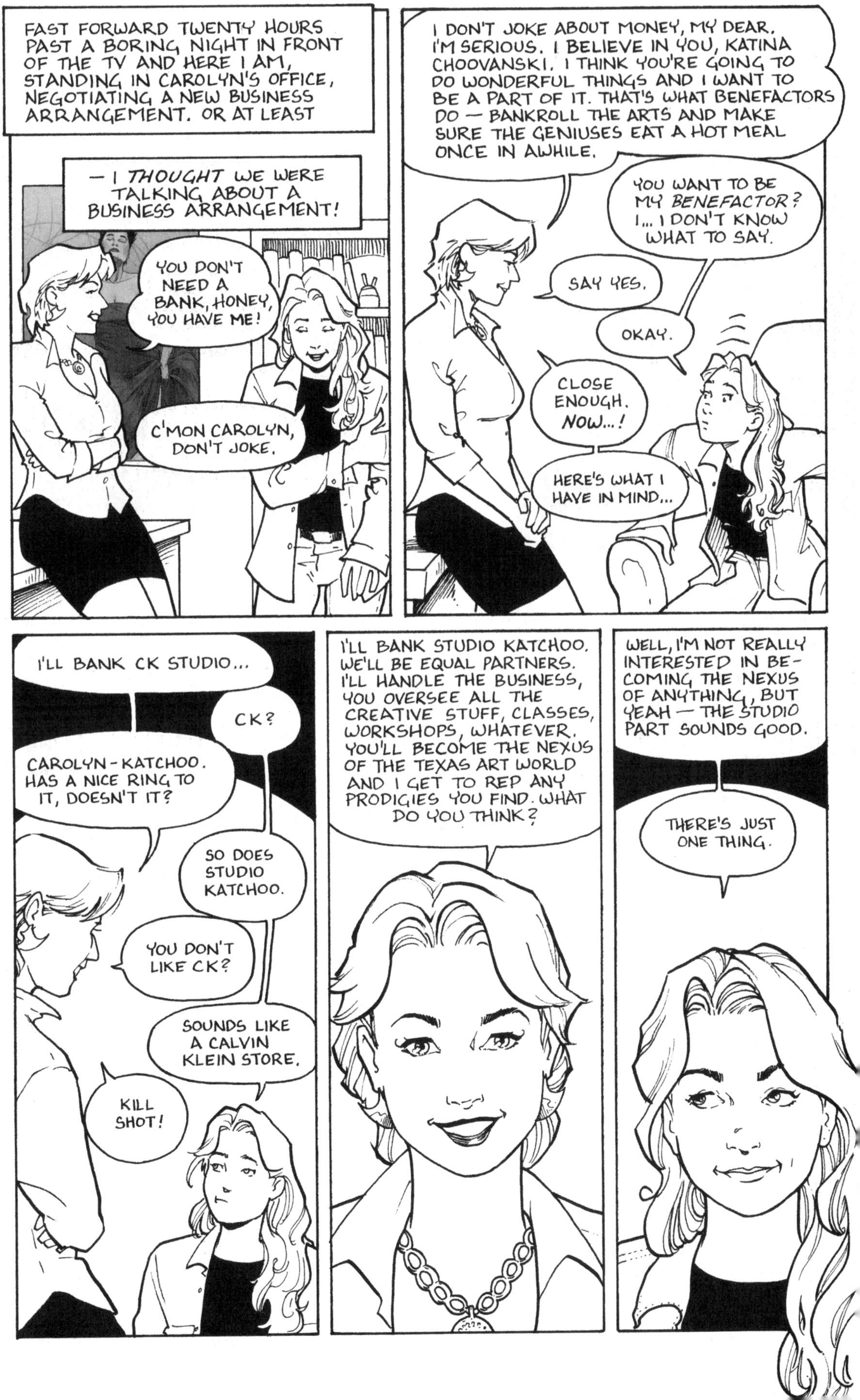
FAST FORWARD TWENTY HOURS PAST A BORING NIGHT IN FRONT OF THE TV AND HERE I AM, STANDING IN CAROLYN'S OFFICE, NEGOTIATING A NEW BUSINESS ARRANGEMENT. OR AT LEAST
— I THOUGHT WE WERE TALKING ABOUT A BUSINESS ARRANGEMENT!
YOU DON'T NEED A BANK, HONEY, YOU HAVE ME!
C'MON CAROLYN, DON'T JOKE.
I DON'T JOKE ABOUT MONEY, MY DEAR. I'M SERIOUS. I BELIEVE IN YOU, KATINA CHOOVANSKI. I THINK YOU'RE GOING TO DO WONDERFUL THINGS AND I WANT TO BE A PART OF IT. THAT'S WHAT BENEFACTORS DO — BANKROLL THE ARTS AND MAKE SURE THE GENIUSES EAT A HOT MEAL ONCE IN AWHILE.
YOU WANT TO BE MY BENEFACTOR? I... I DON'T KNOW WHAT TO SAY.
SAY YES.
OKAY.
CLOSE ENOUGH. NOW...!
HERE'S WHAT I HAVE IN MIND...
I'LL BANK CK STUDIO...
CK?
CAROLYN-KATCHOO. HAS A NICE RING TO IT, DOESN'T IT?
SO DOES STUDIO KATCHOO.
YOU DON'T LIKE CK?
SOUNDS LIKE A CALVIN KLEIN STORE.
KILL SHOT!
I'LL BANK STUDIO KATCHOO. WE'LL BE EQUAL PARTNERS. I'LL HANDLE THE BUSINESS, YOU OVERSEE ALL THE CREATIVE STUFF, CLASSES, WORKSHOPS, WHATEVER. YOU'LL BECOME THE NEXUS OF THE TEXAS ART WORLD AND I GET TO REP ANY PRODIGIES YOU FIND. WHAT DO YOU THINK?
WELL, I'M NOT REALLY INTERESTED IN BECOMING THE NEXUS OF ANYTHING, BUT YEAH — THE STUDIO PART SOUNDS GOOD.
THERE'S JUST ONE THING.

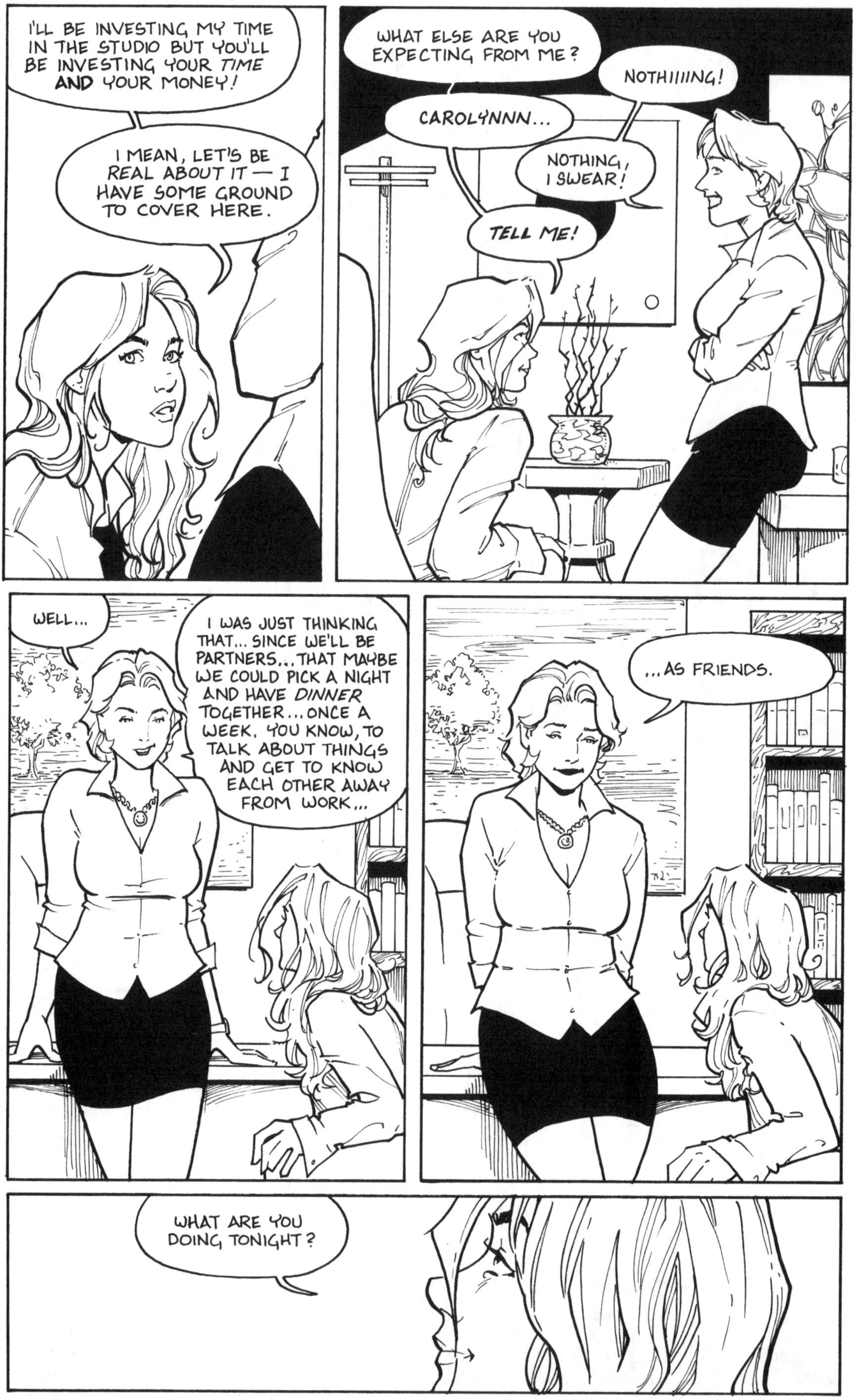

I'LL BE INVESTING MY TIME IN THE STUDIO BUT YOU'LL BE INVESTING YOUR *TIME* **AND** YOUR MONEY!
I MEAN, LET'S BE REAL ABOUT IT — I HAVE SOME GROUND TO COVER HERE.
WHAT ELSE ARE YOU EXPECTING FROM ME?
NOTHIIIING!
CAROLYNNN...
NOTHING, I SWEAR!
TELL ME!
WELL...
I WAS JUST THINKING THAT... SINCE WE'LL BE PARTNERS... THAT MAYBE WE COULD PICK A NIGHT AND HAVE *DINNER* TOGETHER... ONCE A WEEK. YOU KNOW, TO TALK ABOUT THINGS AND GET TO KNOW EACH OTHER AWAY FROM WORK...
...AS FRIENDS.
WHAT ARE YOU DOING TONIGHT?

I hate that word...relationship. It's overused. Everybody's always talking about relationship, relationship, relationship. It's just a word. It's doesn't mean anything. It doesn't describe what you
have to do or how to do it. But people use it as a catch-all phrase because it makes them sound like
they've carefully considered all aspects of the matter and the summation comes down to one
word...relationship. Bull. You can't sum up life in a word and you sure can't sum up what happens
between a man and a woman in a few words.

All I've ever wanted is a good woman who will stand by me. Period. Call that what you want but
don't waste my time with catch phrases you picked up from books and television. And speaking of
television, have you noticed we haven't had any Shakespeares show up since that sqwak box
arrived on the scene? Now we got a country full of illiterate liberals who don't know their butt
from a...

Hey! How about another beer over here?! Jeeze, sweetheart, this isn't rocket science, okay? You
bring 'em, I drink 'em. Can you do that? Yeah? Well, try to keep up, okay? What's that tattoo say
on your shoulder there? What is that, Japanese? Is that supposed to be some sort of liberal slo-
gan in code? What do you mean, I'll never know? I'll go look it up on the net. Hey, I can read you
like a book, baby...I got your number! You hear what I'm sayin'? I'm a lawyer, don't screw with me.
I was drivin' my first Porsche when you were pickin' tofu out of your liberal braces!
                                                                        -Freddie, happy hour

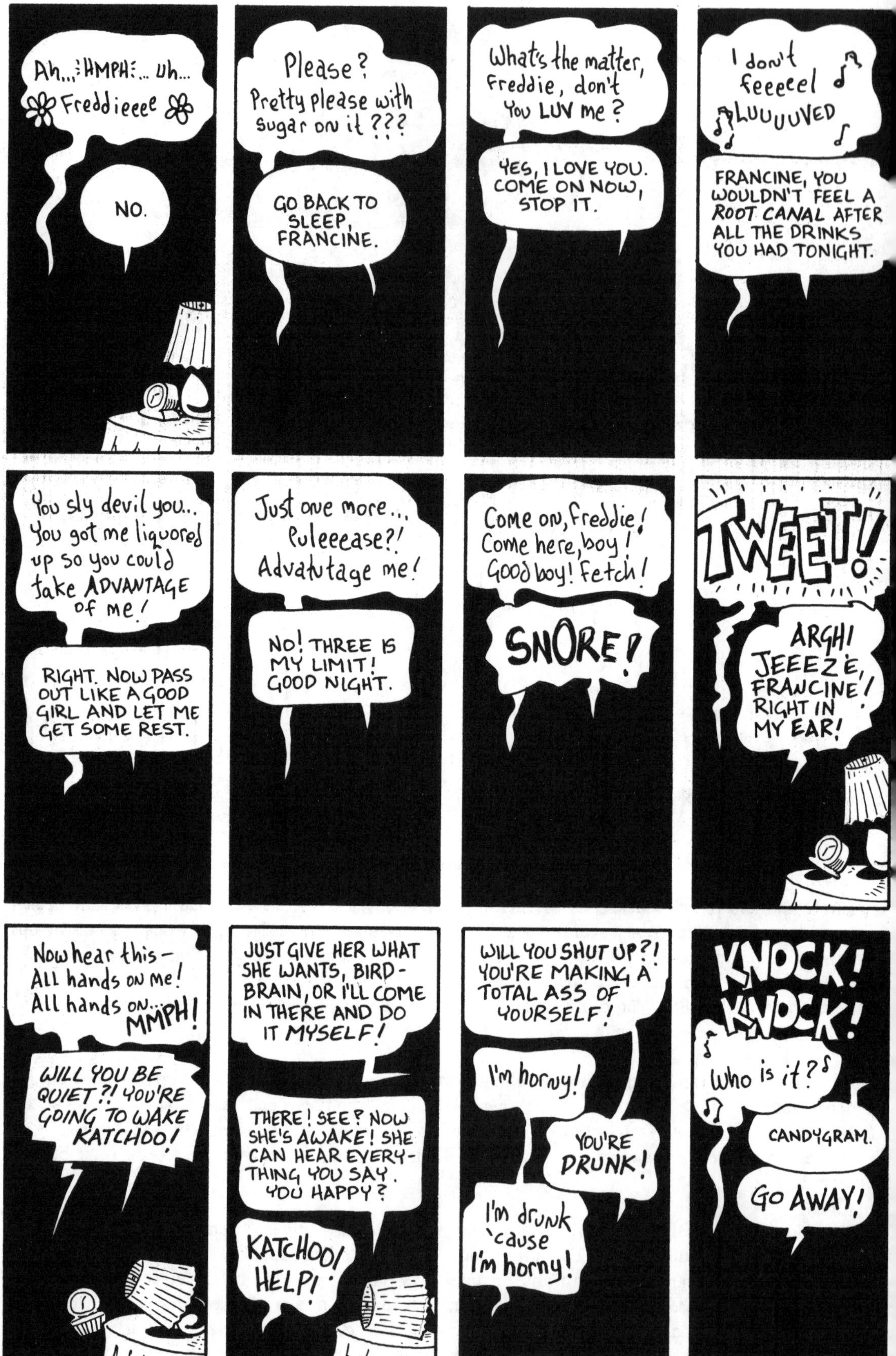
Ah...HMPH... uh... Freddieeee
NO.
Please? Pretty please with sugar on it???
GO BACK TO SLEEP, FRANCINE.
What's the matter, Freddie, don't you LUV me?
YES, I LOVE YOU. COME ON NOW, STOP IT.
I don't feeeeel LUUUUVED
FRANCINE, YOU WOULDN'T FEEL A ROOT CANAL AFTER ALL THE DRINKS YOU HAD TONIGHT.
You sly devil you... You got me liquored up so you could take ADVANTAGE of me!
RIGHT. NOW PASS OUT LIKE A GOOD GIRL AND LET ME GET SOME REST.
Just one more... Puleeease?! Advatutage me!
NO! THREE IS MY LIMIT! GOOD NIGHT.
Come on, Freddie! Come here, boy! Good boy! Fetch!
SNORE!
TWEET!
ARGH! JEEEZE, FRANCINE! RIGHT IN MY EAR!
Now hear this - All hands on me! All hands on... MMPH!
WILL YOU BE QUIET?! YOU'RE GOING TO WAKE KATCHOO!
JUST GIVE HER WHAT SHE WANTS, BIRD-BRAIN, OR I'LL COME IN THERE AND DO IT MYSELF!
THERE! SEE? NOW SHE'S AWAKE! SHE CAN HEAR EVERYTHING YOU SAY. YOU HAPPY?
KATCHOO! HELP!
WILL YOU SHUT UP?! YOU'RE MAKING A TOTAL ASS OF YOURSELF!
I'm horny!
YOU'RE DRUNK!
I'm drunk 'cause I'm horny!
KNOCK! KNOCK!
Who is it?
CANDYGRAM.
GO AWAY!

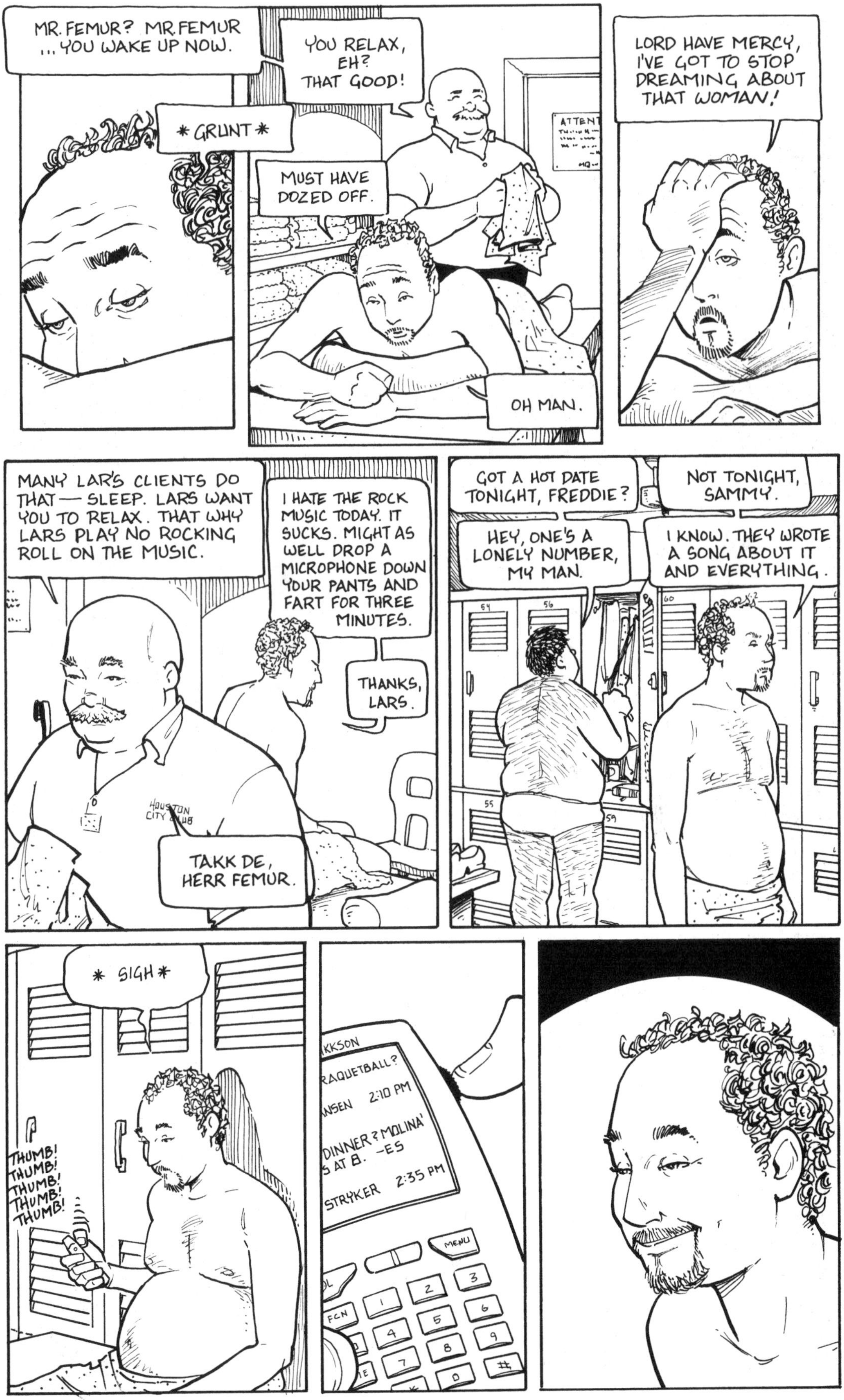

MR. FEMUR? MR. FEMUR ... YOU WAKE UP NOW.
* GRUNT *
YOU RELAX, EH? THAT GOOD!
MUST HAVE DOZED OFF.
OH MAN.
LORD HAVE MERCY, I'VE GOT TO STOP DREAMING ABOUT THAT WOMAN!
MANY LAR'S CLIENTS DO THAT — SLEEP. LARS WANT YOU TO RELAX. THAT WHY LARS PLAY NO ROCKING ROLL ON THE MUSIC.
I HATE THE ROCK MUSIC TODAY. IT SUCKS. MIGHT AS WELL DROP A MICROPHONE DOWN YOUR PANTS AND FART FOR THREE MINUTES.
THANKS, LARS.
HOUSTON CITY CLUB
TAKK DE, HERR FEMUR.
GOT A HOT DATE TONIGHT, FREDDIE?
NOT TONIGHT, SAMMY.
HEY, ONE'S A LONELY NUMBER, MY MAN.
I KNOW. THEY WROTE A SONG ABOUT IT AND EVERYTHING.
* SIGH *
THUMB! THUMB! THUMB! THUMB! THUMB!
RAQUETBALL?
2:10 PM
DINNER? MOLINA'
STRYKER 2:35 PM
MENU

My name is Emily Stryker. I am a criminal pathologist at the Houston forensic center. I met Freddie a few weeks ago when he walked into my examining room with Det. Mike Walsh. I've known Mike for years and he rarely brought lawyers with him to examine bodies, but this case was different. Freddie was like many people who are forced to witness a body on my table, nervous, putting on a brave face, then when the bag is unzipped, *plop* on the floor he goes. We gave the poor man a sedative and let him sleep through the exam. When I woke him up he told me I had beautiful eyes and asked me out. He was so cute about it, like a little boy. I said yes and we've been going out ever since.

Monday was a long one. Four autopsies and a staff meeting about the new computers. I didn't have a chance to eat lunch so I was looking forward to dinner and a couple of cold margaritas. During a quick break I sent Freddie a text message to meet me at Molina's at eight.

I had no idea our dinner would be interrupted by the start of one of the most horrifying crime waves ever to strike Houston.

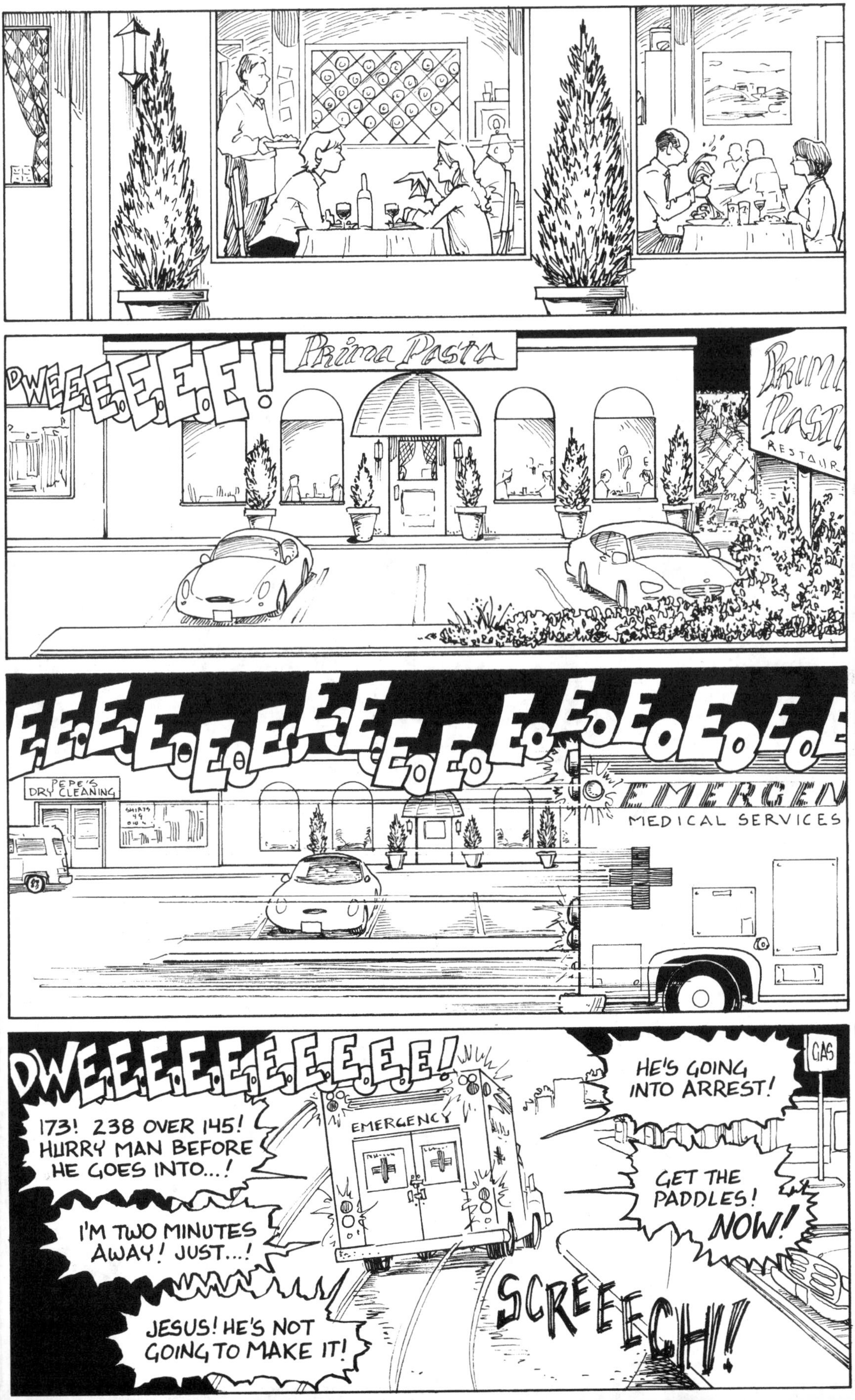
Prima Pasta
DWEEEEEEEEE!
PRIMA PASTA
RESTAURANT
PEPE'S DRY CLEANING
EEEEEEEEEEEEEEEEEEEEE
EMERGENCY
MEDICAL SERVICES
DWEEEEEEEEEEEE!
173! 238 OVER 145! HURRY MAN BEFORE HE GOES INTO...!
I'M TWO MINUTES AWAY! JUST...!
JESUS! HE'S NOT GOING TO MAKE IT!
EMERGENCY
HE'S GOING INTO ARREST!
GET THE PADDLES! NOW!
GAS
SCREEECH!!

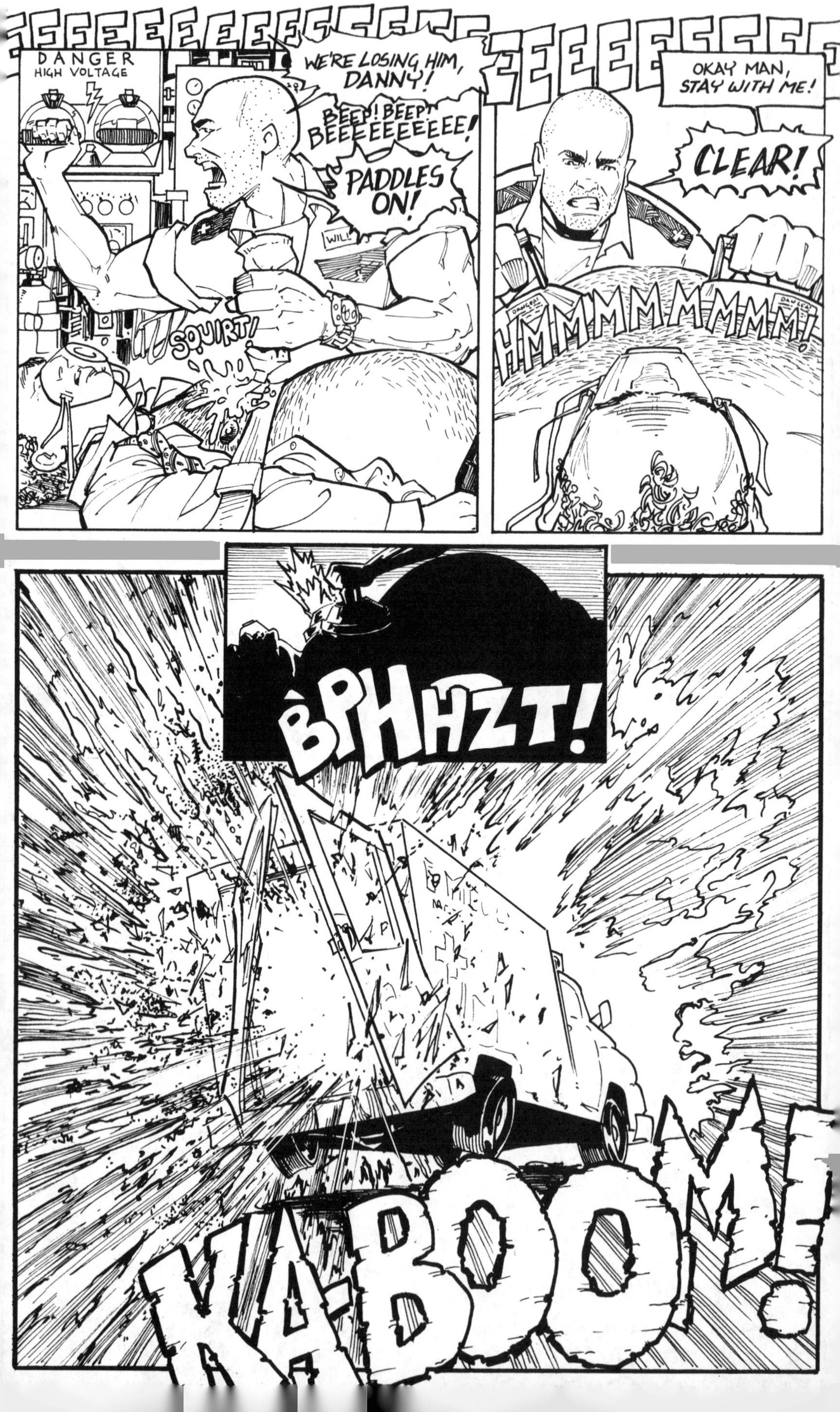
EEEEEEEEEEEEEEEEEEEEE
DANGER
HIGH VOLTAGE
WE'RE LOSING HIM, DANNY!
BEEP! BEEP! BEEEEEEEEEEE!
PADDLES ON!
WIL
SQUIRT!
OKAY MAN, STAY WITH ME!
CLEAR!
DANGER
DANGER
HMMMMMMMMMM!
BPHHZT!
KA-BOOM!

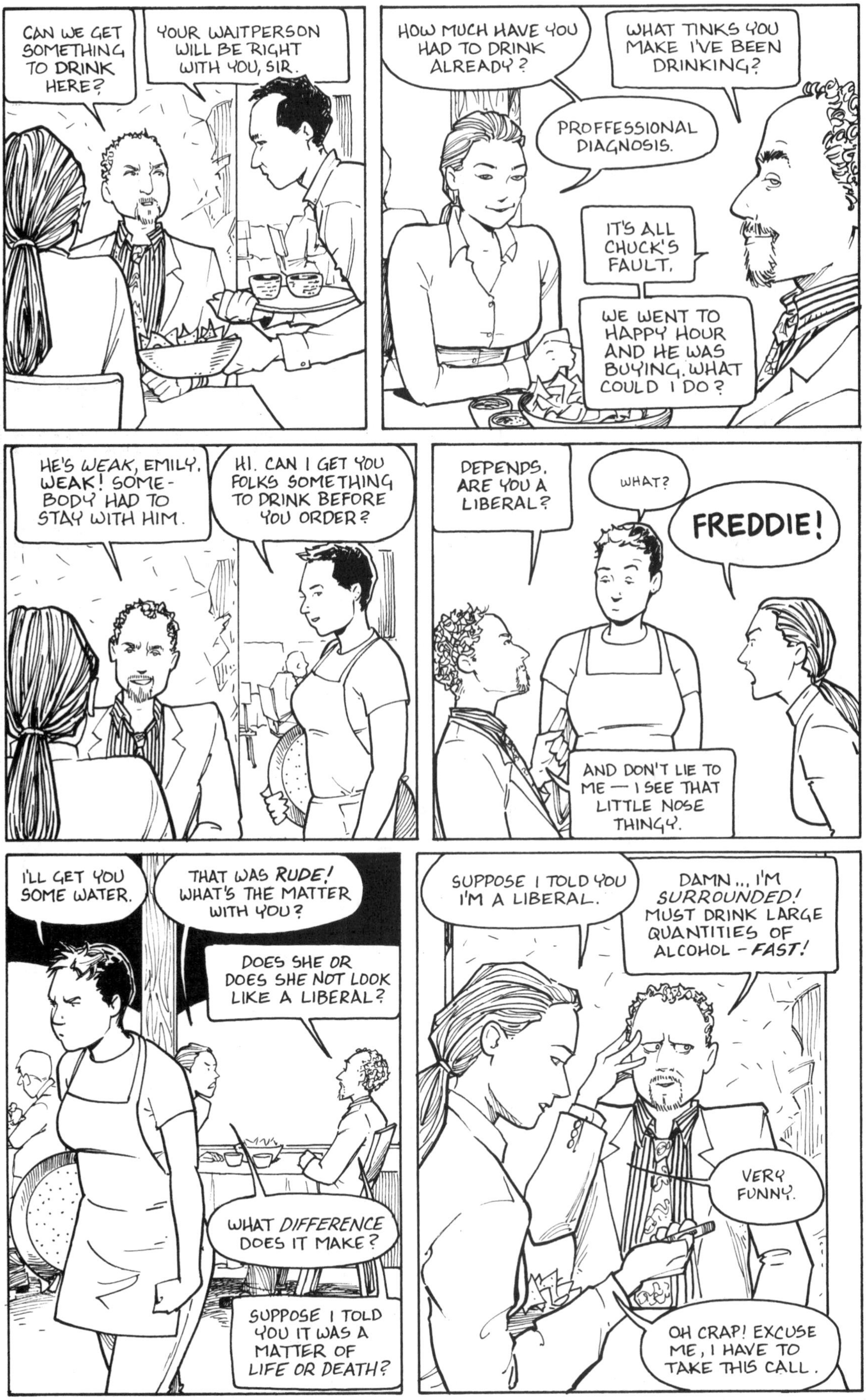

CAN WE GET SOMETHING TO DRINK HERE?
YOUR WAITPERSON WILL BE RIGHT WITH YOU, SIR.
HOW MUCH HAVE YOU HAD TO DRINK ALREADY?
WHAT TINKS YOU MAKE I'VE BEEN DRINKING?
PROFFESSIONAL DIAGNOSIS.
IT'S ALL CHUCK'S FAULT.
WE WENT TO HAPPY HOUR AND HE WAS BUYING. WHAT COULD I DO?
HE'S *WEAK*, EMILY. **WEAK**! SOMEBODY HAD TO STAY WITH HIM.
HI. CAN I GET YOU FOLKS SOMETHING TO DRINK BEFORE YOU ORDER?
DEPENDS. ARE YOU A LIBERAL?
WHAT?
FREDDIE!
AND DON'T LIE TO ME — I SEE THAT LITTLE NOSE THINGY.
I'LL GET YOU SOME WATER.
THAT WAS *RUDE!* WHAT'S THE MATTER WITH YOU?
DOES SHE OR DOES SHE NOT LOOK LIKE A LIBERAL?
WHAT *DIFFERENCE* DOES IT MAKE?
SUPPOSE I TOLD YOU IT WAS A MATTER OF *LIFE OR DEATH?*
SUPPOSE I TOLD YOU I'M A LIBERAL.
DAMN... I'M *SURROUNDED!* MUST DRINK LARGE QUANTITIES OF ALCOHOL – *FAST!*
VERY FUNNY.
OH CRAP! EXCUSE ME, I HAVE TO TAKE THIS CALL.

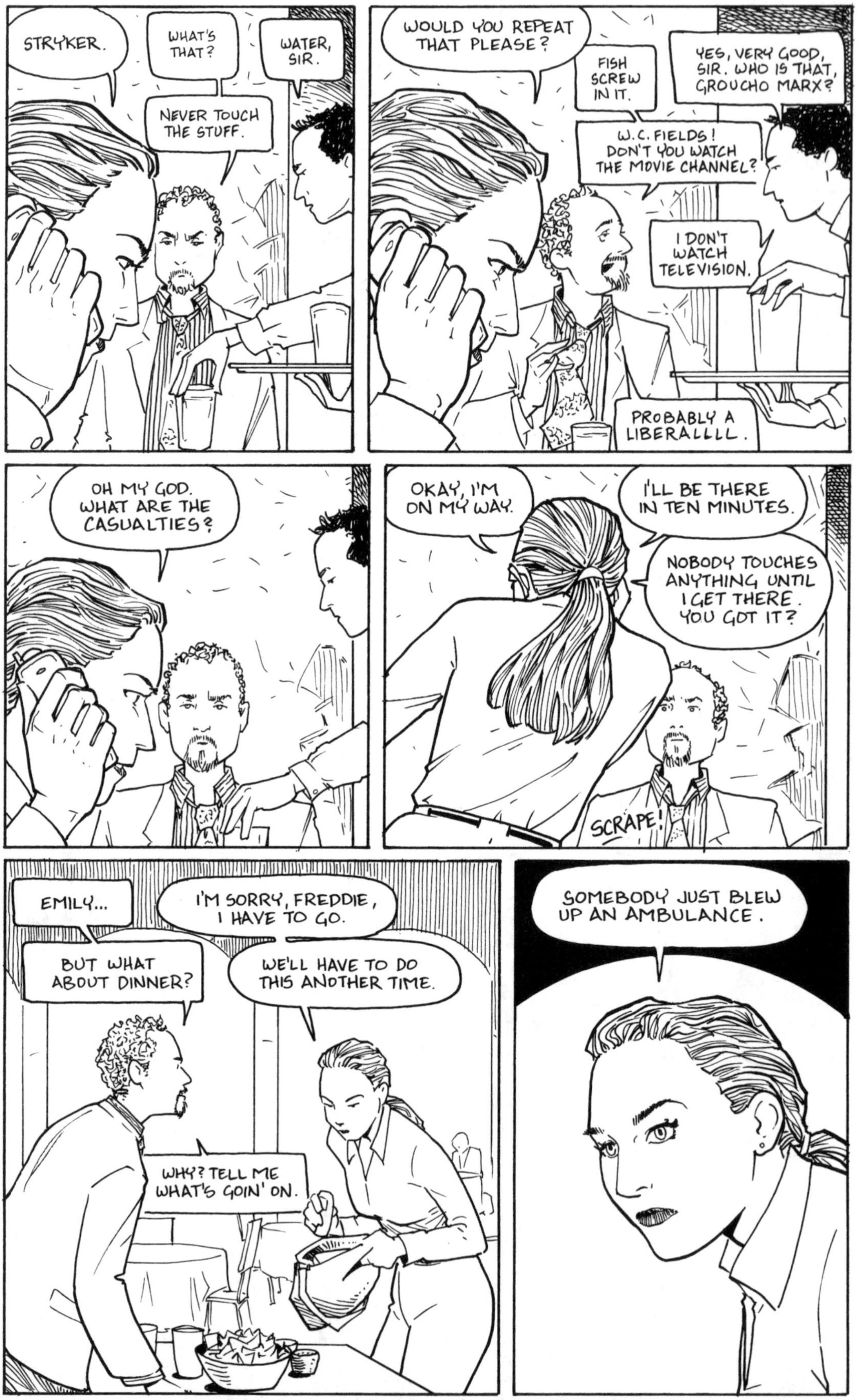
STRYKER.
WHAT'S THAT?
NEVER TOUCH THE STUFF.
WATER, SIR.
WOULD YOU REPEAT THAT PLEASE?
FISH SCREW IN IT.
W.C. FIELDS! DON'T YOU WATCH THE MOVIE CHANNEL?
YES, VERY GOOD, SIR. WHO IS THAT, GROUCHO MARX?
I DON'T WATCH TELEVISION.
PROBABLY A LIBERALLLL.
OH MY GOD. WHAT ARE THE CASUALTIES?
OKAY, I'M ON MY WAY.
I'LL BE THERE IN TEN MINUTES.
NOBODY TOUCHES ANYTHING UNTIL I GET THERE. YOU GOT IT?
SCRAPE!
EMILY...
I'M SORRY, FREDDIE, I HAVE TO GO.
BUT WHAT ABOUT DINNER?
WE'LL HAVE TO DO THIS ANOTHER TIME.
WHY? TELL ME WHAT'S GOIN' ON.
SOMEBODY JUST BLEW UP AN AMBULANCE.

TONIGHT ON AUSTIN CITY LIMITS — *GRIFFIN SILVER!*

1...
2...
3...

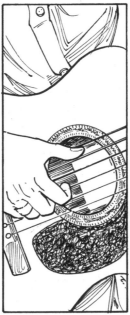

EVERYBODY PACKED AND MOVED AWAY...

TRUDGIN' THROUGH THE SNOW YESTERDAY... I CAN'T BELIEVE I'VE LOST THE ONE...

WHO SAID SHE'D *SAVE ME FROM THE STORM*

FAMILY TIES ARE STRONGER THAN A BOY — SHE HAD TO LEAVE SHE HAD NO CHOICE

IF I HAD KNOWN SHE WAS TO LEAVE... I WOULDN'T HAVE KNOWN HER FROM THE START

INSTEAD SHE WINDS UP WITH MY HEART.

Everybody Packed and Moved Away
— Griffin Silver —

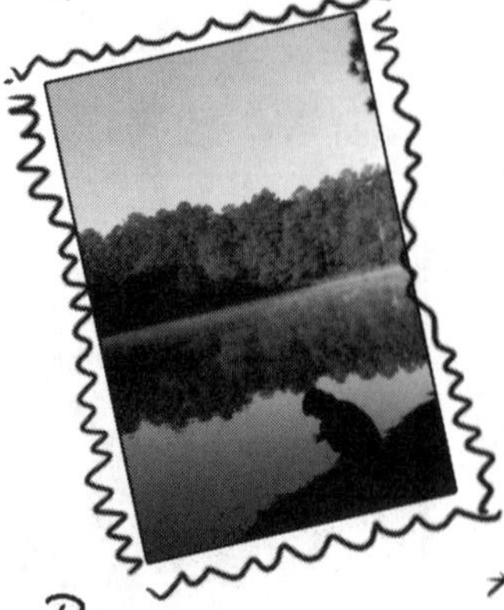

```
D
Everybody packed and moved away
                              A     A/Bb  Bm
trudging thru the snow yesterday
          F#7               Em7
I can't believe I've lost the one
            F#7                       Bm  D  Gmaj7  Em7  D
Who said she'd save me from the storm
   | Bm | D | Gmaj7 | Em7 | D
```

```
D
Family ties are stronger than a boy
                              A     A/Bb  Bm
She had to leave she had no choice
Bm        F#7             Em7
If I had known she was to leave
                F#7                Bm    D
I wouldn't have known her from the start
Gmaj7          Em7           D     Gmaj7  Em7  A7  D
Instead she winds up with my heart
[: Gmaj7 | Em7 | A7 | D :]
```

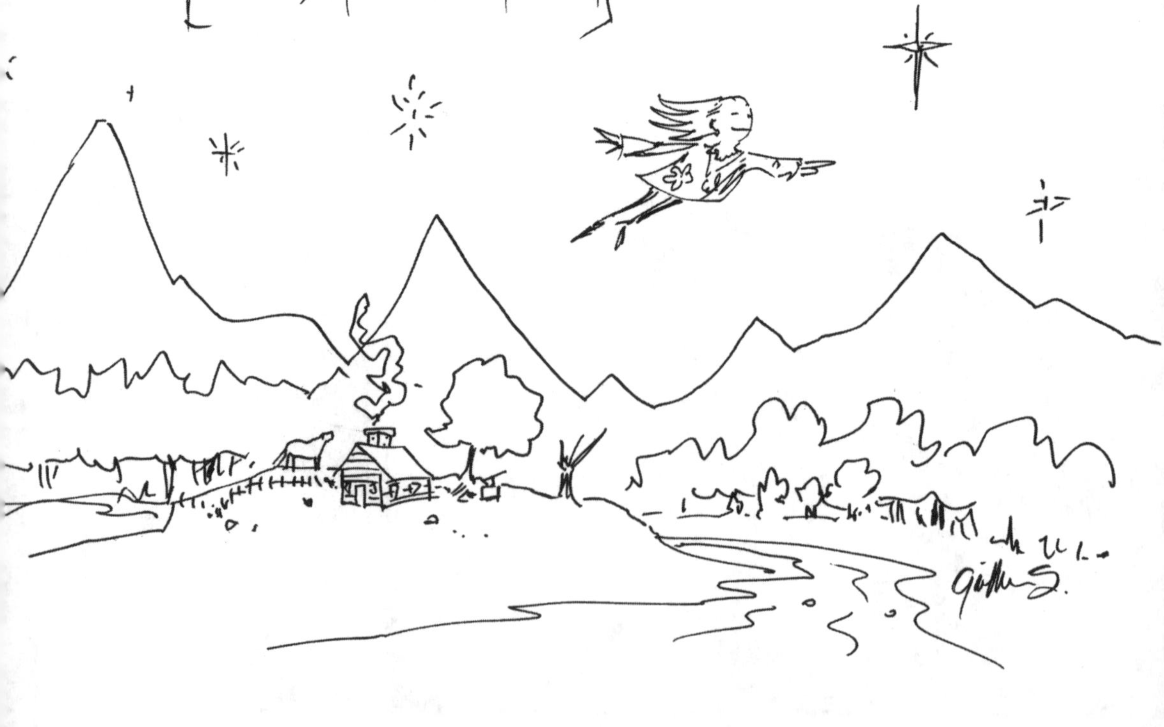

Griffin S.

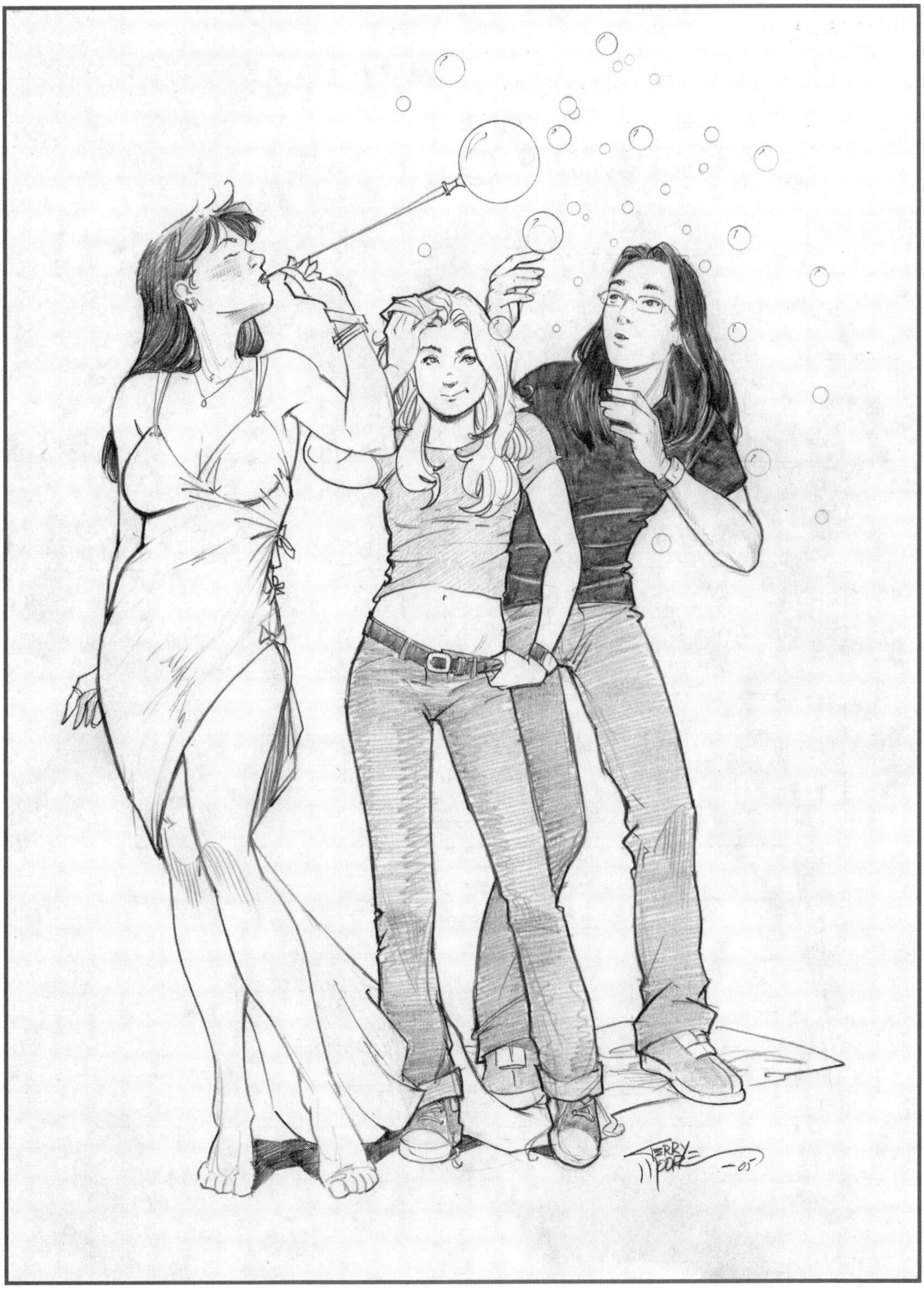

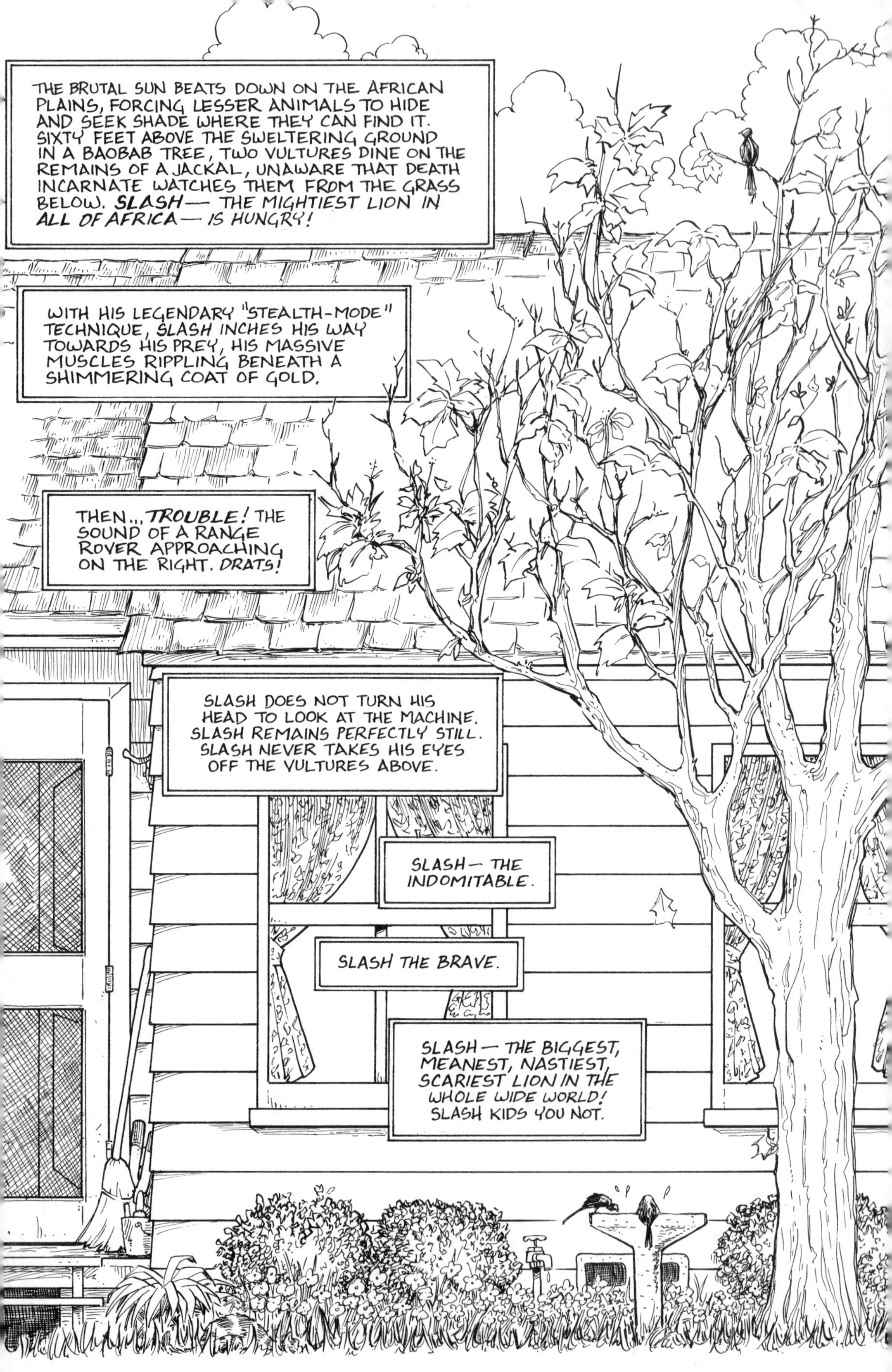
THE BRUTAL SUN BEATS DOWN ON THE AFRICAN PLAINS, FORCING LESSER ANIMALS TO HIDE AND SEEK SHADE WHERE THEY CAN FIND IT. SIXTY FEET ABOVE THE SWELTERING GROUND IN A BAOBAB TREE, TWO VULTURES DINE ON THE REMAINS OF A JACKAL, UNAWARE THAT DEATH INCARNATE WATCHES THEM FROM THE GRASS BELOW. SLASH— THE MIGHTIEST LION IN ALL OF AFRICA— IS HUNGRY!
WITH HIS LEGENDARY "STEALTH-MODE" TECHNIQUE, SLASH INCHES HIS WAY TOWARDS HIS PREY, HIS MASSIVE MUSCLES RIPPLING BENEATH A SHIMMERING COAT OF GOLD.
THEN... TROUBLE! THE SOUND OF A RANGE ROVER APPROACHING ON THE RIGHT. DRATS!
SLASH DOES NOT TURN HIS HEAD TO LOOK AT THE MACHINE. SLASH REMAINS PERFECTLY STILL. SLASH NEVER TAKES HIS EYES OFF THE VULTURES ABOVE.
SLASH— THE INDOMITABLE.
SLASH THE BRAVE.
SLASH— THE BIGGEST, MEANEST, NASTIEST, SCARIEST LION IN THE WHOLE WIDE WORLD! SLASH KIDS YOU NOT.

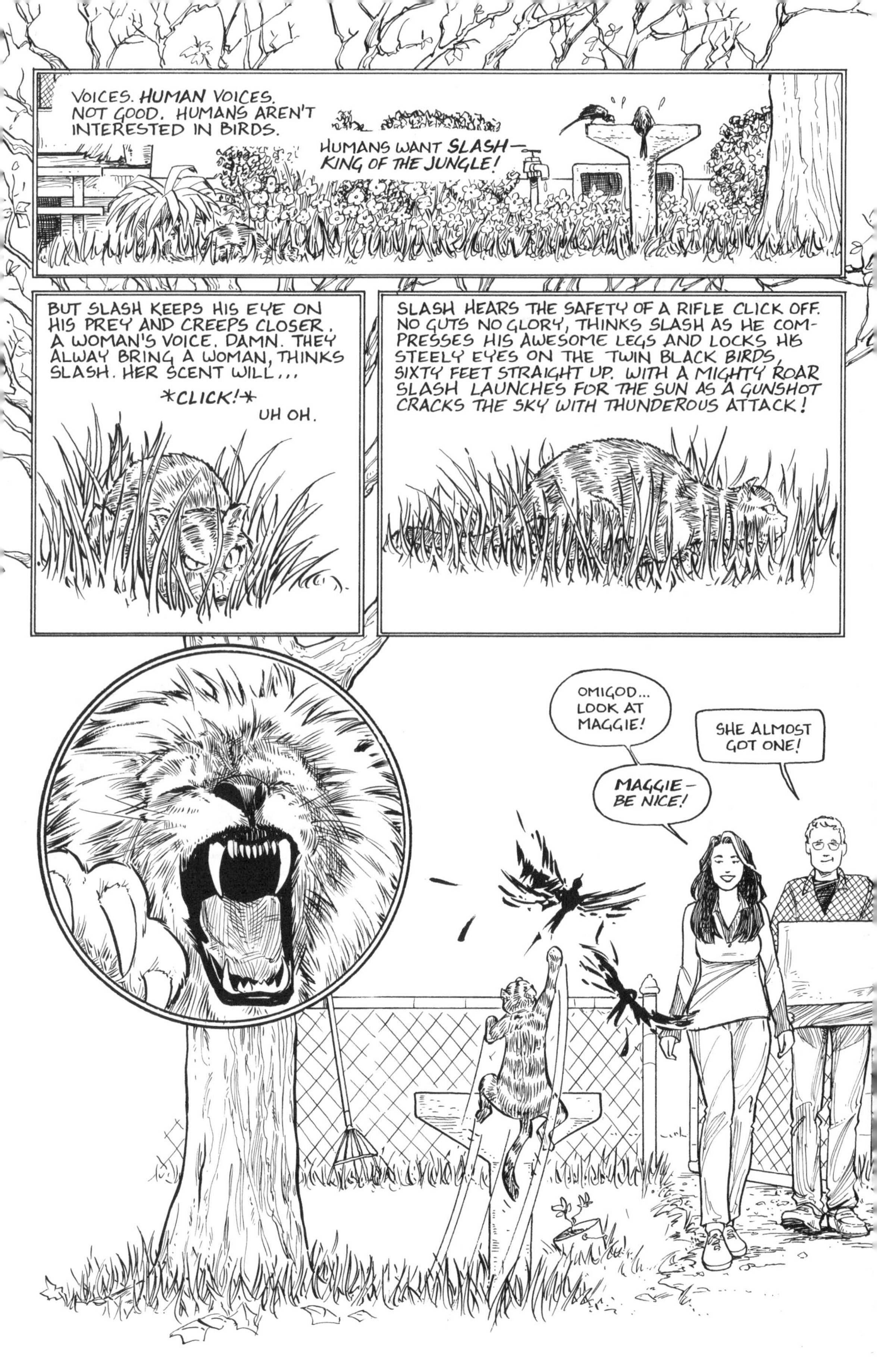

VOICES. HUMAN VOICES. NOT GOOD. HUMANS AREN'T INTERESTED IN BIRDS.
HUMANS WANT SLASH— KING OF THE JUNGLE!
BUT SLASH KEEPS HIS EYE ON HIS PREY AND CREEPS CLOSER. A WOMAN'S VOICE. DAMN. THEY ALWAY BRING A WOMAN, THINKS SLASH. HER SCENT WILL...
CLICK!
UH OH.
SLASH HEARS THE SAFETY OF A RIFLE CLICK OFF. NO GUTS NO GLORY, THINKS SLASH AS HE COMPRESSES HIS AWESOME LEGS AND LOCKS HIS STEELY EYES ON THE TWIN BLACK BIRDS, SIXTY FEET STRAIGHT UP. WITH A MIGHTY ROAR SLASH LAUNCHES FOR THE SUN AS A GUNSHOT CRACKS THE SKY WITH THUNDEROUS ATTACK!
OMIGOD... LOOK AT MAGGIE!
MAGGIE— BE NICE!
SHE ALMOST GOT ONE!

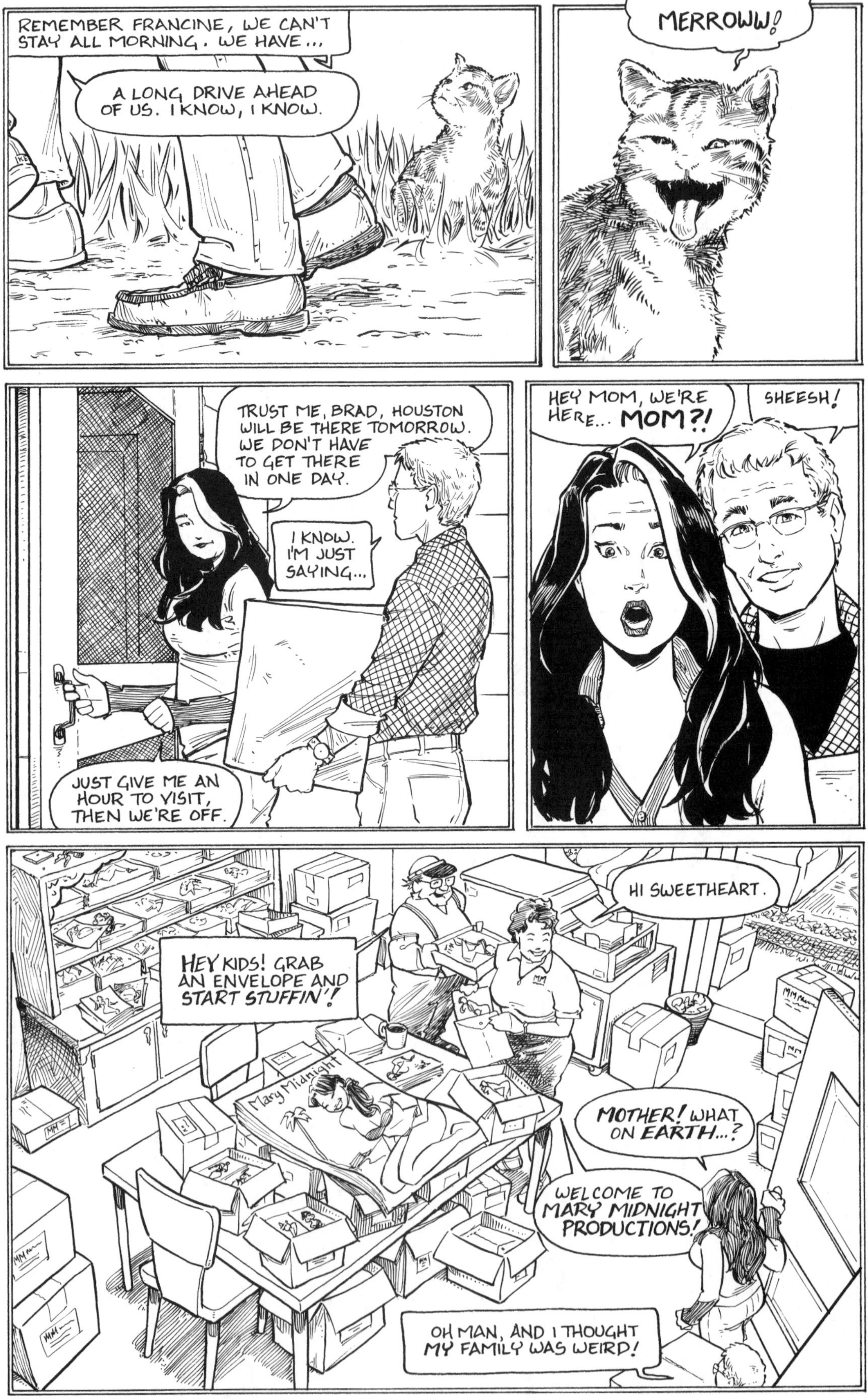
REMEMBER FRANCINE, WE CAN'T STAY ALL MORNING. WE HAVE...
A LONG DRIVE AHEAD OF US. I KNOW, I KNOW.
MERROWW!
TRUST ME, BRAD, HOUSTON WILL BE THERE TOMORROW. WE DON'T HAVE TO GET THERE IN ONE DAY.
I KNOW. I'M JUST SAYING...
JUST GIVE ME AN HOUR TO VISIT, THEN WE'RE OFF.
HEY MOM, WE'RE HERE... MOM?!
SHEESH!
HI SWEETHEART.
HEY KIDS! GRAB AN ENVELOPE AND START STUFFIN'!
Mary Midnight
MOTHER! WHAT ON EARTH...?
WELCOME TO MARY MIDNIGHT PRODUCTIONS!
OH MAN, AND I THOUGHT MY FAMILY WAS WEIRD!

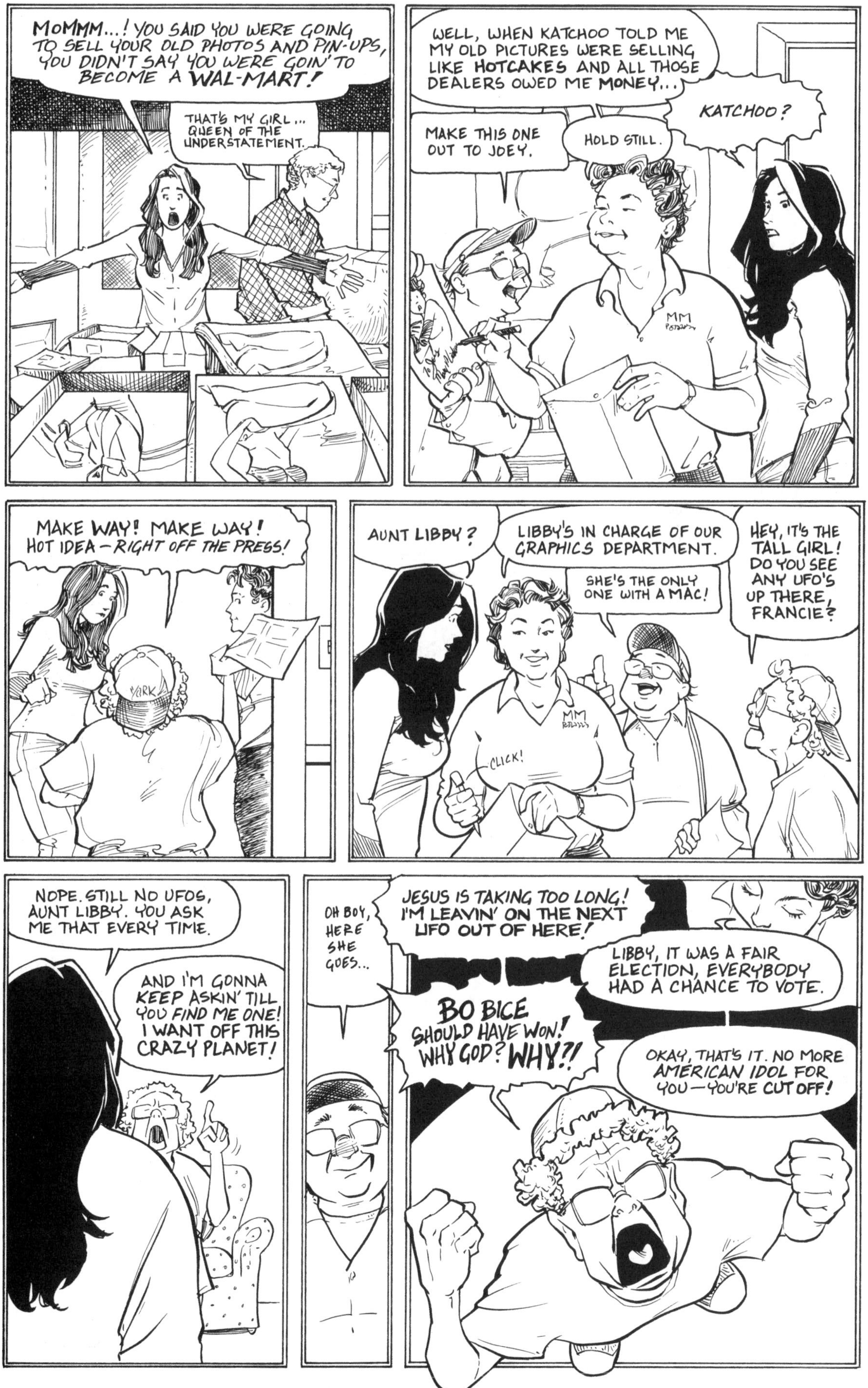
MOMMM...! YOU SAID YOU WERE GOING TO SELL YOUR OLD PHOTOS AND PIN-UPS, YOU DIDN'T SAY YOU WERE GOIN' TO BECOME A WAL-MART!
THAT'S MY GIRL... QUEEN OF THE UNDERSTATEMENT.
WELL, WHEN KATCHOO TOLD ME MY OLD PICTURES WERE SELLING LIKE HOTCAKES AND ALL THOSE DEALERS OWED ME MONEY...
KATCHOO?
MAKE THIS ONE OUT TO JOEY.
HOLD STILL.
MAKE WAY! MAKE WAY! HOT IDEA—RIGHT OFF THE PRESS!
YARK
AUNT LIBBY?
LIBBY'S IN CHARGE OF OUR GRAPHICS DEPARTMENT.
SHE'S THE ONLY ONE WITH A MAC!
HEY, IT'S THE TALL GIRL! DO YOU SEE ANY UFO'S UP THERE, FRANCIE?
CLICK!
NOPE. STILL NO UFOS, AUNT LIBBY. YOU ASK ME THAT EVERY TIME.
AND I'M GONNA KEEP ASKIN' TILL YOU FIND ME ONE! I WANT OFF THIS CRAZY PLANET!
OH BOY, HERE SHE GOES...
JESUS IS TAKING TOO LONG! I'M LEAVIN' ON THE NEXT UFO OUT OF HERE!
LIBBY, IT WAS A FAIR ELECTION, EVERYBODY HAD A CHANCE TO VOTE.
BO BICE SHOULD HAVE WON! WHY GOD? WHY?!
OKAY, THAT'S IT. NO MORE AMERICAN IDOL FOR YOU—YOU'RE CUT OFF!

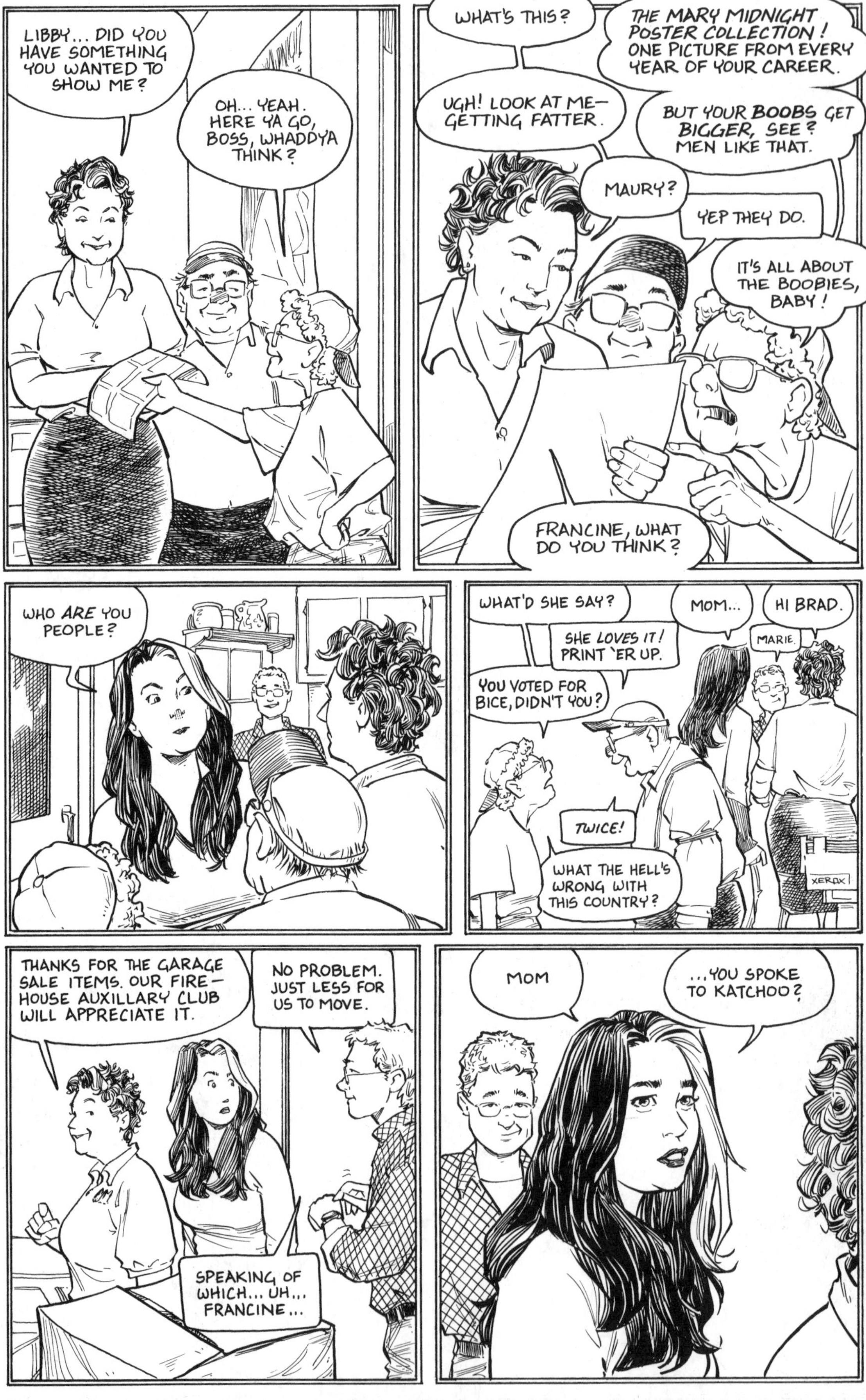

LIBBY... DID YOU HAVE SOMETHING YOU WANTED TO SHOW ME?
OH... YEAH. HERE YA GO, BOSS, WHADDYA THINK?
WHAT'S THIS?
THE MARY MIDNIGHT POSTER COLLECTION! ONE PICTURE FROM EVERY YEAR OF YOUR CAREER.
UGH! LOOK AT ME— GETTING FATTER.
BUT YOUR BOOBS GET BIGGER, SEE? MEN LIKE THAT.
MAURY?
YEP THEY DO.
IT'S ALL ABOUT THE BOOBIES, BABY!
FRANCINE, WHAT DO YOU THINK?
WHO ARE YOU PEOPLE?
WHAT'D SHE SAY?
SHE LOVES IT! PRINT 'ER UP.
MOM...
HI BRAD.
MARIE.
YOU VOTED FOR BICE, DIDN'T YOU?
TWICE!
WHAT THE HELL'S WRONG WITH THIS COUNTRY?
XEROX
THANKS FOR THE GARAGE SALE ITEMS. OUR FIRE-HOUSE AUXILLARY CLUB WILL APPRECIATE IT.
NO PROBLEM. JUST LESS FOR US TO MOVE.
SPEAKING OF WHICH... UH... FRANCINE...
MOM
...YOU SPOKE TO KATCHOO?

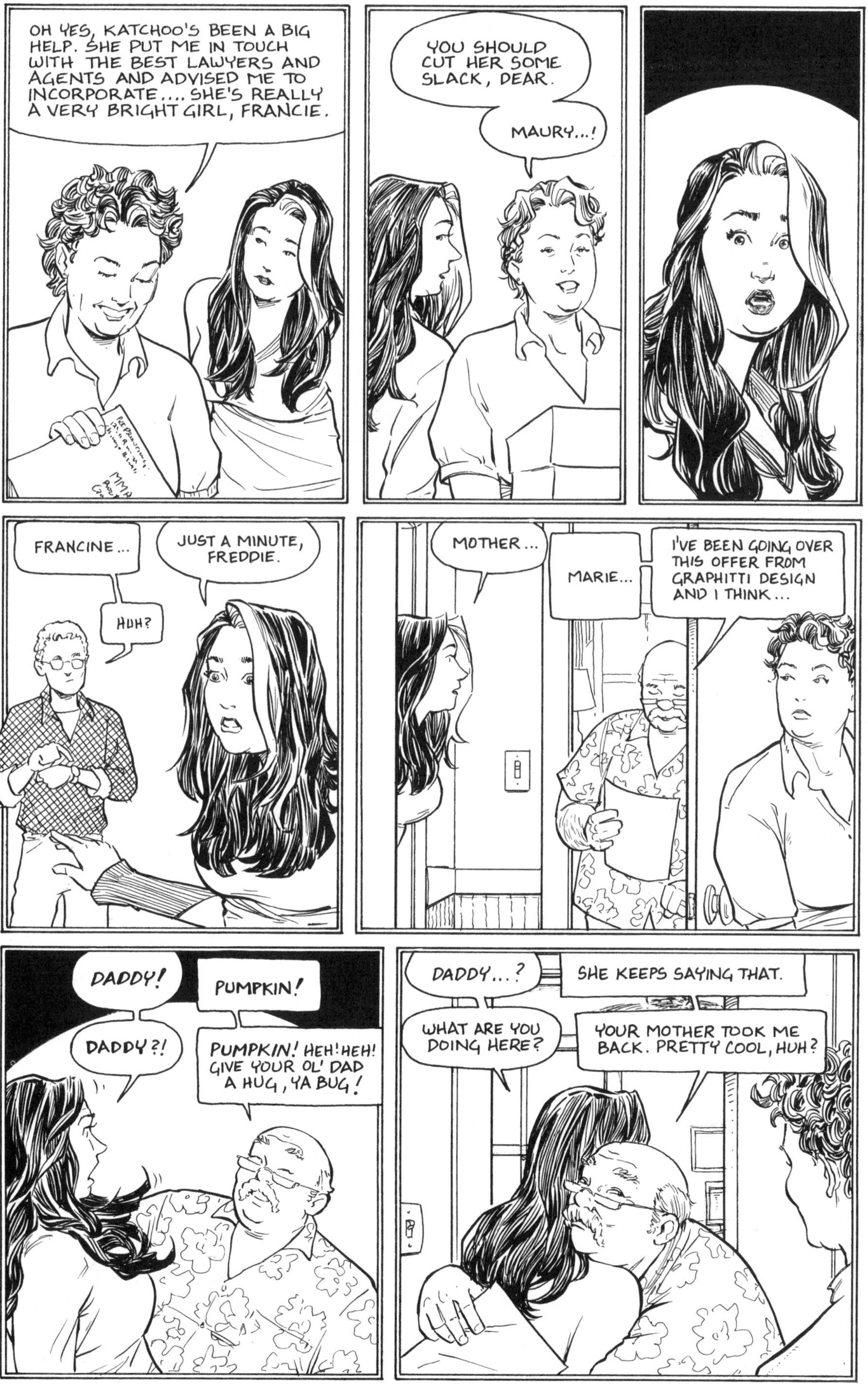
OH YES, KATCHOO'S BEEN A BIG HELP. SHE PUT ME IN TOUCH WITH THE BEST LAWYERS AND AGENTS AND ADVISED ME TO INCORPORATE.... SHE'S REALLY A VERY BRIGHT GIRL, FRANCIE.
YOU SHOULD CUT HER SOME SLACK, DEAR.
MAURY...!
FRANCINE...
JUST A MINUTE, FREDDIE.
HUH?
MOTHER...
MARIE...
I'VE BEEN GOING OVER THIS OFFER FROM GRAPHITTI DESIGN AND I THINK...
DADDY!
PUMPKIN!
DADDY?!
PUMPKIN! HEH! HEH! GIVE YOUR OL' DAD A HUG, YA BUG!
DADDY...?
SHE KEEPS SAYING THAT.
WHAT ARE YOU DOING HERE?
YOUR MOTHER TOOK ME BACK. PRETTY COOL, HUH?

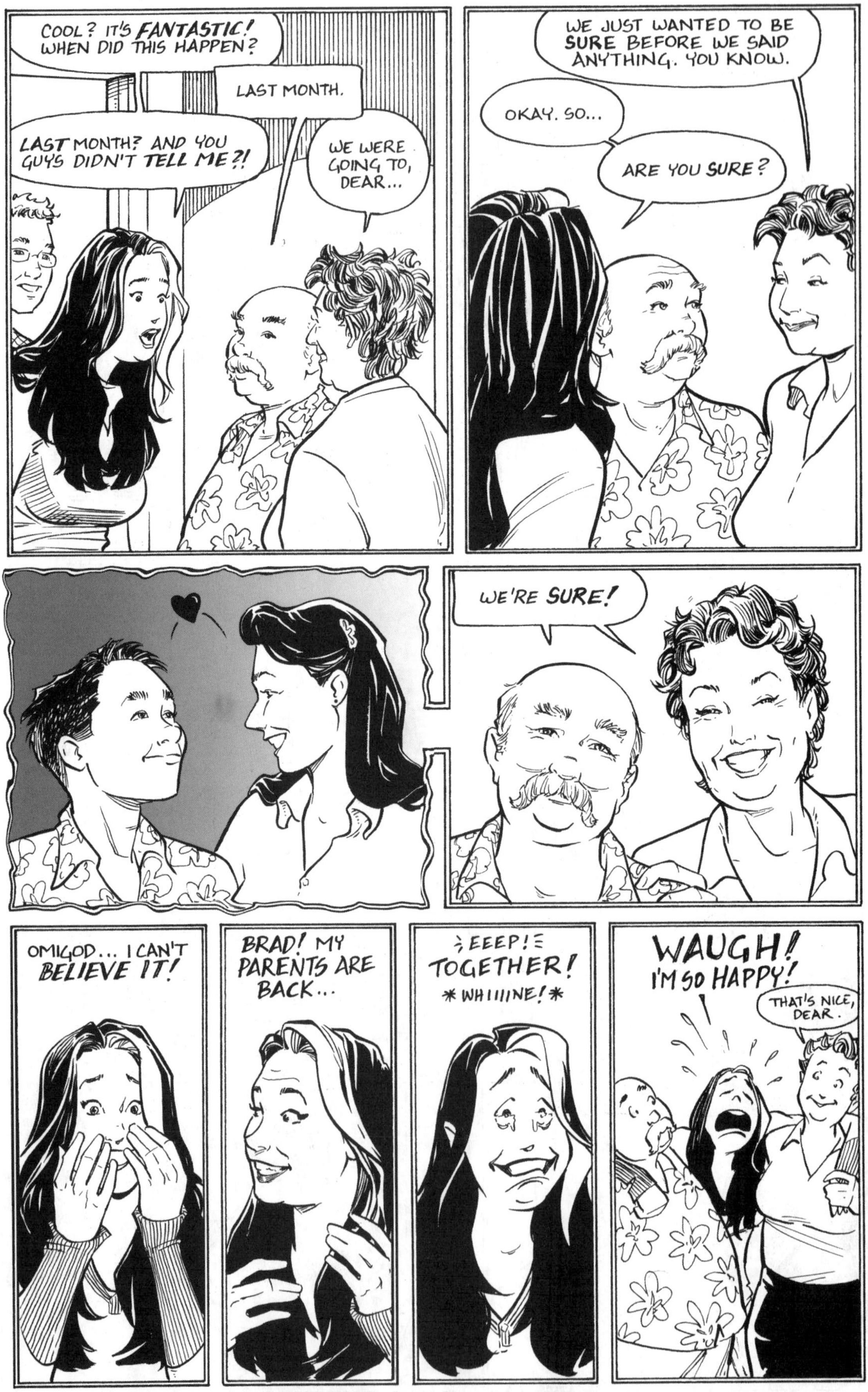
COOL? IT'S FANTASTIC! WHEN DID THIS HAPPEN?
LAST MONTH.
LAST MONTH? AND YOU GUYS DIDN'T TELL ME?!
WE WERE GOING TO, DEAR...
WE JUST WANTED TO BE SURE BEFORE WE SAID ANYTHING. YOU KNOW.
OKAY. SO...
ARE YOU SURE?
WE'RE SURE!
OMIGOD... I CAN'T BELIEVE IT!
BRAD! MY PARENTS ARE BACK...
EEEP! TOGETHER!
WHIIIINE!
WAUGH! I'M SO HAPPY!
THAT'S NICE, DEAR.

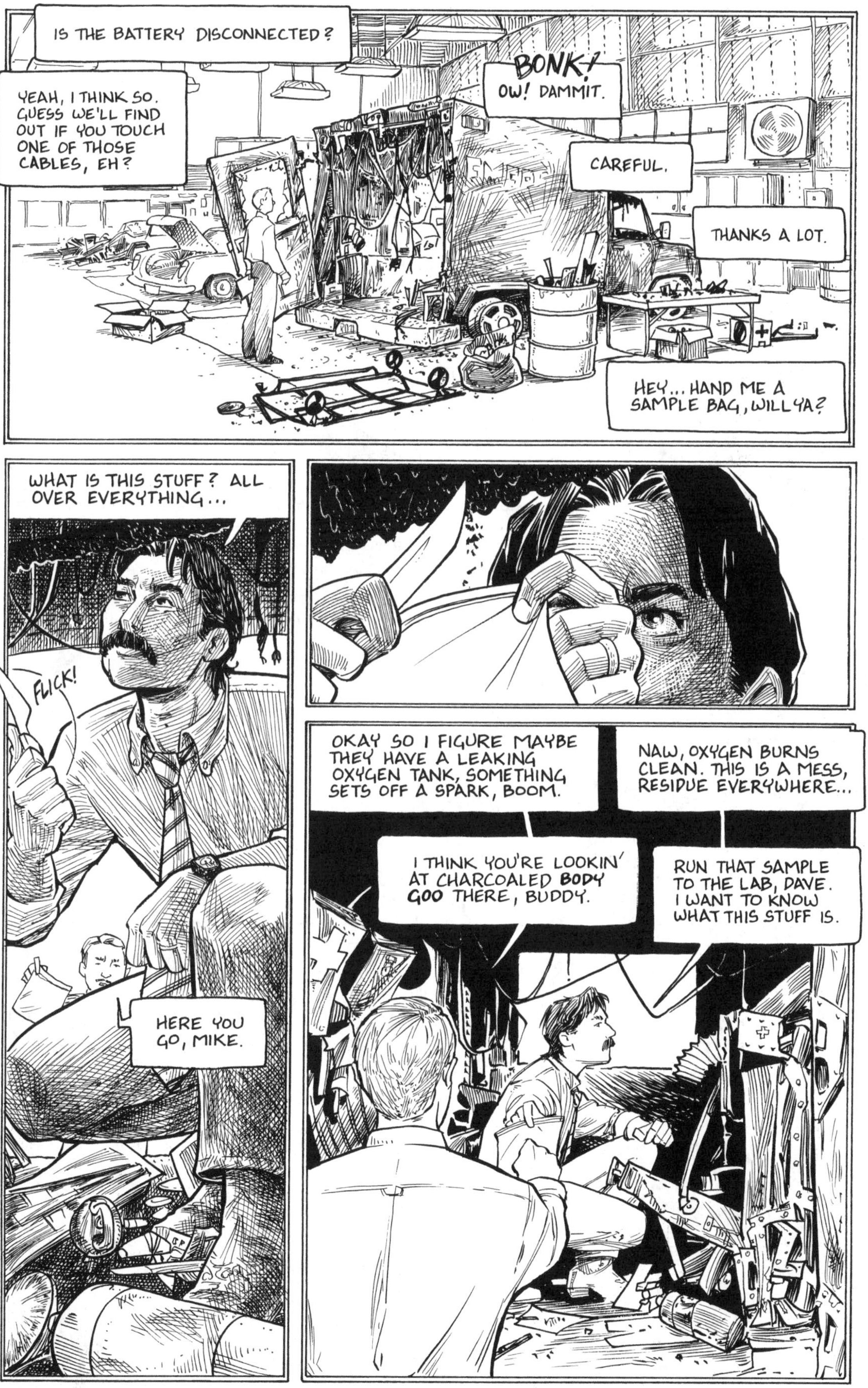
IS THE BATTERY DISCONNECTED?
YEAH, I THINK SO. GUESS WE'LL FIND OUT IF YOU TOUCH ONE OF THOSE CABLES, EH?
BONK!
OW! DAMMIT.
CAREFUL.
THANKS A LOT.
HEY... HAND ME A SAMPLE BAG, WILLYA?
WHAT IS THIS STUFF? ALL OVER EVERYTHING...
FLICK!
HERE YOU GO, MIKE.
OKAY SO I FIGURE MAYBE THEY HAVE A LEAKING OXYGEN TANK, SOMETHING SETS OFF A SPARK, BOOM.
NAW, OXYGEN BURNS CLEAN. THIS IS A MESS, RESIDUE EVERYWHERE...
I THINK YOU'RE LOOKIN' AT CHARCOALED **BODY GOO** THERE, BUDDY.
RUN THAT SAMPLE TO THE LAB, DAVE. I WANT TO KNOW WHAT THIS STUFF IS.

WHAT IS THIS STUFF?

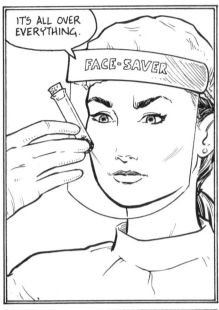

IT'S ALL OVER EVERYTHING.

FACE-SAVER

CHRIS... RUN THIS SAMPLE TO THE LAB, PLEASE.

I'M MOUNTING SAMPLES.

PLEASE, IT'S IMPORTANT.

YOU POOR MAN... WHAT IS YOUR STORY? HOW DID YOU GO FROM A BABE IN A WOMB TO THIS— A BURNED OUT SHELL ON MY TABLE?

WHO DID THIS TO YOU?

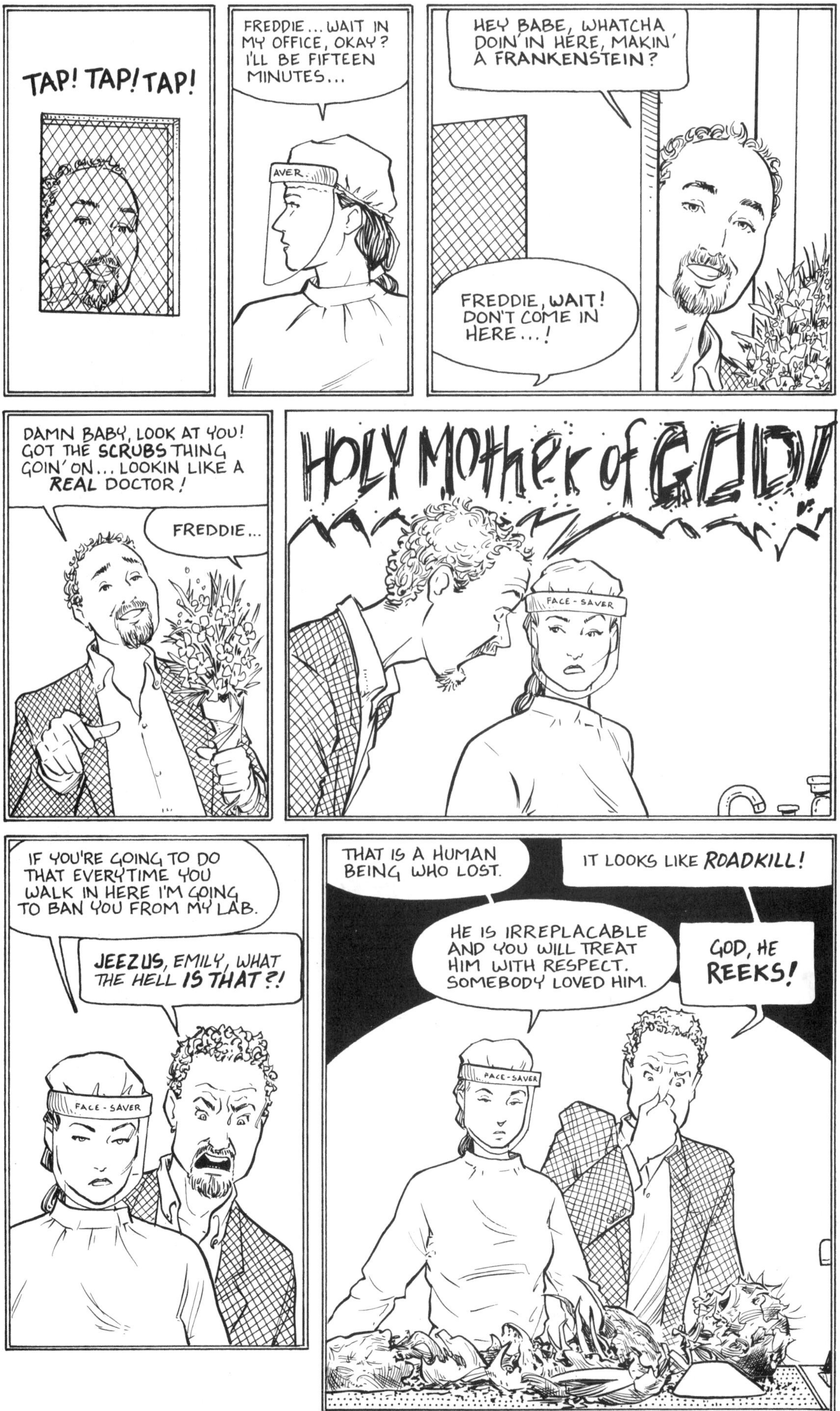
TAP! TAP! TAP!
FREDDIE... WAIT IN MY OFFICE, OKAY? I'LL BE FIFTEEN MINUTES...
AVER
HEY BABE, WHATCHA DOIN' IN HERE, MAKIN' A FRANKENSTEIN?
FREDDIE, WAIT! DON'T COME IN HERE...!
DAMN BABY, LOOK AT YOU! GOT THE SCRUBS THING GOIN' ON... LOOKIN LIKE A REAL DOCTOR!
FREDDIE...
HOLY MOTHER OF GOD!
FACE-SAVER
IF YOU'RE GOING TO DO THAT EVERYTIME YOU WALK IN HERE I'M GOING TO BAN YOU FROM MY LAB.
JEEZUS, EMILY, WHAT THE HELL IS THAT?!
FACE-SAVER
THAT IS A HUMAN BEING WHO LOST.
IT LOOKS LIKE ROADKILL!
HE IS IRREPLACABLE AND YOU WILL TREAT HIM WITH RESPECT. SOMEBODY LOVED HIM.
GOD, HE REEKS!
FACE-SAVER

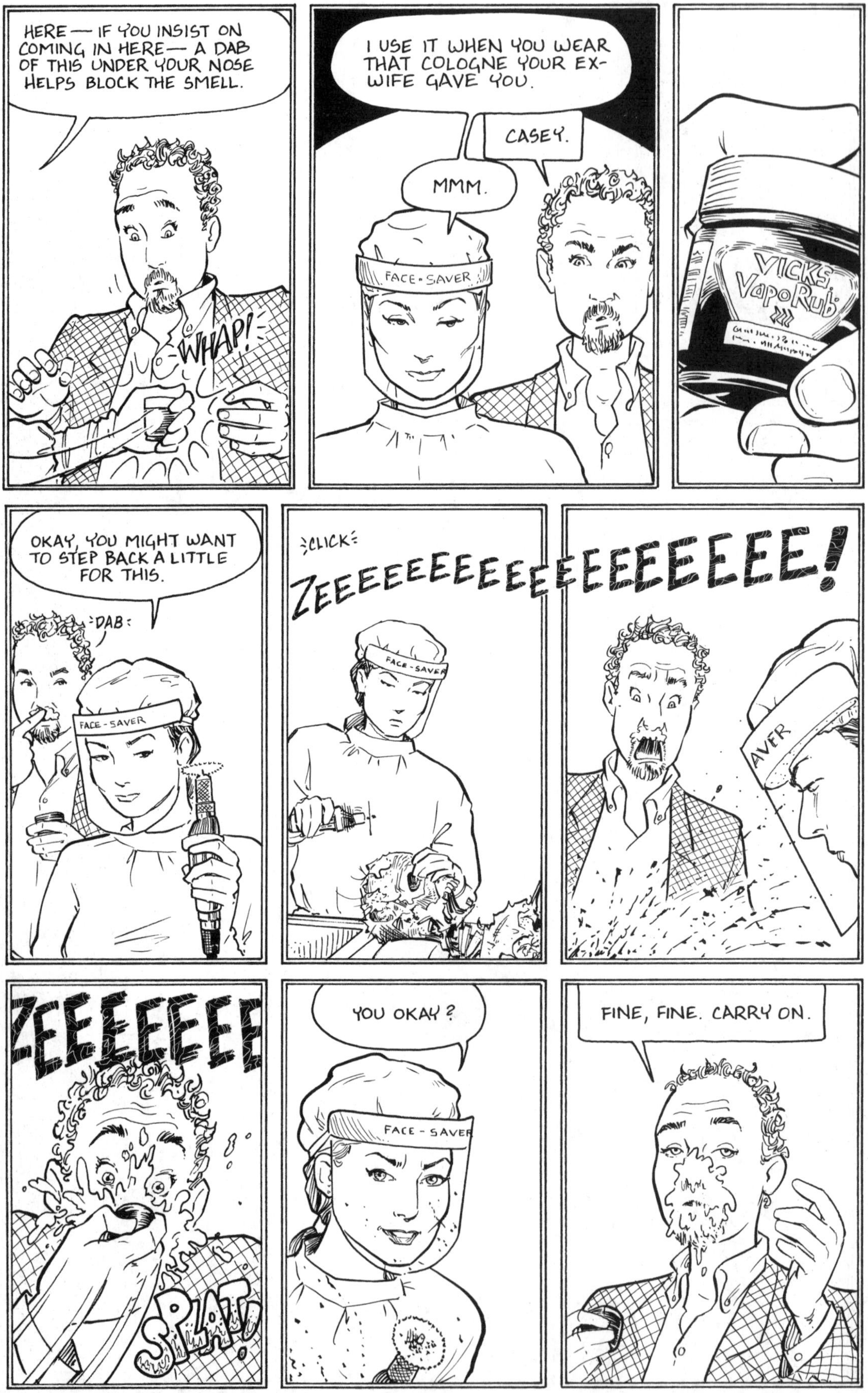
HERE— IF YOU INSIST ON COMING IN HERE— A DAB OF THIS UNDER YOUR NOSE HELPS BLOCK THE SMELL.
WHAP!
I USE IT WHEN YOU WEAR THAT COLOGNE YOUR EX-WIFE GAVE YOU.
MMM.
CASEY.
FACE-SAVER
VICKS VapoRub
OKAY, YOU MIGHT WANT TO STEP BACK A LITTLE FOR THIS.
DAB
FACE-SAVER
CLICK
ZEEEEEEEEEEEEEEEEEEE!
FACE-SAVER
AVER
ZEEEEEEE
SPLAT!
YOU OKAY?
FACE-SAVER
FINE, FINE. CARRY ON.

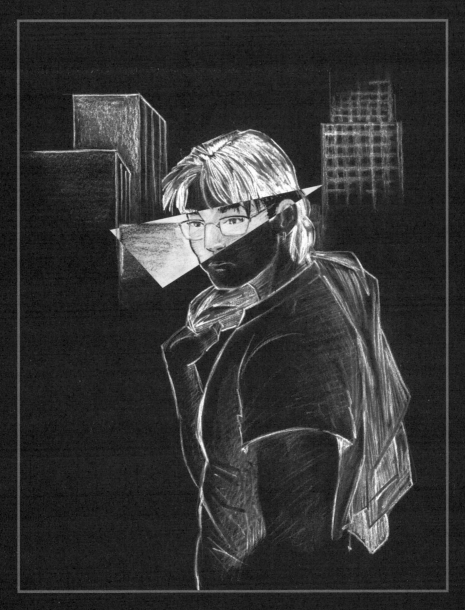

I left Japan to come to New York. I had a layover in Houston and decided on a whim to go see Katchoo's paintings at the Hobbs Gallery. I didn't know she would be there, but she was and, well, next thing I know we're in Las Vegas with a wedding application. I guess we both got carried away. Vegas does that to you. A couple of days later Katchoo woke up from the dream, kissed me and left me standing on the balcony of the Bellagio. It wasn't a goodbye kiss, it was a thank you and I'll meet you back in Houston kiss. That night I had dinner with Casey and caught a plane to New York in the morning.

A couple of years ago Katchoo and I were among a handful of people lucky enough to survive a plane crash. All of us had trouble coping with the reality of that. Many of us continue to have physical problems and, for some of us, the fight to survive continues. That's why I came to New York.

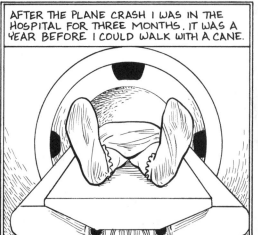
AFTER THE PLANE CRASH I WAS IN THE HOSPITAL FOR THREE MONTHS. IT WAS A YEAR BEFORE I COULD WALK WITH A CANE.

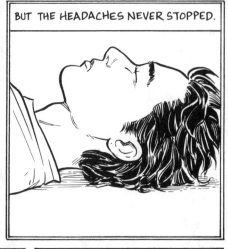
BUT THE HEADACHES NEVER STOPPED.

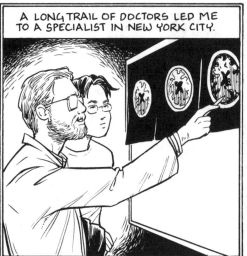
A LONG TRAIL OF DOCTORS LED ME TO A SPECIALIST IN NEW YORK CITY.

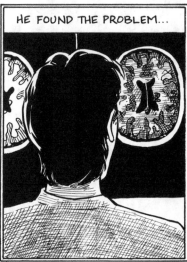
HE FOUND THE PROBLEM...

BUT HE DIDN'T HAVE A SOLUTION.

SOMETIMES LIFE IS BLACK AND WHITE.

OPEN

SOMETIMES THE ANSWER TO YOUR PRAYER IS NO.

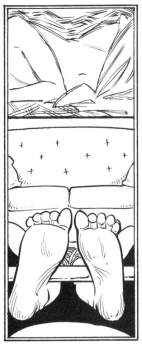

BULL.

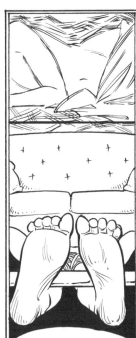

LIAR!

BLAH, BLAH BLAH BLAH!

OFF 4.1³ GM -3.1 GPO +1.⁷ NEWS

DING! DONG!

I GUESS THEY JUST THINK WE'RE ALL IDIOTS.

DING! DONG!

I'M BACK!

ZZZ

CASEY...!

WHAP!

SMOOCHIES!

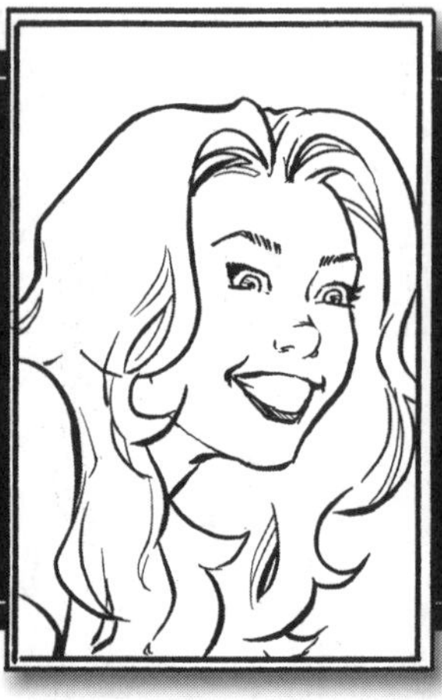

If there is a person who loves life more than Gwynnethina Casey Bullocks-Femur, I have yet to meet them. I think it crosses her mind a hundred times a day, "God I love being alive!"

Wish I could say the same.

I mean, I like it...just not with the fervor Casey has for it. I think everybody should have at least one cheerleader friend.

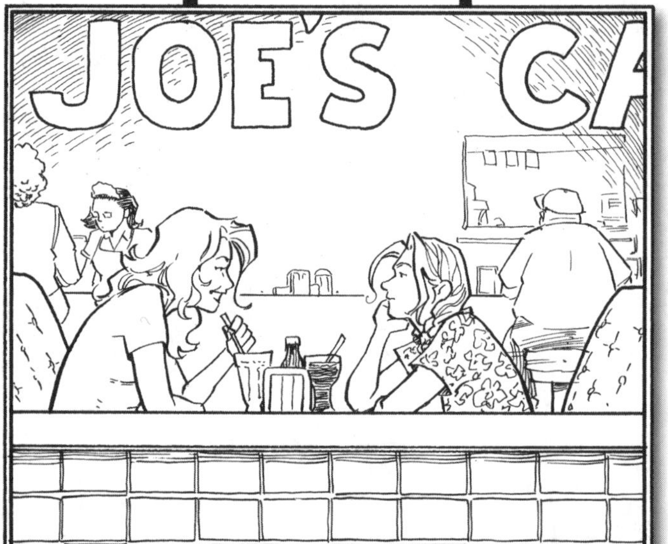
JOE'S CA

Casey is the best friend I've ever had—without her I would be a sour dissident. She reminds me that life can be fun. And it's not like she's completely oblivious to the awful things in this world, she just doesn't seem to absorb them like I do. They don't stick in her belly and light a fire of outrage within her that can't be put out. She doesn't yell at the stupidity on TV like I do, she doesn't yell at politicians and celebrities. Bless her heart, she doesn't yell at anybody. She hugs them.

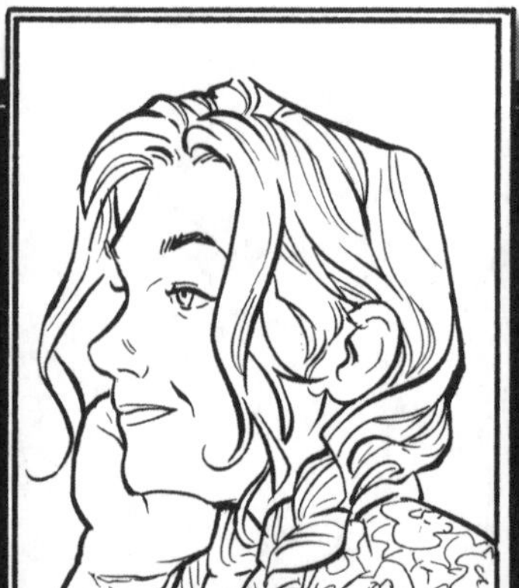

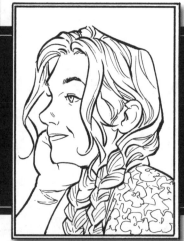

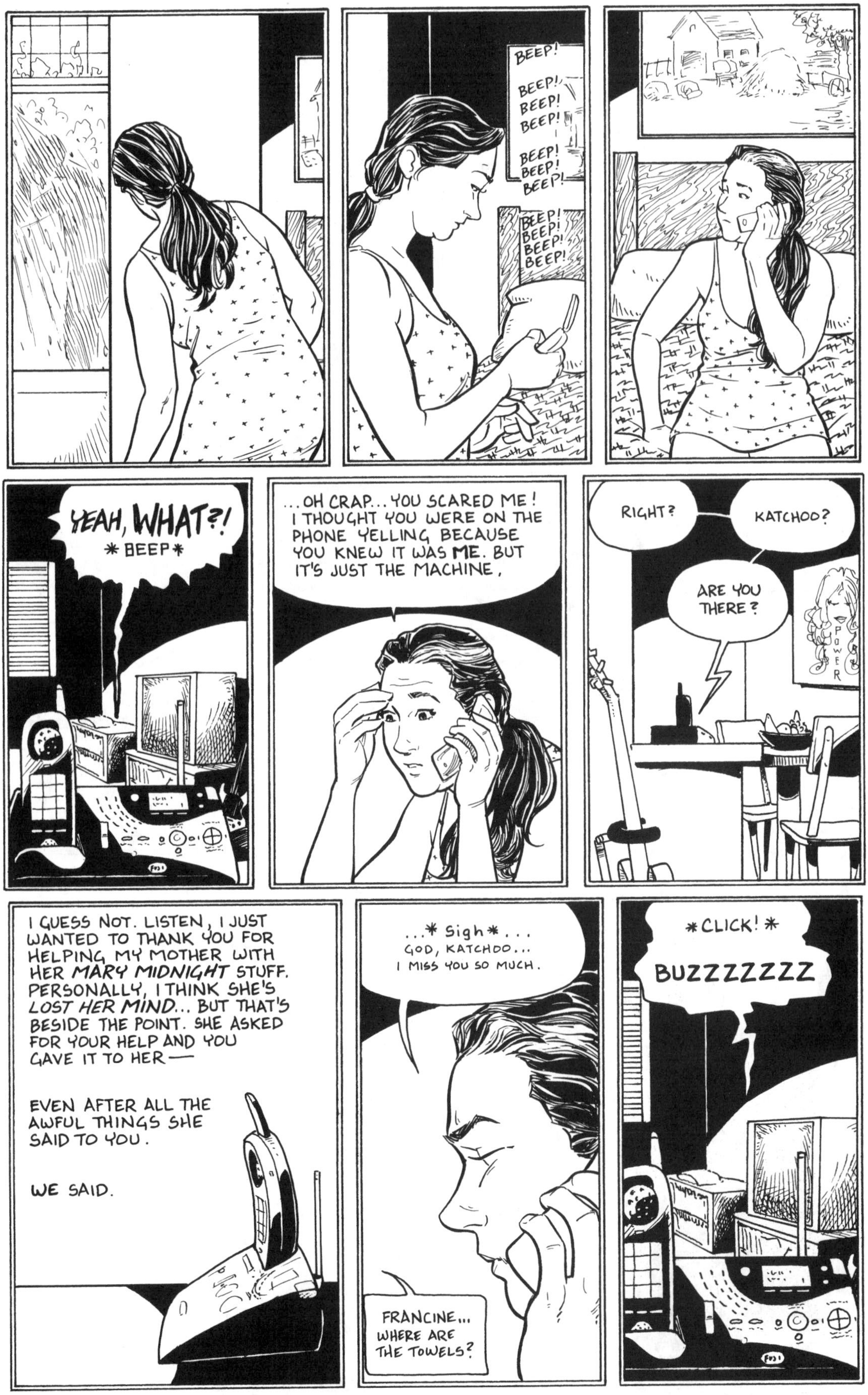
BEEP!
BEEP! BEEP! BEEP!
BEEP! BEEP! BEEP!
BEEP! BEEP! BEEP! BEEP!
YEAH, WHAT?!
BEEP
...OH CRAP...YOU SCARED ME! I THOUGHT YOU WERE ON THE PHONE YELLING BECAUSE YOU KNEW IT WAS ME. BUT IT'S JUST THE MACHINE,
RIGHT?
KATCHOO?
ARE YOU THERE?
POWER
I GUESS NOT. LISTEN, I JUST WANTED TO THANK YOU FOR HELPING MY MOTHER WITH HER MARY MIDNIGHT STUFF. PERSONALLY, I THINK SHE'S LOST HER MIND... BUT THAT'S BESIDE THE POINT. SHE ASKED FOR YOUR HELP AND YOU GAVE IT TO HER—
EVEN AFTER ALL THE AWFUL THINGS SHE SAID TO YOU.
WE SAID.
...*Sigh*... GOD, KATCHOO... I MISS YOU SO MUCH.
FRANCINE... WHERE ARE THE TOWELS?
CLICK!
BUZZZZZZZ

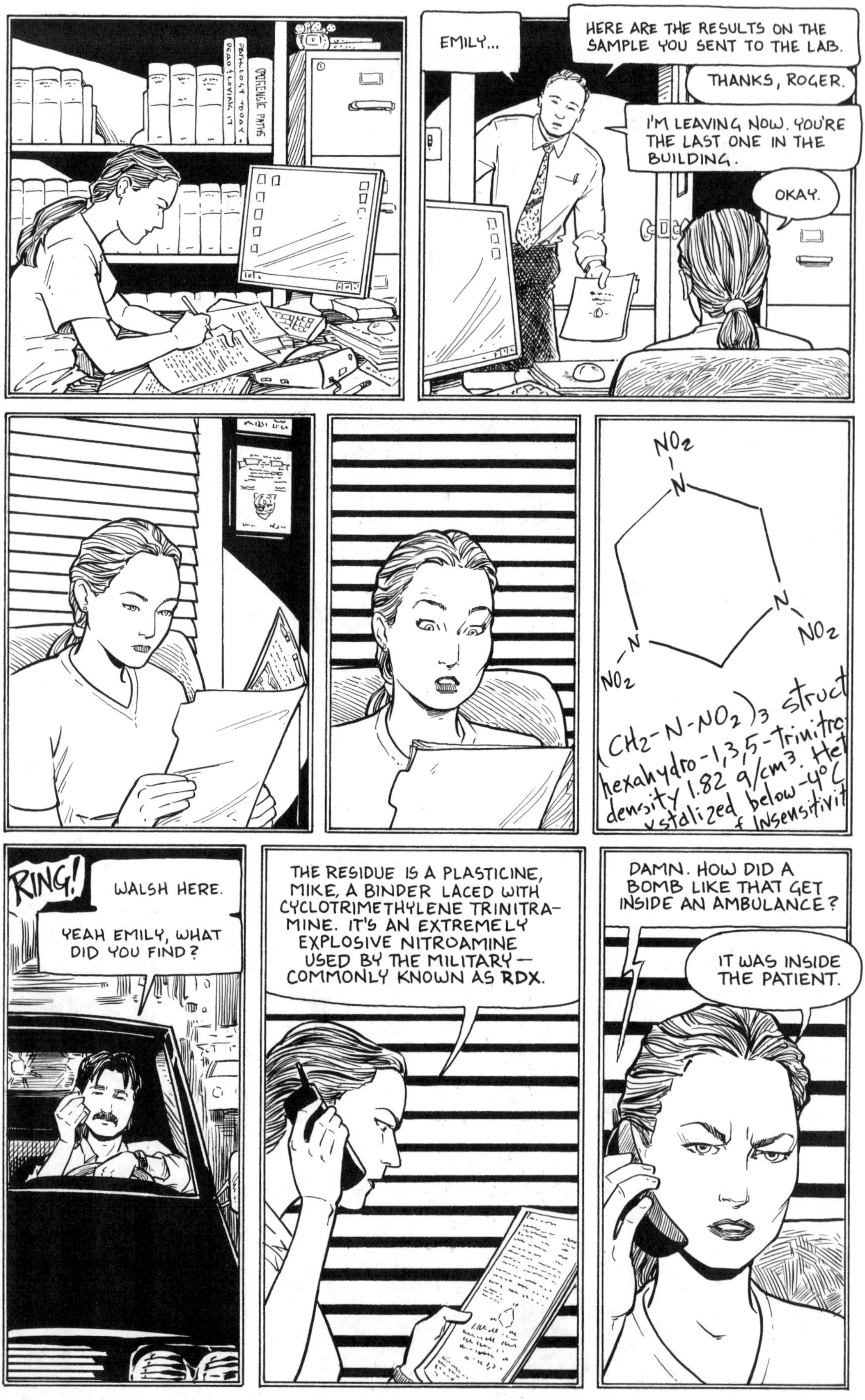
EMILY...
HERE ARE THE RESULTS ON THE SAMPLE YOU SENT TO THE LAB.
THANKS, ROGER.
I'M LEAVING NOW. YOU'RE THE LAST ONE IN THE BUILDING.
OKAY.
NO2
N
N
NO2
N
NO2
(CH2-N-NO2)3 struct
hexahydro-1,3,5-trinitro
density 1.82 g/cm3. Het
xstalized below -4°C
f Insensitivit
RING!
WALSH HERE.
YEAH EMILY, WHAT DID YOU FIND?
THE RESIDUE IS A PLASTICINE, MIKE, A BINDER LACED WITH CYCLOTRIMETHYLENE TRINITRAMINE. IT'S AN EXTREMELY EXPLOSIVE NITROAMINE USED BY THE MILITARY— COMMONLY KNOWN AS RDX.
DAMN. HOW DID A BOMB LIKE THAT GET INSIDE AN AMBULANCE?
IT WAS INSIDE THE PATIENT.

BLINK!

BLINK!

BLINK!

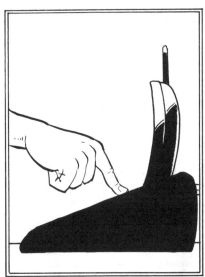

OH CRAP... YOU SCARED ME! I THOUGHT YOU WERE ON THE PHONE YELLING BECAUSE YOU KNEW IT WAS ME. BUT IT'S JUST THE MACHINE.

RIGHT?

KATCHOO?

ARE YOU THERE?

I GUESS NOT. LISTEN, I JUST WANTED TO THANK YOU FOR HELPING MY MOTHER WITH HER MARY MIDNIGHT STUFF. PERSONALLY, I THINK SHE'S LOST HER MIND... BUT THAT'S BESIDE THE POINT. SHE ASKED FOR YOUR HELP AND YOU GAVE IT TO HER —

EVEN AFTER ALL THE AWFUL THINGS SHE SAID TO YOU.

WE SAID.

* SIGH *

GOD, KATCHOO...

I MISS YOU SO MUCH.

* CLICK! *

BZZZZZZZ

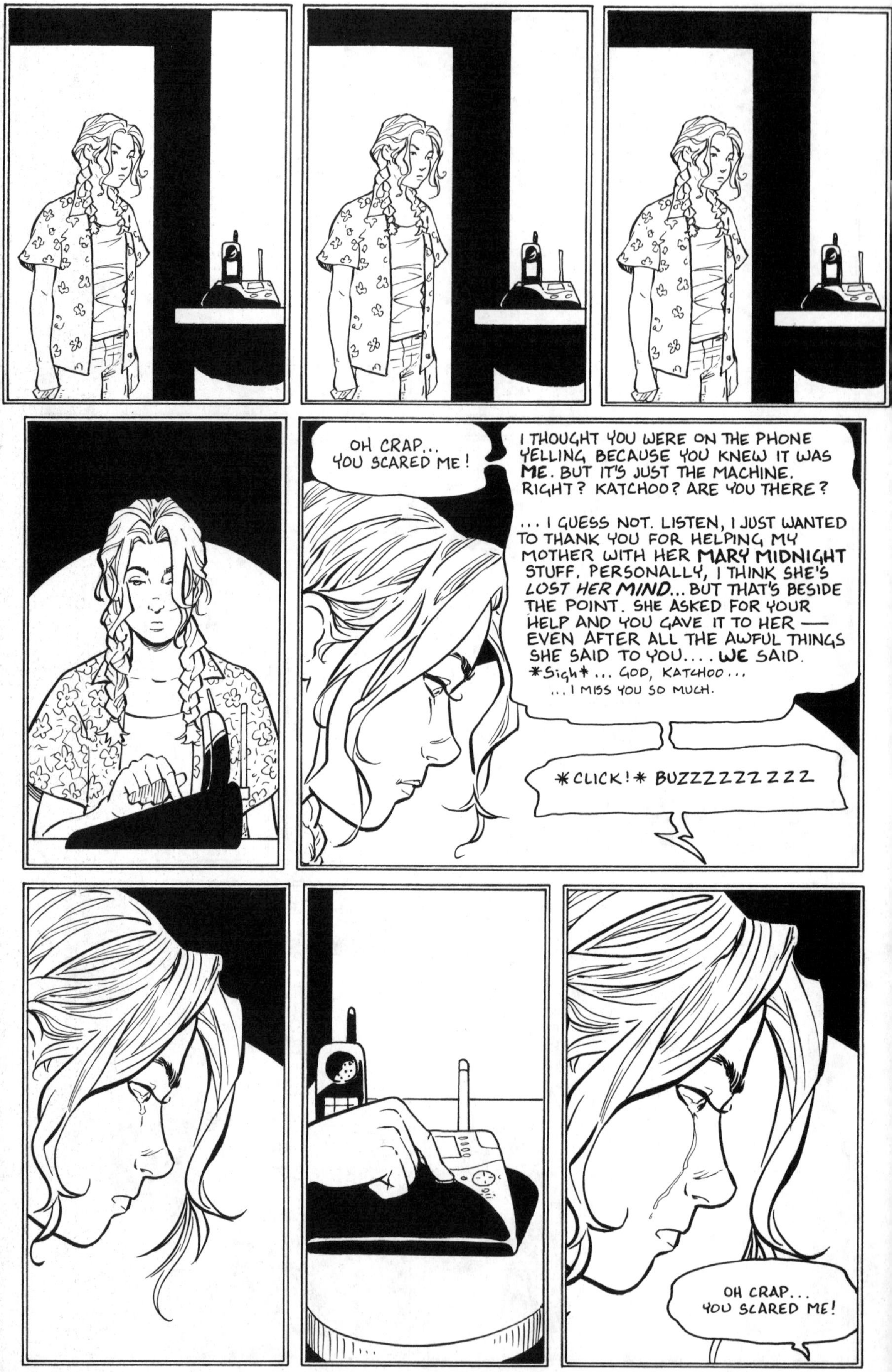
OH CRAP... YOU SCARED ME!
I THOUGHT YOU WERE ON THE PHONE YELLING BECAUSE YOU KNEW IT WAS ME. BUT IT'S JUST THE MACHINE. RIGHT? KATCHOO? ARE YOU THERE?
... I GUESS NOT. LISTEN, I JUST WANTED TO THANK YOU FOR HELPING MY MOTHER WITH HER MARY MIDNIGHT STUFF. PERSONALLY, I THINK SHE'S LOST HER MIND... BUT THAT'S BESIDE THE POINT. SHE ASKED FOR YOUR HELP AND YOU GAVE IT TO HER — EVEN AFTER ALL THE AWFUL THINGS SHE SAID TO YOU.... WE SAID. *Sigh*... GOD, KATCHOO... ...I MISS YOU SO MUCH.
CLICK! BUZZZZZZZZZ
OH CRAP... YOU SCARED ME!

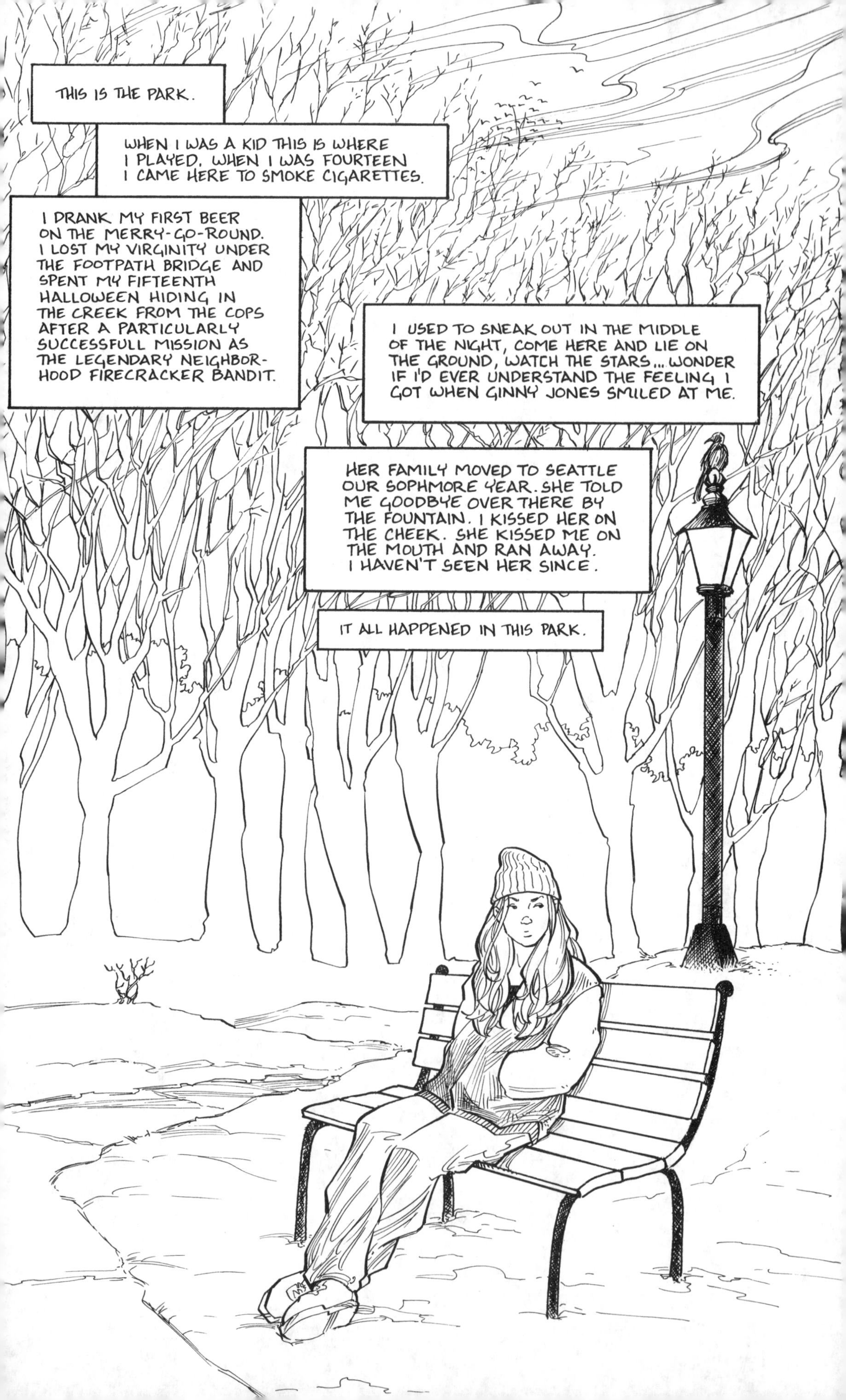
THIS IS THE PARK.
WHEN I WAS A KID THIS IS WHERE I PLAYED. WHEN I WAS FOURTEEN I CAME HERE TO SMOKE CIGARETTES.
I DRANK MY FIRST BEER ON THE MERRY-GO-ROUND. I LOST MY VIRGINITY UNDER THE FOOTPATH BRIDGE AND SPENT MY FIFTEENTH HALLOWEEN HIDING IN THE CREEK FROM THE COPS AFTER A PARTICULARLY SUCCESSFULL MISSION AS THE LEGENDARY NEIGHBOR-HOOD FIRECRACKER BANDIT.
I USED TO SNEAK OUT IN THE MIDDLE OF THE NIGHT, COME HERE AND LIE ON THE GROUND, WATCH THE STARS... WONDER IF I'D EVER UNDERSTAND THE FEELING I GOT WHEN GINNY JONES SMILED AT ME.
HER FAMILY MOVED TO SEATTLE OUR SOPHMORE YEAR. SHE TOLD ME GOODBYE OVER THERE BY THE FOUNTAIN. I KISSED HER ON THE CHEEK. SHE KISSED ME ON THE MOUTH AND RAN AWAY. I HAVEN'T SEEN HER SINCE.
IT ALL HAPPENED IN THIS PARK.

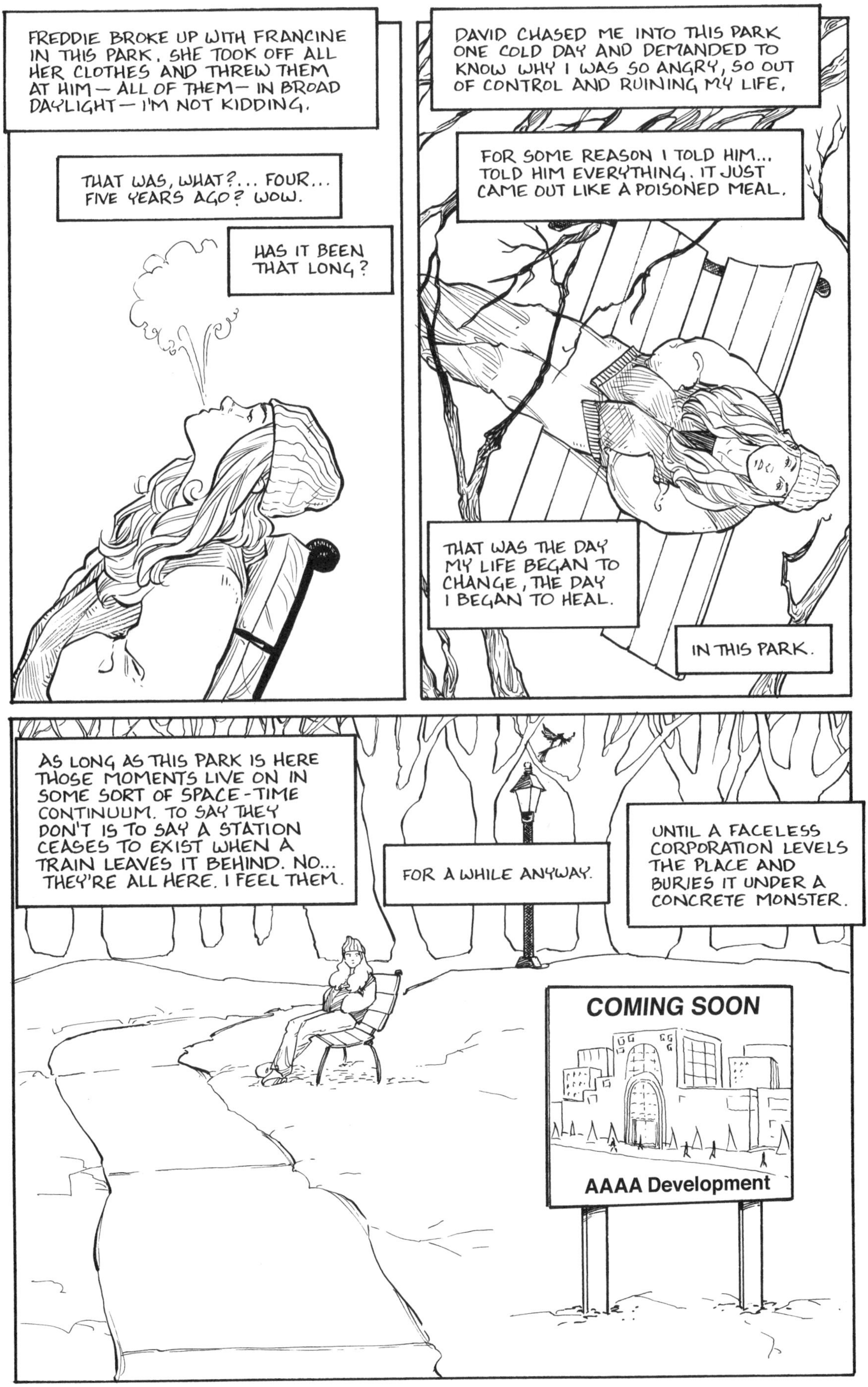
FREDDIE BROKE UP WITH FRANCINE IN THIS PARK. SHE TOOK OFF ALL HER CLOTHES AND THREW THEM AT HIM — ALL OF THEM — IN BROAD DAYLIGHT — I'M NOT KIDDING.
THAT WAS, WHAT?... FOUR... FIVE YEARS AGO? WOW.
HAS IT BEEN THAT LONG?
DAVID CHASED ME INTO THIS PARK ONE COLD DAY AND DEMANDED TO KNOW WHY I WAS SO ANGRY, SO OUT OF CONTROL AND RUINING MY LIFE.
FOR SOME REASON I TOLD HIM... TOLD HIM EVERYTHING. IT JUST CAME OUT LIKE A POISONED MEAL.
THAT WAS THE DAY MY LIFE BEGAN TO CHANGE, THE DAY I BEGAN TO HEAL.
IN THIS PARK.
AS LONG AS THIS PARK IS HERE THOSE MOMENTS LIVE ON IN SOME SORT OF SPACE-TIME CONTINUUM. TO SAY THEY DON'T IS TO SAY A STATION CEASES TO EXIST WHEN A TRAIN LEAVES IT BEHIND. NO... THEY'RE ALL HERE. I FEEL THEM.
FOR A WHILE ANYWAY.
UNTIL A FACELESS CORPORATION LEVELS THE PLACE AND BURIES IT UNDER A CONCRETE MONSTER.
COMING SOON
AAAA Development

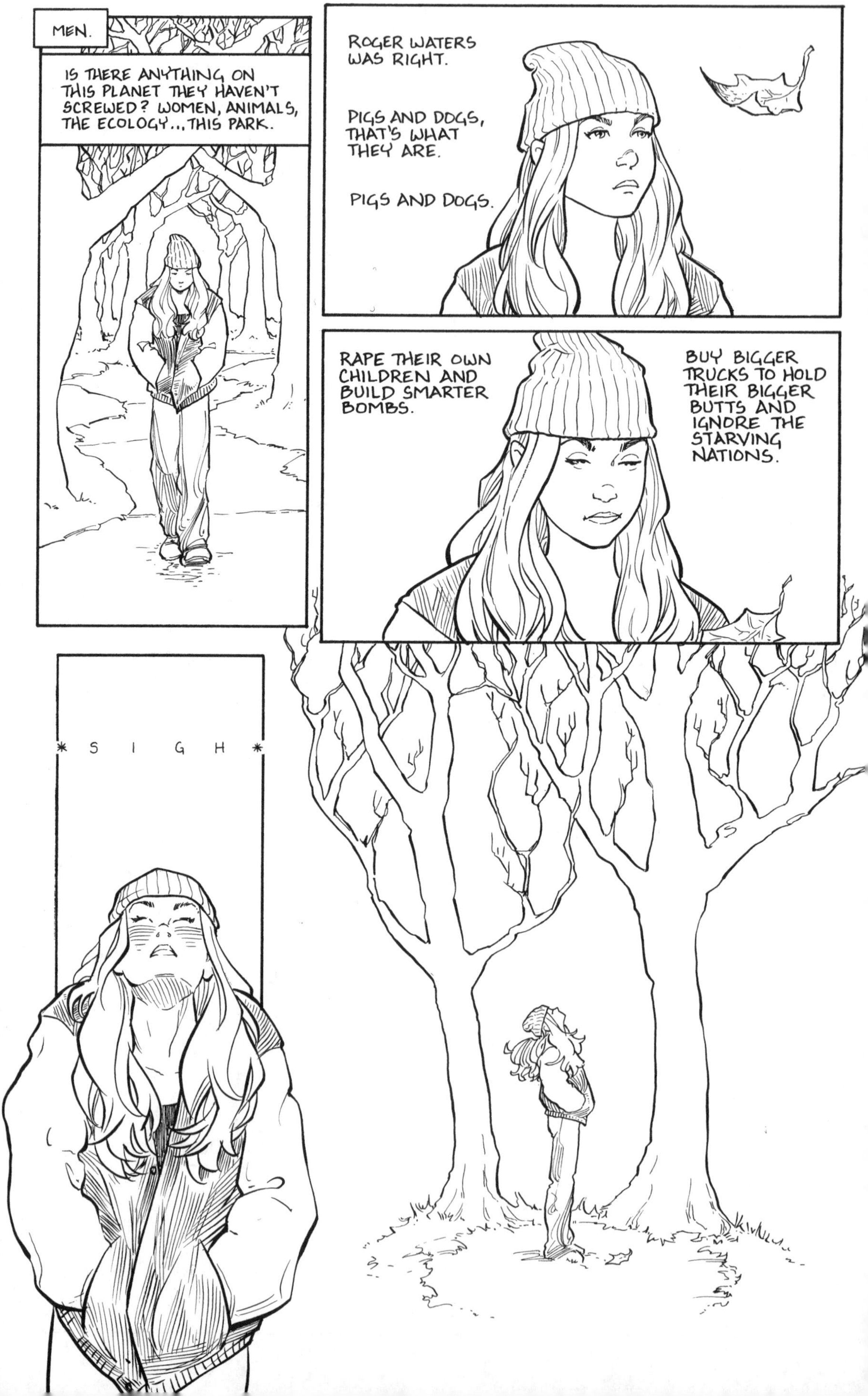

MEN.
IS THERE ANYTHING ON THIS PLANET THEY HAVEN'T SCREWED? WOMEN, ANIMALS, THE ECOLOGY..., THIS PARK.
ROGER WATERS WAS RIGHT.
PIGS AND DOGS, THAT'S WHAT THEY ARE.
PIGS AND DOGS.
RAPE THEIR OWN CHILDREN AND BUILD SMARTER BOMBS.
BUY BIGGER TRUCKS TO HOLD THEIR BIGGER BUTTS AND IGNORE THE STARVING NATIONS.
SIGH

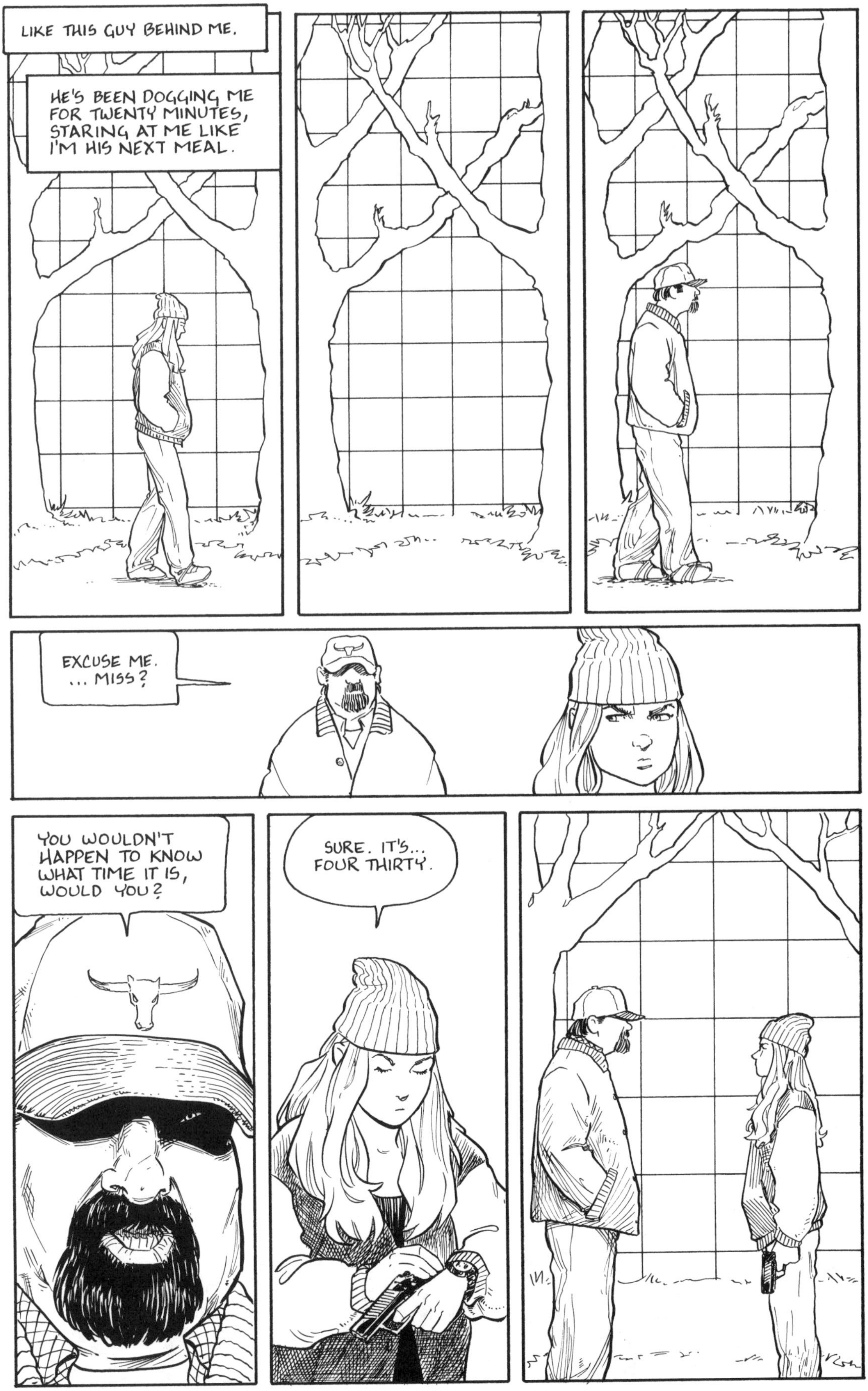
LIKE THIS GUY BEHIND ME.
HE'S BEEN DOGGING ME FOR TWENTY MINUTES, STARING AT ME LIKE I'M HIS NEXT MEAL.
EXCUSE ME. ... MISS?
YOU WOULDN'T HAPPEN TO KNOW WHAT TIME IT IS, WOULD YOU?
SURE. IT'S... FOUR THIRTY.

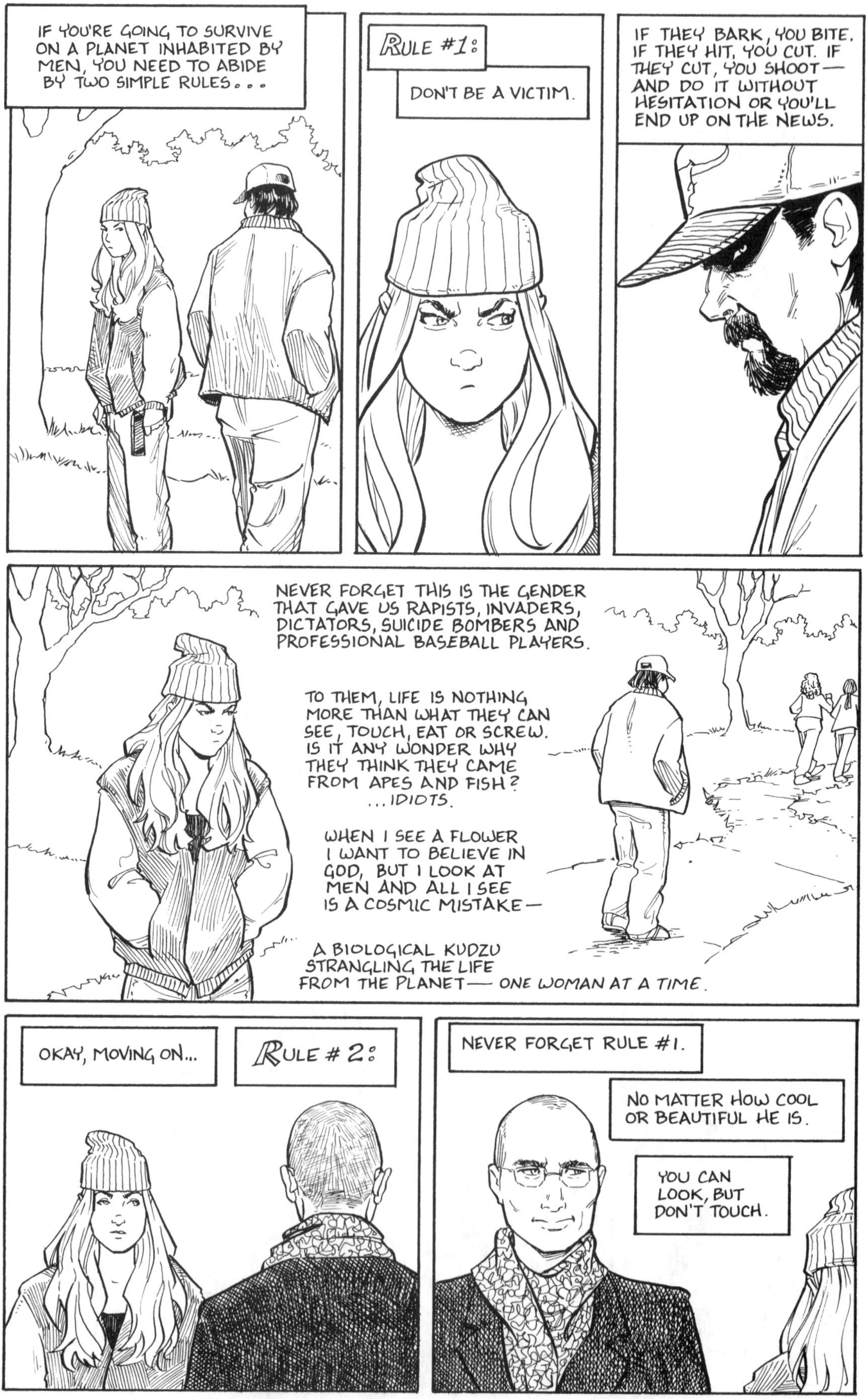

IF YOU'RE GOING TO SURVIVE ON A PLANET INHABITED BY MEN, YOU NEED TO ABIDE BY TWO SIMPLE RULES...
RULE #1:
DON'T BE A VICTIM.
IF THEY BARK, YOU BITE. IF THEY HIT, YOU CUT. IF THEY CUT, YOU SHOOT— AND DO IT WITHOUT HESITATION OR YOU'LL END UP ON THE NEWS.
NEVER FORGET THIS IS THE GENDER THAT GAVE US RAPISTS, INVADERS, DICTATORS, SUICIDE BOMBERS AND PROFESSIONAL BASEBALL PLAYERS.
TO THEM, LIFE IS NOTHING MORE THAN WHAT THEY CAN SEE, TOUCH, EAT OR SCREW. IS IT ANY WONDER WHY THEY THINK THEY CAME FROM APES AND FISH? ...IDIOTS.
WHEN I SEE A FLOWER I WANT TO BELIEVE IN GOD, BUT I LOOK AT MEN AND ALL I SEE IS A COSMIC MISTAKE—
A BIOLOGICAL KUDZU STRANGLING THE LIFE FROM THE PLANET— ONE WOMAN AT A TIME.
OKAY, MOVING ON...
RULE #2:
NEVER FORGET RULE #1.
NO MATTER HOW COOL OR BEAUTIFUL HE IS.
YOU CAN LOOK, BUT DON'T TOUCH.

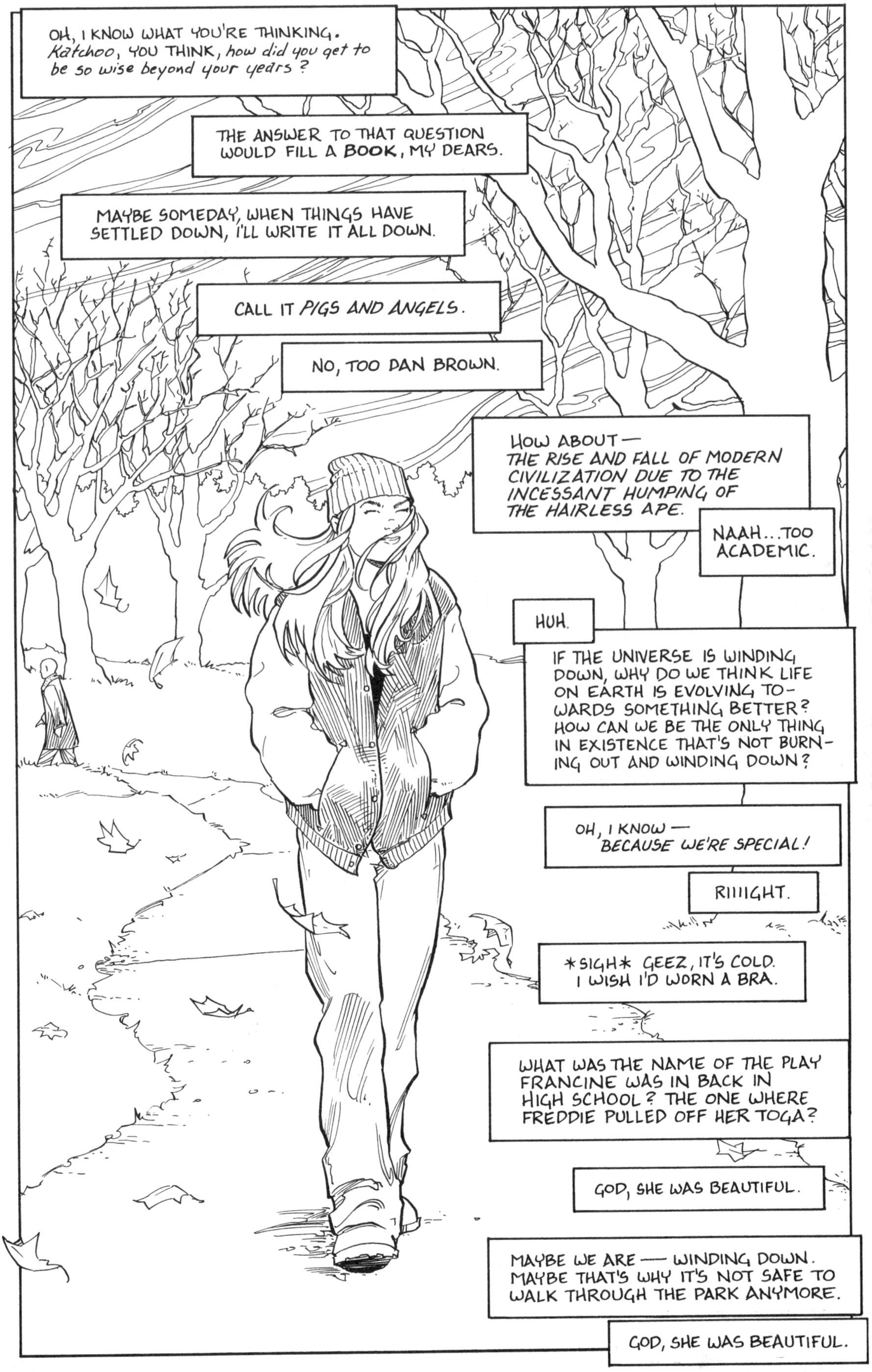
OH, I KNOW WHAT YOU'RE THINKING. *Katchoo,* YOU THINK, *how did you get to be so wise beyond your years?*
THE ANSWER TO THAT QUESTION WOULD FILL A **BOOK**, MY DEARS.
MAYBE SOMEDAY, WHEN THINGS HAVE SETTLED DOWN, I'LL WRITE IT ALL DOWN.
CALL IT *PIGS AND ANGELS*.
NO, TOO DAN BROWN.
HOW ABOUT— *THE RISE AND FALL OF MODERN CIVILIZATION DUE TO THE INCESSANT HUMPING OF THE HAIRLESS APE.*
NAAH...TOO ACADEMIC.
HUH.
IF THE UNIVERSE IS WINDING DOWN, WHY DO WE THINK LIFE ON EARTH IS EVOLVING TOWARDS SOMETHING BETTER? HOW CAN WE BE THE ONLY THING IN EXISTENCE THAT'S NOT BURNING OUT AND WINDING DOWN?
OH, I KNOW— *BECAUSE WE'RE SPECIAL!*
RIIIIGHT.
SIGH GEEZ, IT'S COLD. I WISH I'D WORN A BRA.
WHAT WAS THE NAME OF THE PLAY FRANCINE WAS IN BACK IN HIGH SCHOOL? THE ONE WHERE FREDDIE PULLED OFF HER TOGA?
GOD, SHE WAS BEAUTIFUL.
MAYBE WE ARE — WINDING DOWN. MAYBE THAT'S WHY IT'S NOT SAFE TO WALK THROUGH THE PARK ANYMORE.
GOD, SHE WAS BEAUTIFUL.

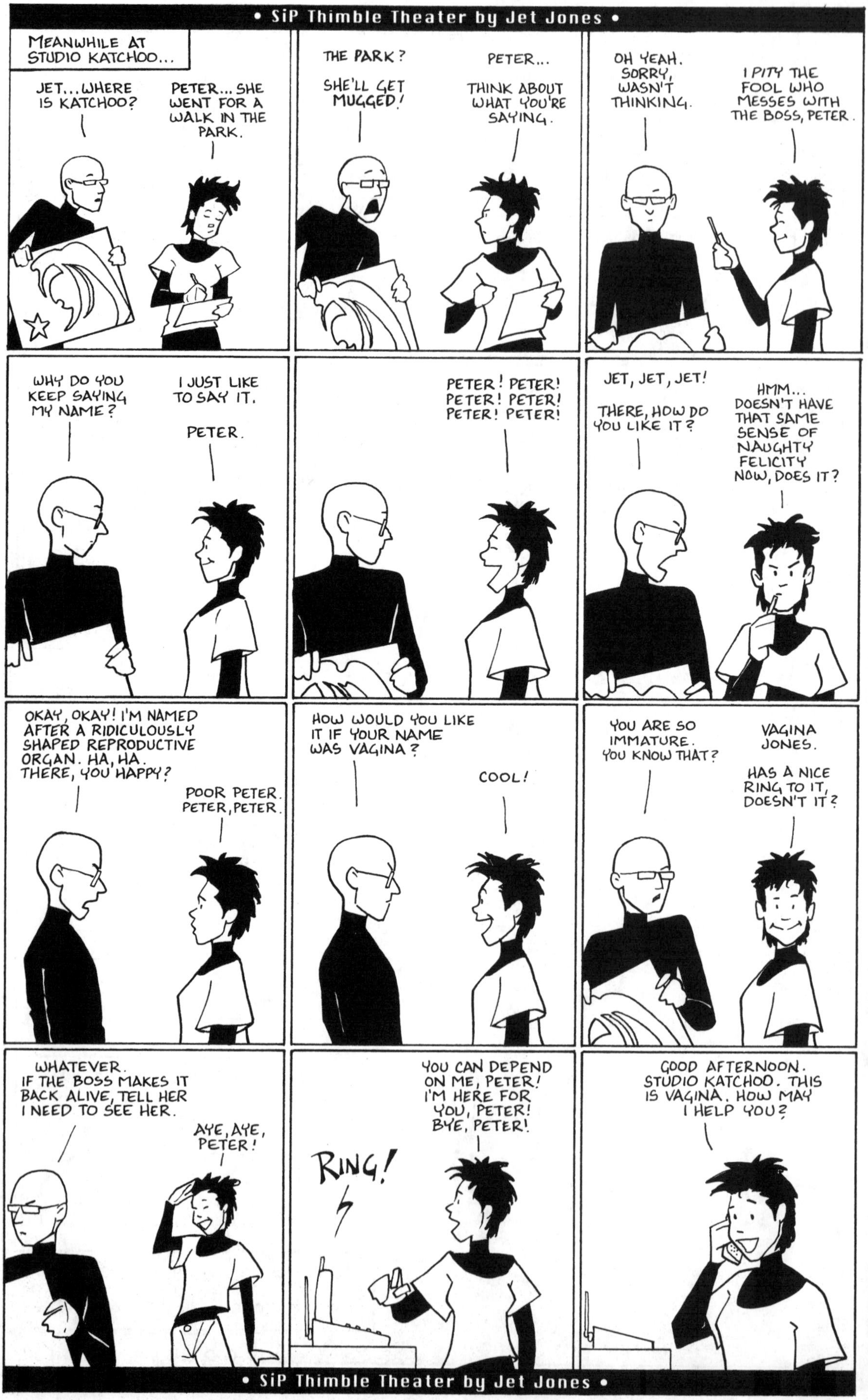
• SiP Thimble Theater by Jet Jones •
MEANWHILE AT STUDIO KATCHOO...
JET... WHERE IS KATCHOO?
PETER... SHE WENT FOR A WALK IN THE PARK.
THE PARK?
SHE'LL GET MUGGED!
PETER...
THINK ABOUT WHAT YOU'RE SAYING.
OH YEAH. SORRY, WASN'T THINKING.
I PITY THE FOOL WHO MESSES WITH THE BOSS, PETER.
WHY DO YOU KEEP SAYING MY NAME?
I JUST LIKE TO SAY IT.
PETER.
PETER! PETER! PETER! PETER! PETER! PETER!
JET, JET, JET!
THERE, HOW DO YOU LIKE IT?
HMM... DOESN'T HAVE THAT SAME SENSE OF NAUGHTY FELICITY NOW, DOES IT?
OKAY, OKAY! I'M NAMED AFTER A RIDICULOUSLY SHAPED REPRODUCTIVE ORGAN. HA, HA. THERE, YOU HAPPY?
POOR PETER. PETER, PETER.
HOW WOULD YOU LIKE IT IF YOUR NAME WAS VAGINA?
COOL!
YOU ARE SO IMMATURE. YOU KNOW THAT?
VAGINA JONES.
HAS A NICE RING TO IT, DOESN'T IT?
WHATEVER. IF THE BOSS MAKES IT BACK ALIVE, TELL HER I NEED TO SEE HER.
AYE, AYE, PETER!
YOU CAN DEPEND ON ME, PETER! I'M HERE FOR YOU, PETER! BYE, PETER!
RING!
GOOD AFTERNOON. STUDIO KATCHOO. THIS IS VAGINA. HOW MAY I HELP YOU?
• SiP Thimble Theater by Jet Jones •

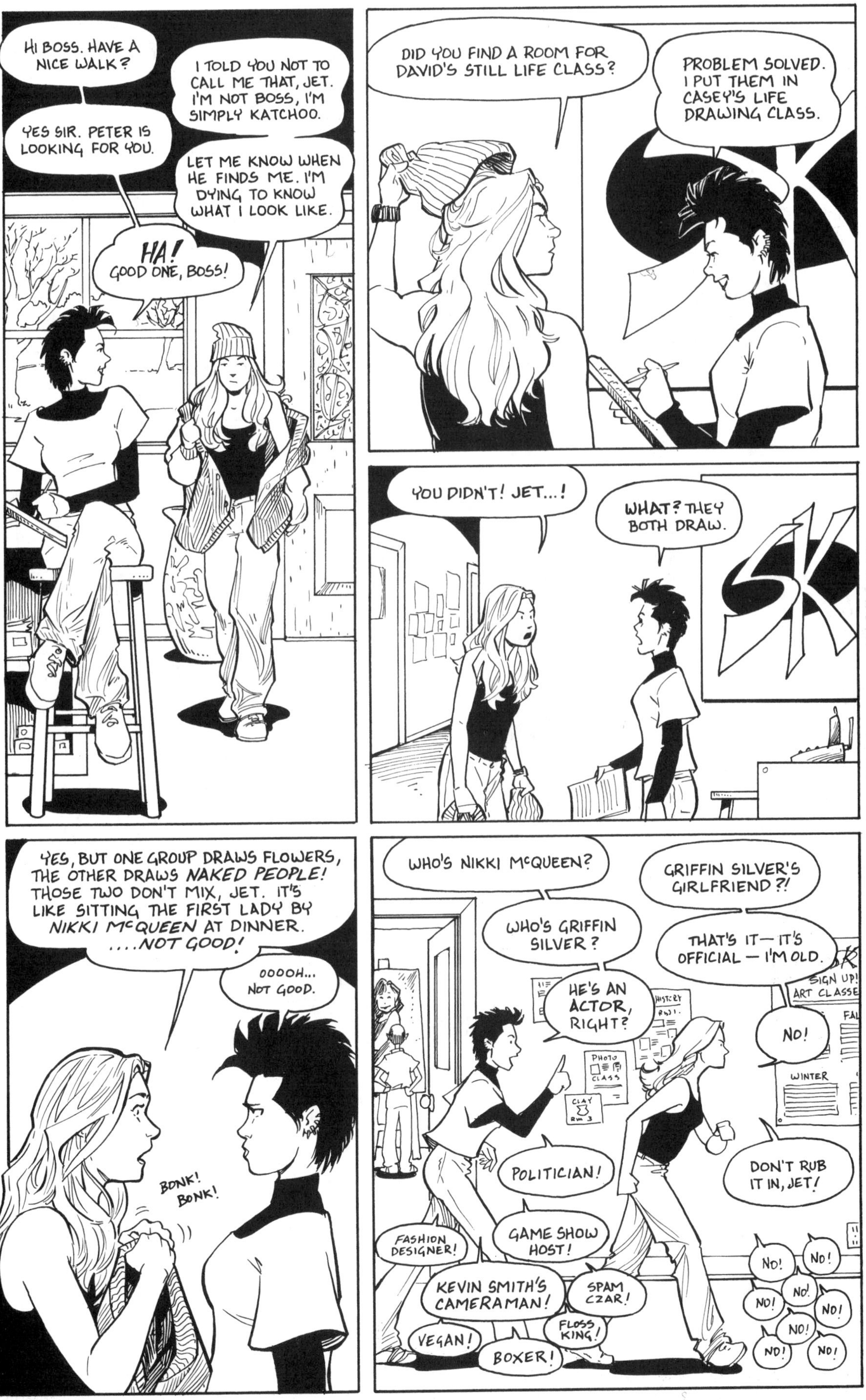
HI BOSS. HAVE A NICE WALK?
I TOLD YOU NOT TO CALL ME THAT, JET. I'M NOT BOSS, I'M SIMPLY KATCHOO.
YES SIR. PETER IS LOOKING FOR YOU.
LET ME KNOW WHEN HE FINDS ME. I'M DYING TO KNOW WHAT I LOOK LIKE.
HA! GOOD ONE, BOSS!
DID YOU FIND A ROOM FOR DAVID'S STILL LIFE CLASS?
PROBLEM SOLVED. I PUT THEM IN CASEY'S LIFE DRAWING CLASS.
YOU DIDN'T! JET...!
WHAT? THEY BOTH DRAW.
YES, BUT ONE GROUP DRAWS FLOWERS, THE OTHER DRAWS NAKED PEOPLE! THOSE TWO DON'T MIX, JET. IT'S LIKE SITTING THE FIRST LADY BY NIKKI McQUEEN AT DINNER. ....NOT GOOD!
OOOOH... NOT GOOD.
BONK! BONK!
WHO'S NIKKI McQUEEN?
GRIFFIN SILVER'S GIRLFRIEND?!
WHO'S GRIFFIN SILVER?
THAT'S IT— IT'S OFFICIAL — I'M OLD.
HE'S AN ACTOR, RIGHT?
SIGN UP! ART CLASSE
HISTORY
PHOTO CLASS
CLAY RM 3
WINTER
NO!
POLITICIAN!
DON'T RUB IT IN, JET!
GAME SHOW HOST!
FASHION DESIGNER!
KEVIN SMITH'S CAMERAMAN!
SPAM CZAR!
FLOSS KING!
VEGAN!
BOXER!
NO! NO! NO! NO! NO! NO! NO! NO!

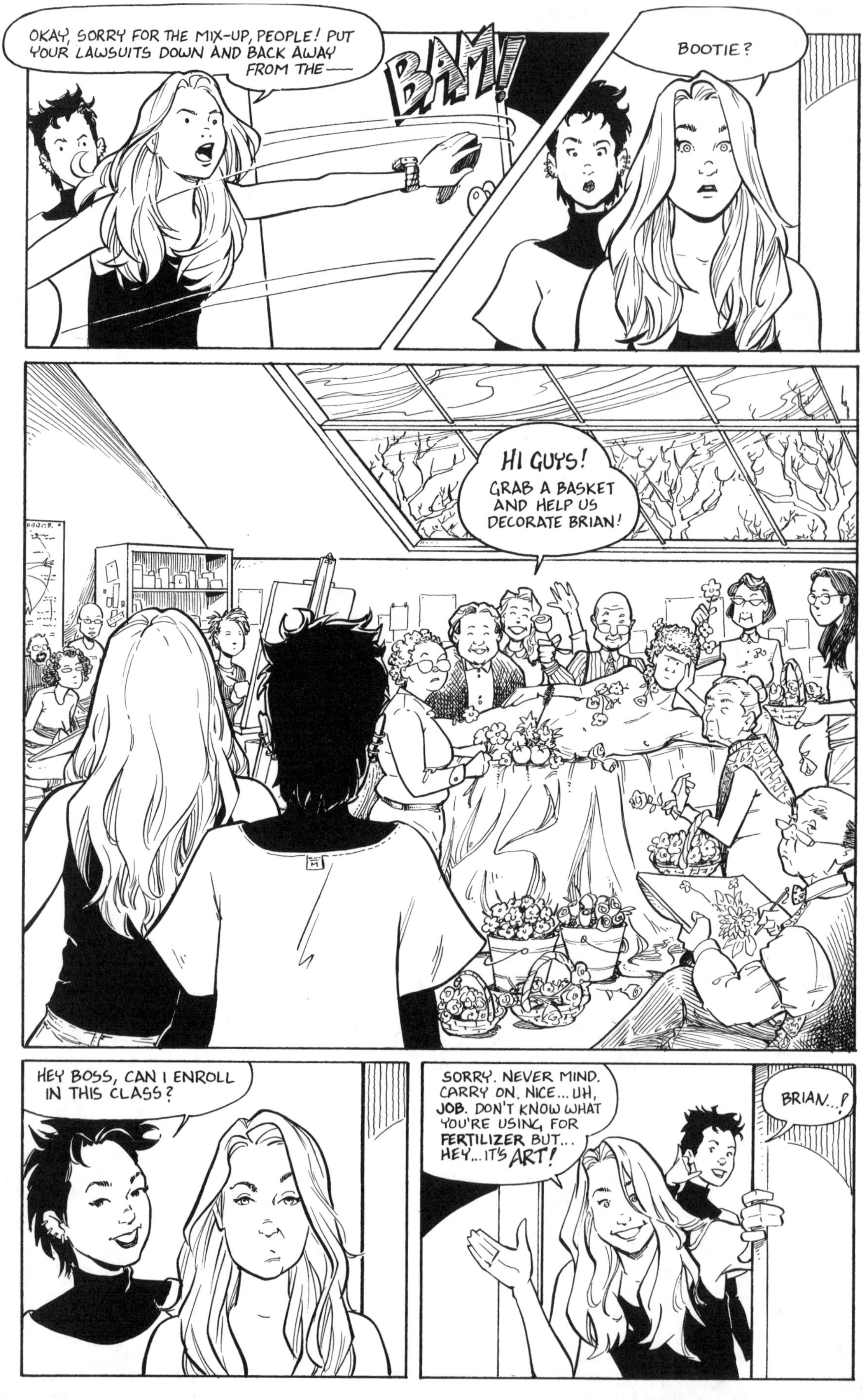
OKAY, SORRY FOR THE MIX-UP, PEOPLE! PUT YOUR LAWSUITS DOWN AND BACK AWAY FROM THE—
BAM!
BOOTIE?
HI GUYS! GRAB A BASKET AND HELP US DECORATE BRIAN!
HEY BOSS, CAN I ENROLL IN THIS CLASS?
SORRY. NEVER MIND. CARRY ON. NICE... UH, JOB. DON'T KNOW WHAT YOU'RE USING FOR FERTILIZER BUT... HEY... IT'S ART!
BRIAN...!

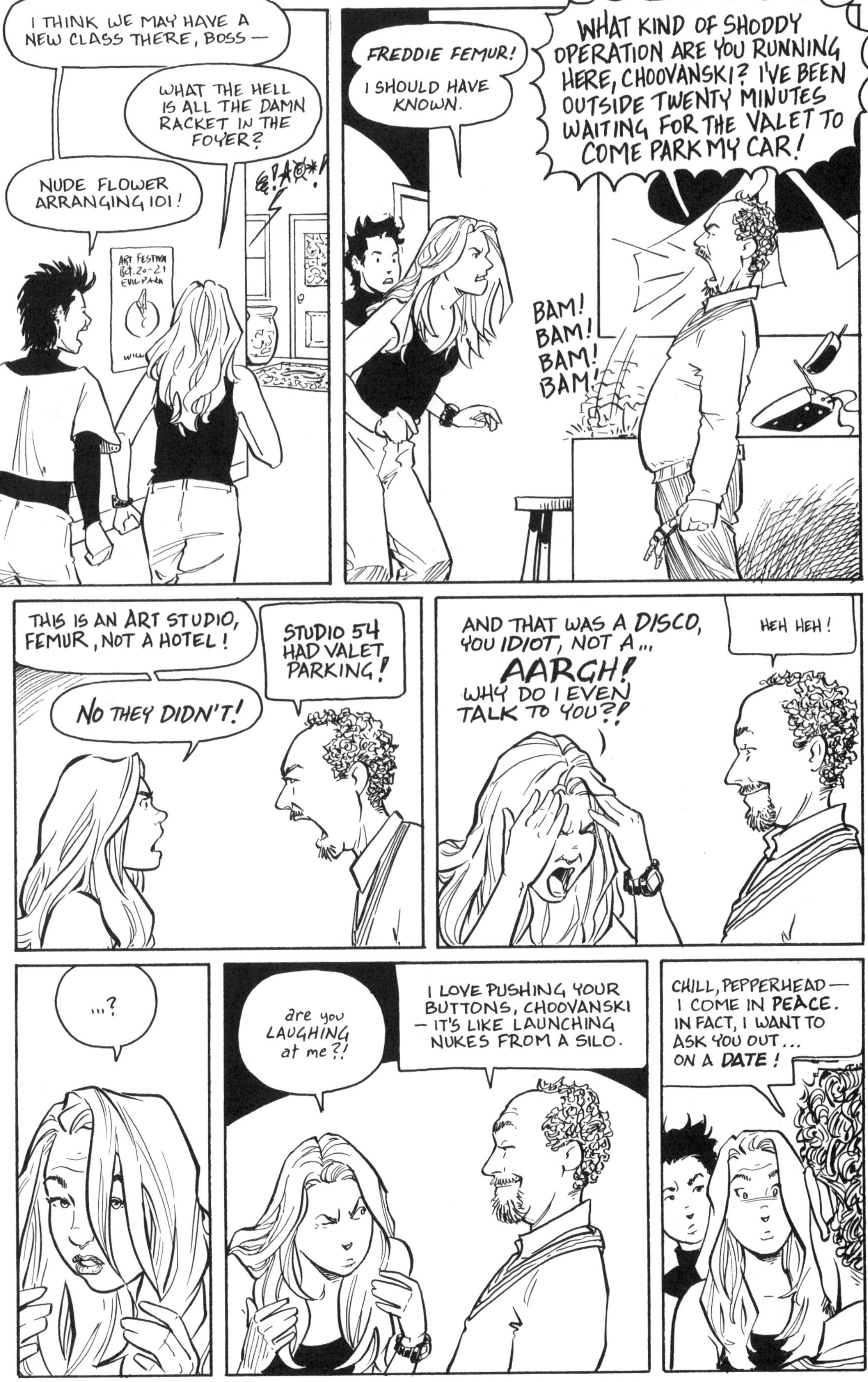
I THINK WE MAY HAVE A NEW CLASS THERE, BOSS —
WHAT THE HELL IS ALL THE DAMN RACKET IN THE FOYER?
NUDE FLOWER ARRANGING 101!
ART FESTIVAL Oct. 20-21 EVIL PARK
FREDDIE FEMUR!
I SHOULD HAVE KNOWN.
WHAT KIND OF SHODDY OPERATION ARE YOU RUNNING HERE, CHOOVANSKI? I'VE BEEN OUTSIDE TWENTY MINUTES WAITING FOR THE VALET TO COME PARK MY CAR!
BAM! BAM! BAM! BAM!
THIS IS AN ART STUDIO, FEMUR, NOT A HOTEL!
STUDIO 54 HAD VALET PARKING!
NO THEY DIDN'T!
AND THAT WAS A DISCO, YOU IDIOT, NOT A... AARGH! WHY DO I EVEN TALK TO YOU?!
HEH HEH!
...?
are you LAUGHING at me?!
I LOVE PUSHING YOUR BUTTONS, CHOOVANSKI — IT'S LIKE LAUNCHING NUKES FROM A SILO.
CHILL, PEPPERHEAD — I COME IN PEACE. IN FACT, I WANT TO ASK YOU OUT... ON A DATE!

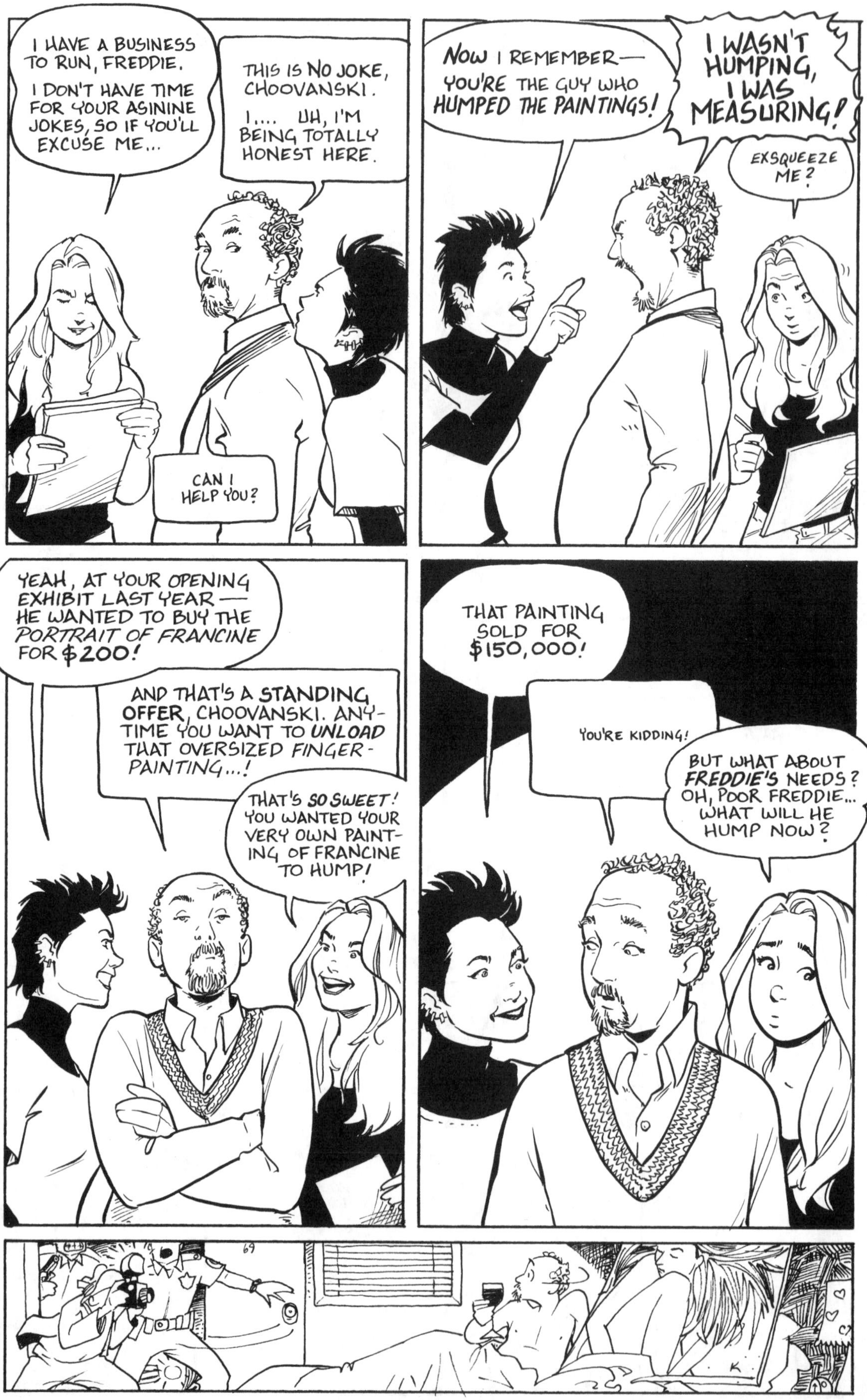
I HAVE A BUSINESS TO RUN, FREDDIE.
I DON'T HAVE TIME FOR YOUR ASININE JOKES, SO IF YOU'LL EXCUSE ME...
THIS IS NO JOKE, CHOOVANSKI.
I.... UH, I'M BEING TOTALLY HONEST HERE.
CAN I HELP YOU?
NOW I REMEMBER— YOU'RE THE GUY WHO HUMPED THE PAINTINGS!
I WASN'T HUMPING, I WAS MEASURING!
EXSQUEEZE ME?
YEAH, AT YOUR OPENING EXHIBIT LAST YEAR— HE WANTED TO BUY THE *PORTRAIT OF FRANCINE* FOR $200!
AND THAT'S A STANDING OFFER, CHOOVANSKI. ANY-TIME YOU WANT TO UNLOAD THAT OVERSIZED FINGER-PAINTING...!
THAT'S SO SWEET! YOU WANTED YOUR VERY OWN PAINT-ING OF FRANCINE TO HUMP!
THAT PAINTING SOLD FOR $150,000!
YOU'RE KIDDING!
BUT WHAT ABOUT FREDDIE'S NEEDS? OH, POOR FREDDIE... WHAT WILL HE HUMP NOW?

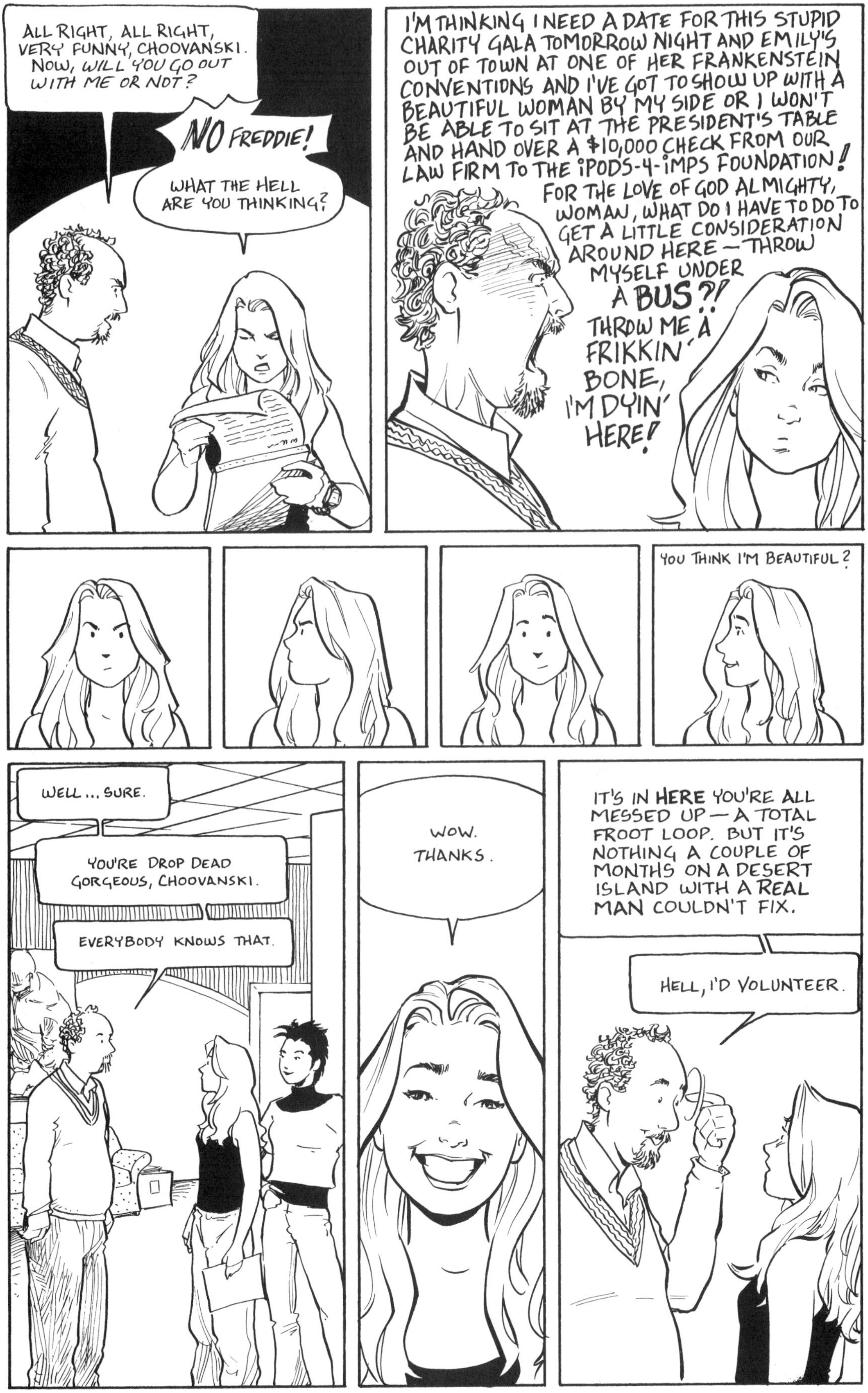
ALL RIGHT, ALL RIGHT, VERY FUNNY, CHOOVANSKI. NOW, WILL YOU GO OUT WITH ME OR NOT?
NO FREDDIE!
WHAT THE HELL ARE YOU THINKING?
I'M THINKING I NEED A DATE FOR THIS STUPID CHARITY GALA TOMORROW NIGHT AND EMILY'S OUT OF TOWN AT ONE OF HER FRANKENSTEIN CONVENTIONS AND I'VE GOT TO SHOW UP WITH A BEAUTIFUL WOMAN BY MY SIDE OR I WON'T BE ABLE TO SIT AT THE PRESIDENT'S TABLE AND HAND OVER A $10,000 CHECK FROM OUR LAW FIRM TO THE iPODS-4-iMPS FOUNDATION!
FOR THE LOVE OF GOD ALMIGHTY, WOMAN, WHAT DO I HAVE TO DO TO GET A LITTLE CONSIDERATION AROUND HERE — THROW MYSELF UNDER A BUS?!
THROW ME A FRIKKIN' BONE, I'M DYIN' HERE!
YOU THINK I'M BEAUTIFUL?
WELL ... SURE.
YOU'RE DROP DEAD GORGEOUS, CHOOVANSKI.
EVERYBODY KNOWS THAT.
WOW. THANKS.
IT'S IN HERE YOU'RE ALL MESSED UP — A TOTAL FROOT LOOP. BUT IT'S NOTHING A COUPLE OF MONTHS ON A DESERT ISLAND WITH A REAL MAN COULDN'T FIX.
HELL, I'D VOLUNTEER.

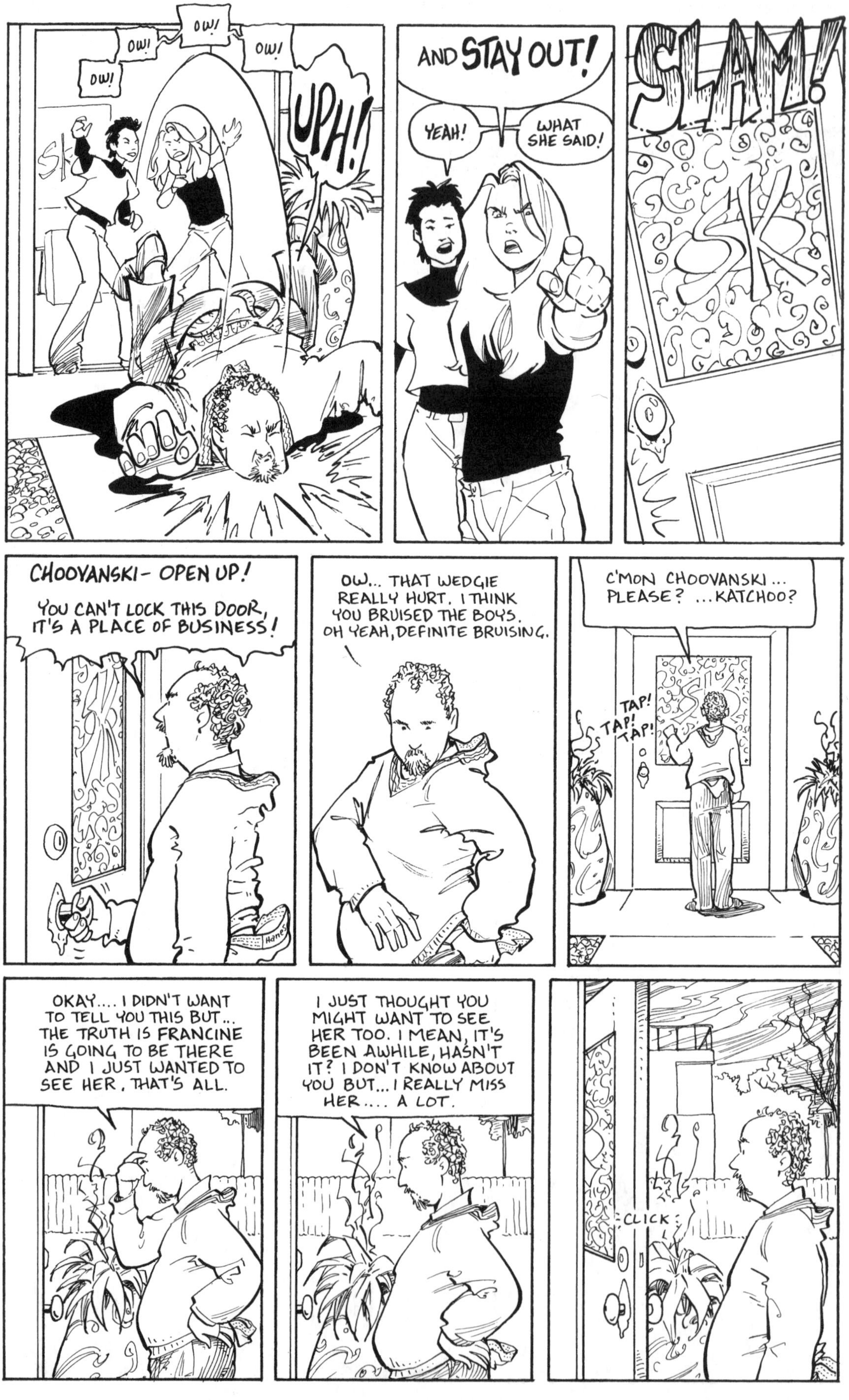
OW!
OW!
OW!
OW!
UPH!
AND STAY OUT!
YEAH!
WHAT SHE SAID!
SLAM!
CHOOVANSKI- OPEN UP!
YOU CAN'T LOCK THIS DOOR, IT'S A PLACE OF BUSINESS!
OW... THAT WEDGIE REALLY HURT. I THINK YOU BRUISED THE BOYS. OH YEAH, DEFINITE BRUISING.
C'MON CHOOVANSKI... PLEASE? ...KATCHOO?
TAP! TAP! TAP!
OKAY.... I DIDN'T WANT TO TELL YOU THIS BUT... THE TRUTH IS FRANCINE IS GOING TO BE THERE AND I JUST WANTED TO SEE HER, THAT'S ALL.
I JUST THOUGHT YOU MIGHT WANT TO SEE HER TOO. I MEAN, IT'S BEEN AWHILE, HASN'T IT? I DON'T KNOW ABOUT YOU BUT... I REALLY MISS HER.... A LOT.
CLICK

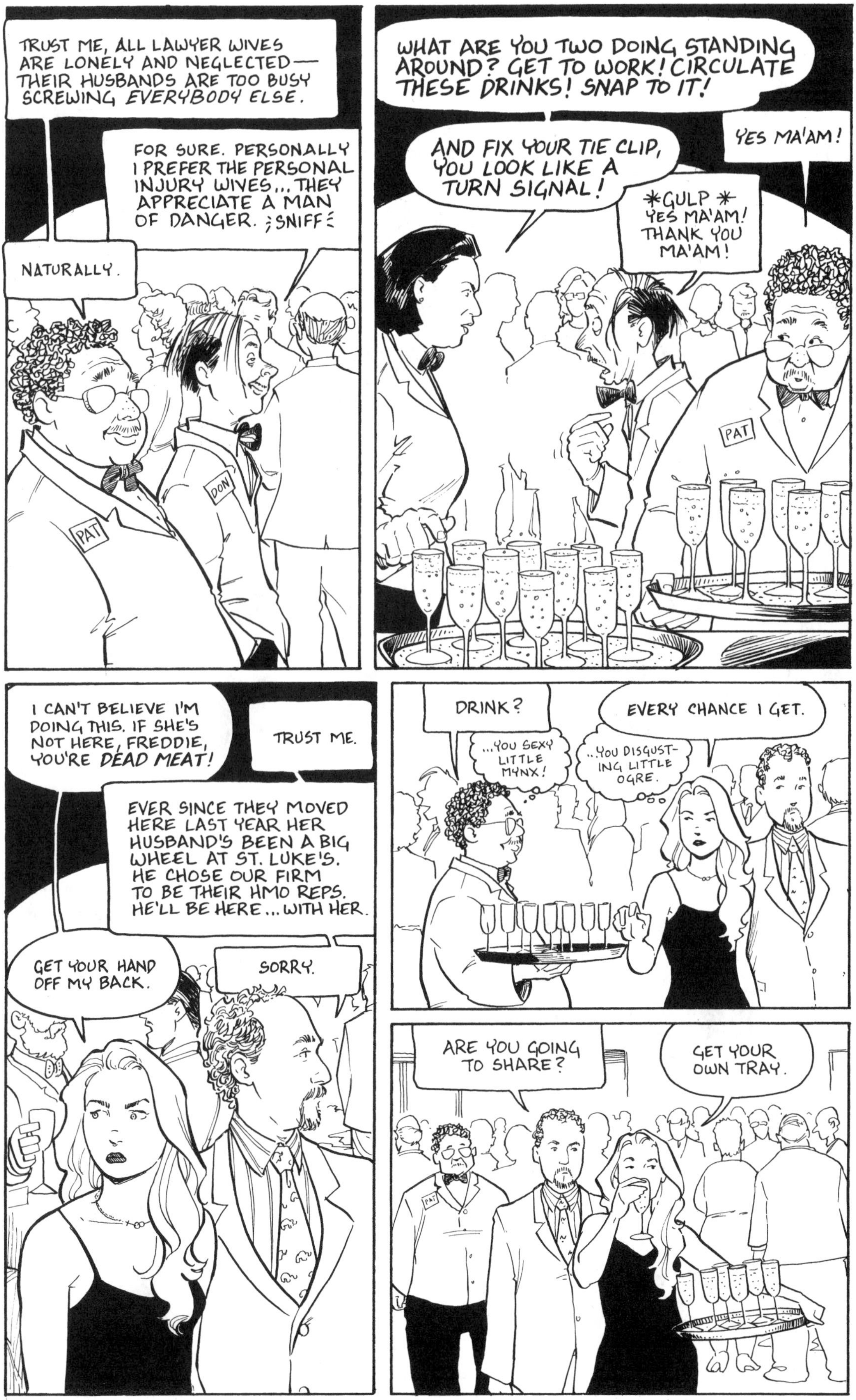
TRUST ME, ALL LAWYER WIVES ARE LONELY AND NEGLECTED— THEIR HUSBANDS ARE TOO BUSY SCREWING EVERYBODY ELSE.
FOR SURE. PERSONALLY I PREFER THE PERSONAL INJURY WIVES... THEY APPRECIATE A MAN OF DANGER. SNIFF
NATURALLY.
DON
PAT
WHAT ARE YOU TWO DOING STANDING AROUND? GET TO WORK! CIRCULATE THESE DRINKS! SNAP TO IT!
AND FIX YOUR TIE CLIP, YOU LOOK LIKE A TURN SIGNAL!
YES MA'AM!
GULP YES MA'AM! THANK YOU MA'AM!
PAT
I CAN'T BELIEVE I'M DOING THIS. IF SHE'S NOT HERE, FREDDIE, YOU'RE DEAD MEAT!
TRUST ME.
EVER SINCE THEY MOVED HERE LAST YEAR HER HUSBAND'S BEEN A BIG WHEEL AT ST. LUKE'S. HE CHOSE OUR FIRM TO BE THEIR HMO REPS. HE'LL BE HERE... WITH HER.
GET YOUR HAND OFF MY BACK.
SORRY.
DRINK?
...YOU SEXY LITTLE MYNX!
EVERY CHANCE I GET.
...YOU DISGUSTING LITTLE OGRE.
ARE YOU GOING TO SHARE?
GET YOUR OWN TRAY.
PAT

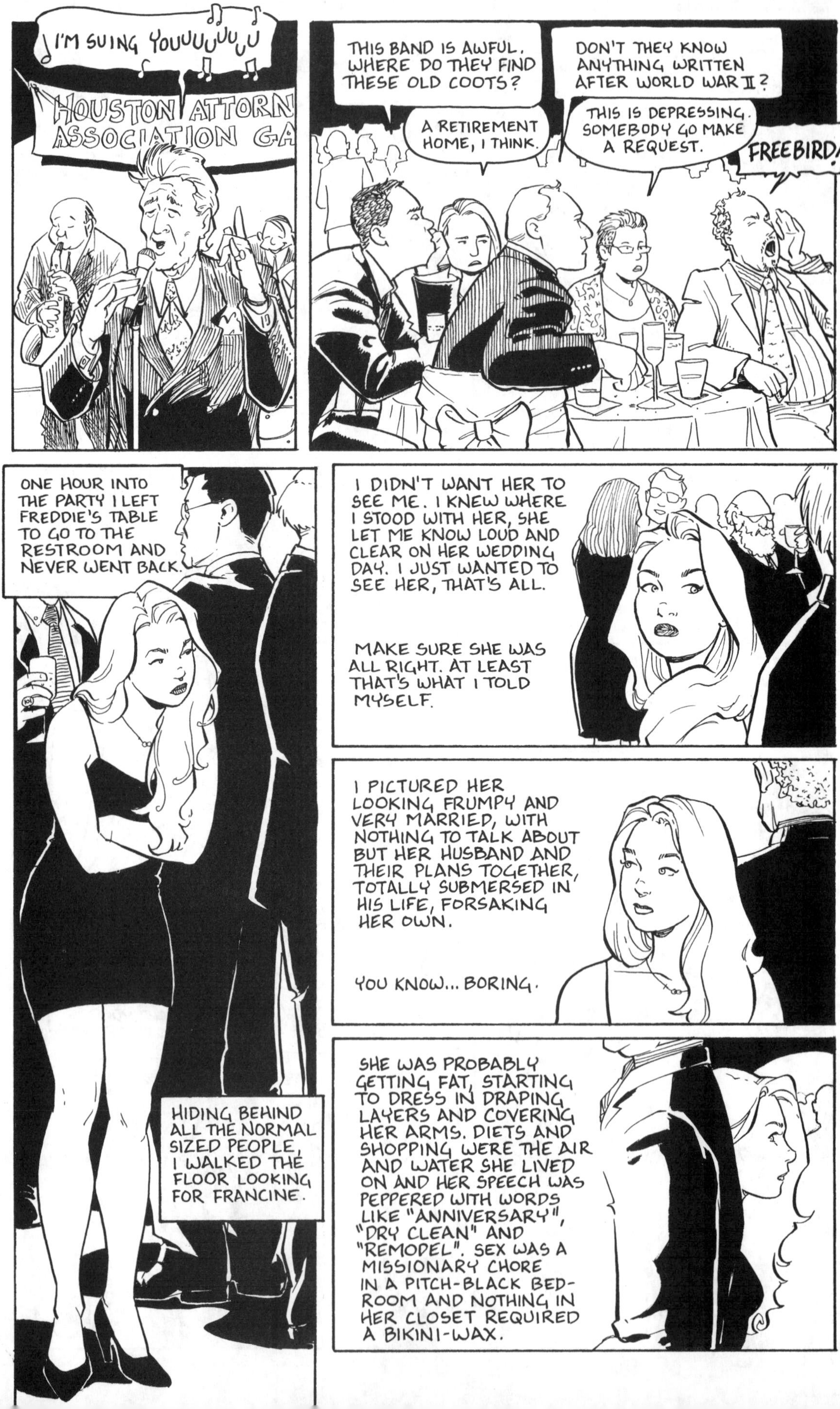
I'M SUING YOUUUUUUUU
HOUSTON ATTORN ASSOCIATION GA
THIS BAND IS AWFUL. WHERE DO THEY FIND THESE OLD COOTS?
A RETIREMENT HOME, I THINK.
DON'T THEY KNOW ANYTHING WRITTEN AFTER WORLD WAR II?
THIS IS DEPRESSING. SOMEBODY GO MAKE A REQUEST.
FREEBIRD!
ONE HOUR INTO THE PARTY I LEFT FREDDIE'S TABLE TO GO TO THE RESTROOM AND NEVER WENT BACK.
HIDING BEHIND ALL THE NORMAL SIZED PEOPLE, I WALKED THE FLOOR LOOKING FOR FRANCINE.
I DIDN'T WANT HER TO SEE ME. I KNEW WHERE I STOOD WITH HER, SHE LET ME KNOW LOUD AND CLEAR ON HER WEDDING DAY. I JUST WANTED TO SEE HER, THAT'S ALL.
MAKE SURE SHE WAS ALL RIGHT. AT LEAST THAT'S WHAT I TOLD MYSELF.
I PICTURED HER LOOKING FRUMPY AND VERY MARRIED, WITH NOTHING TO TALK ABOUT BUT HER HUSBAND AND THEIR PLANS TOGETHER, TOTALLY SUBMERSED IN HIS LIFE, FORSAKING HER OWN.
YOU KNOW... BORING.
SHE WAS PROBABLY GETTING FAT, STARTING TO DRESS IN DRAPING LAYERS AND COVERING HER ARMS. DIETS AND SHOPPING WERE THE AIR AND WATER SHE LIVED ON AND HER SPEECH WAS PEPPERED WITH WORDS LIKE "ANNIVERSARY", "DRY CLEAN" AND "REMODEL". SEX WAS A MISSIONARY CHORE IN A PITCH-BLACK BEDROOM AND NOTHING IN HER CLOSET REQUIRED A BIKINI-WAX.

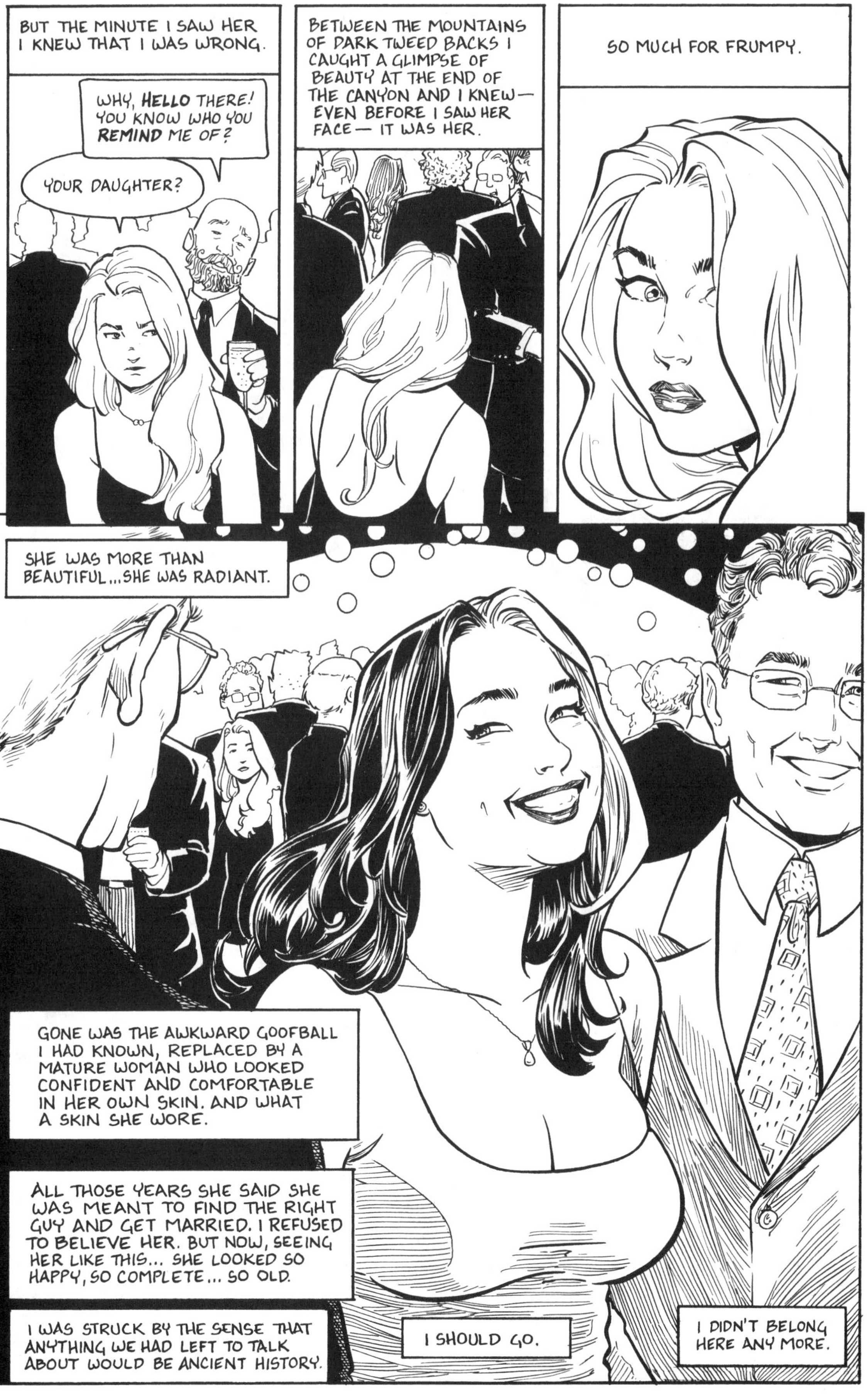
BUT THE MINUTE I SAW HER I KNEW THAT I WAS WRONG.
WHY, HELLO THERE! YOU KNOW WHO YOU REMIND ME OF?
YOUR DAUGHTER?
BETWEEN THE MOUNTAINS OF DARK TWEED BACKS I CAUGHT A GLIMPSE OF BEAUTY AT THE END OF THE CANYON AND I KNEW— EVEN BEFORE I SAW HER FACE— IT WAS HER.
SO MUCH FOR FRUMPY.
SHE WAS MORE THAN BEAUTIFUL...SHE WAS RADIANT.
GONE WAS THE AWKWARD GOOFBALL I HAD KNOWN, REPLACED BY A MATURE WOMAN WHO LOOKED CONFIDENT AND COMFORTABLE IN HER OWN SKIN. AND WHAT A SKIN SHE WORE.
ALL THOSE YEARS SHE SAID SHE WAS MEANT TO FIND THE RIGHT GUY AND GET MARRIED. I REFUSED TO BELIEVE HER. BUT NOW, SEEING HER LIKE THIS... SHE LOOKED SO HAPPY, SO COMPLETE... SO OLD.
I WAS STRUCK BY THE SENSE THAT ANYTHING WE HAD LEFT TO TALK ABOUT WOULD BE ANCIENT HISTORY.
I SHOULD GO.
I DIDN'T BELONG HERE ANY MORE.

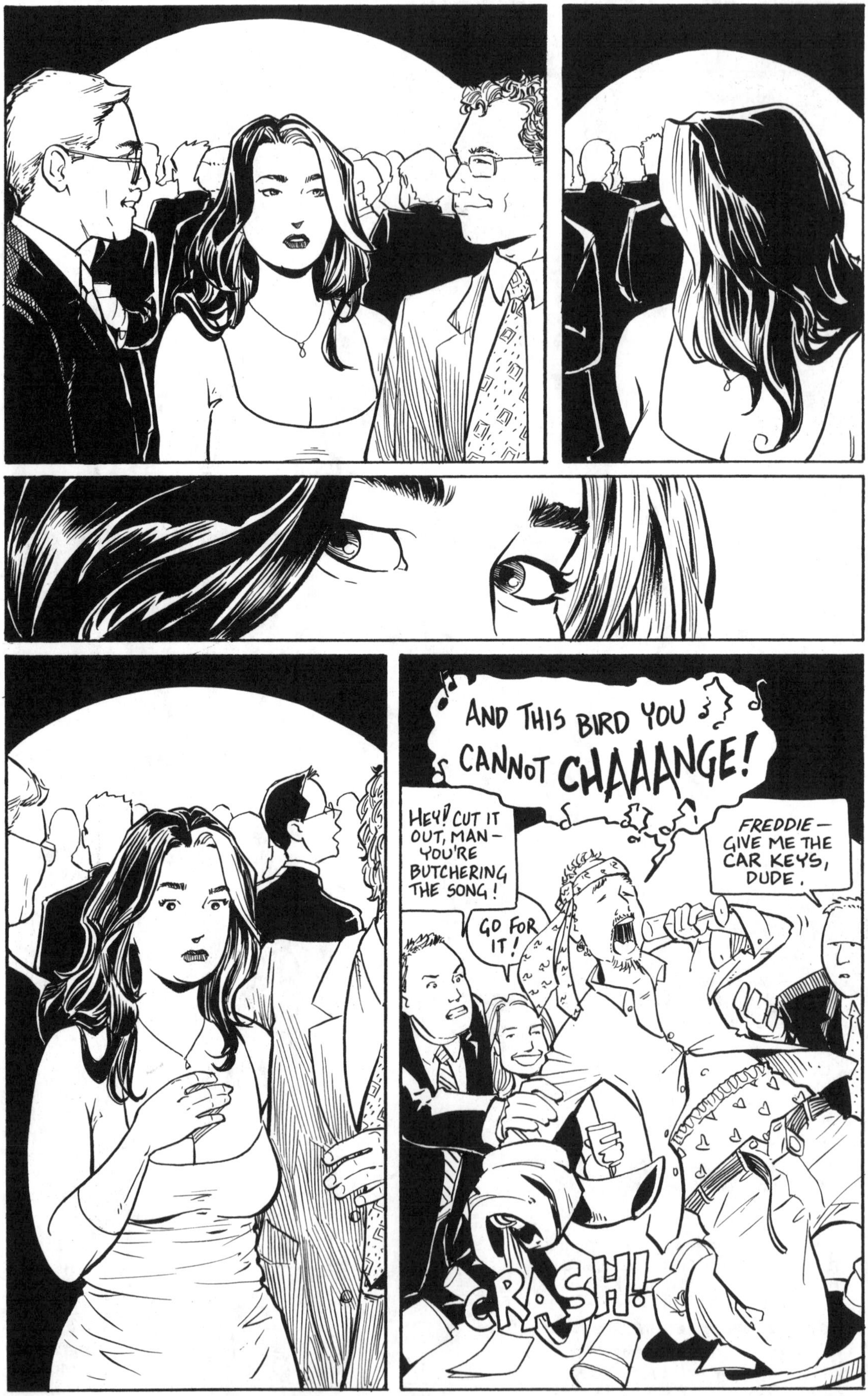

AND THIS BIRD YOU CANNOT CHAAANGE!
HEY! CUT IT OUT, MAN— YOU'RE BUTCHERING THE SONG!
GO FOR IT!
FREDDIE— GIVE ME THE CAR KEYS, DUDE.
CRASH!

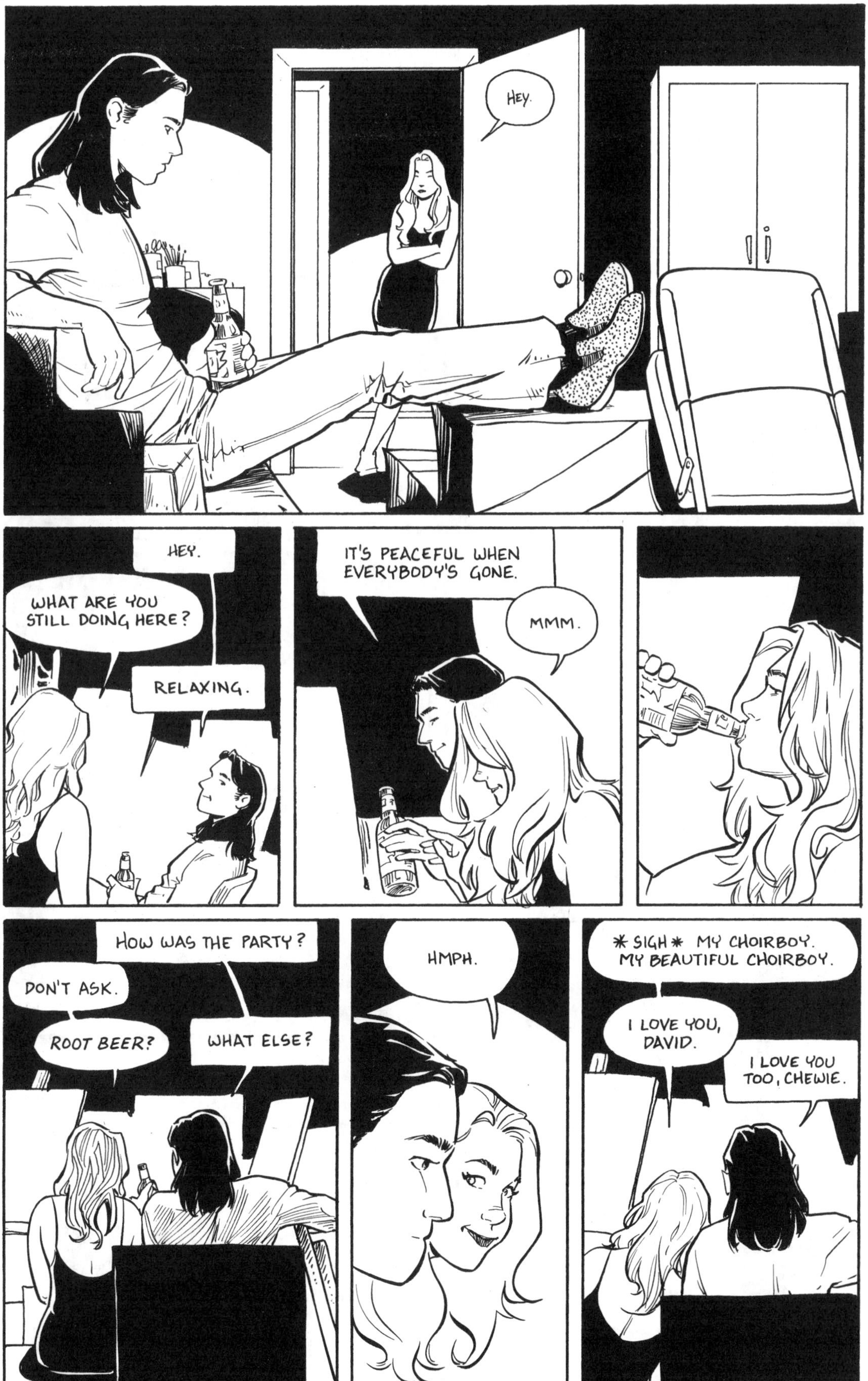
HEY.
HEY.
WHAT ARE YOU STILL DOING HERE?
RELAXING.
IT'S PEACEFUL WHEN EVERYBODY'S GONE.
MMM.
HOW WAS THE PARTY?
DON'T ASK.
ROOT BEER?
WHAT ELSE?
HMPH.
SIGH MY CHOIRBOY. MY BEAUTIFUL CHOIRBOY.
I LOVE YOU, DAVID.
I LOVE YOU TOO, CHEWIE.

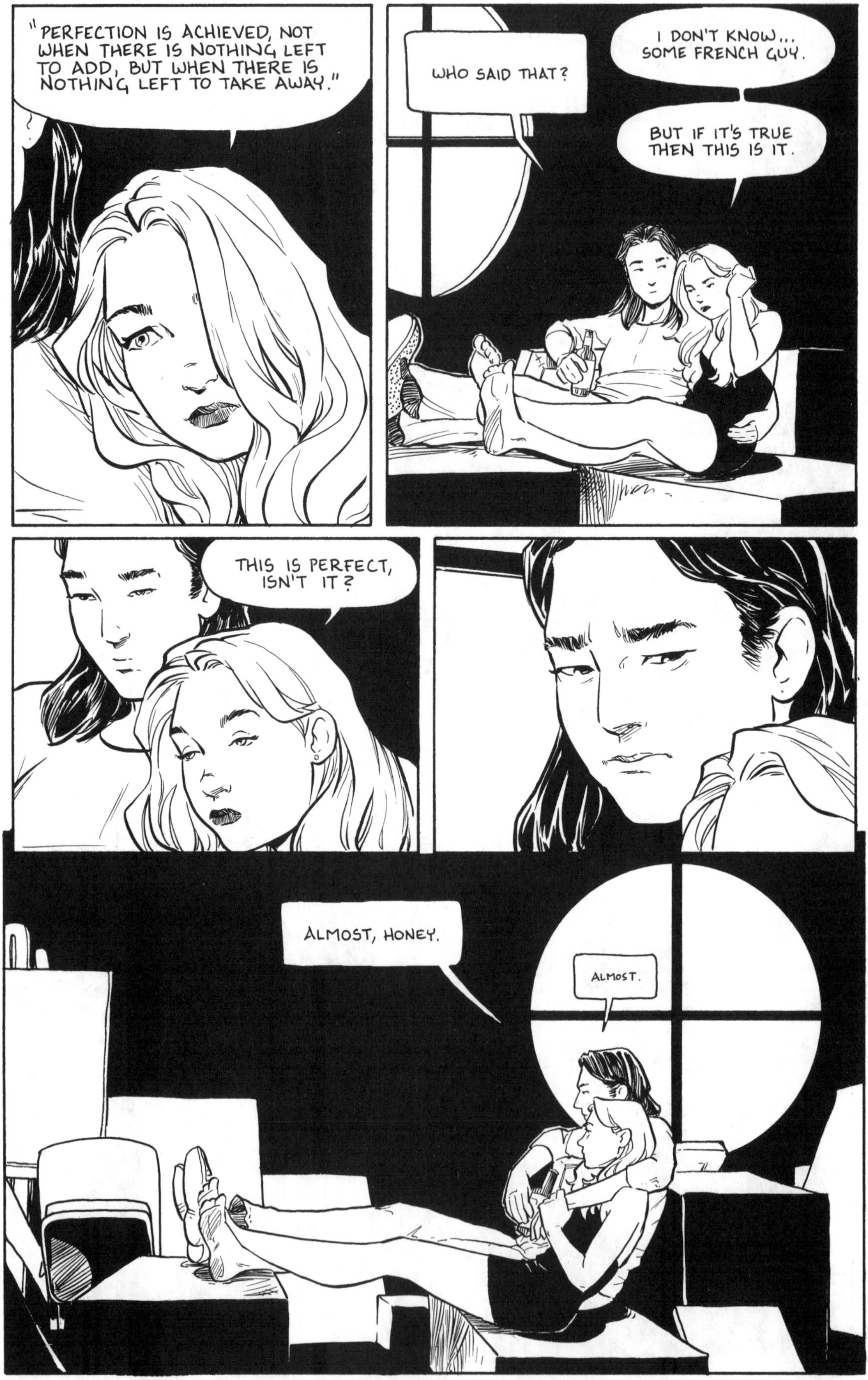
"PERFECTION IS ACHIEVED, NOT WHEN THERE IS NOTHING LEFT TO ADD, BUT WHEN THERE IS NOTHING LEFT TO TAKE AWAY."
WHO SAID THAT?
I DON'T KNOW... SOME FRENCH GUY.
BUT IF IT'S TRUE THEN THIS IS IT.
THIS IS PERFECT, ISN'T IT?
ALMOST, HONEY.
ALMOST.

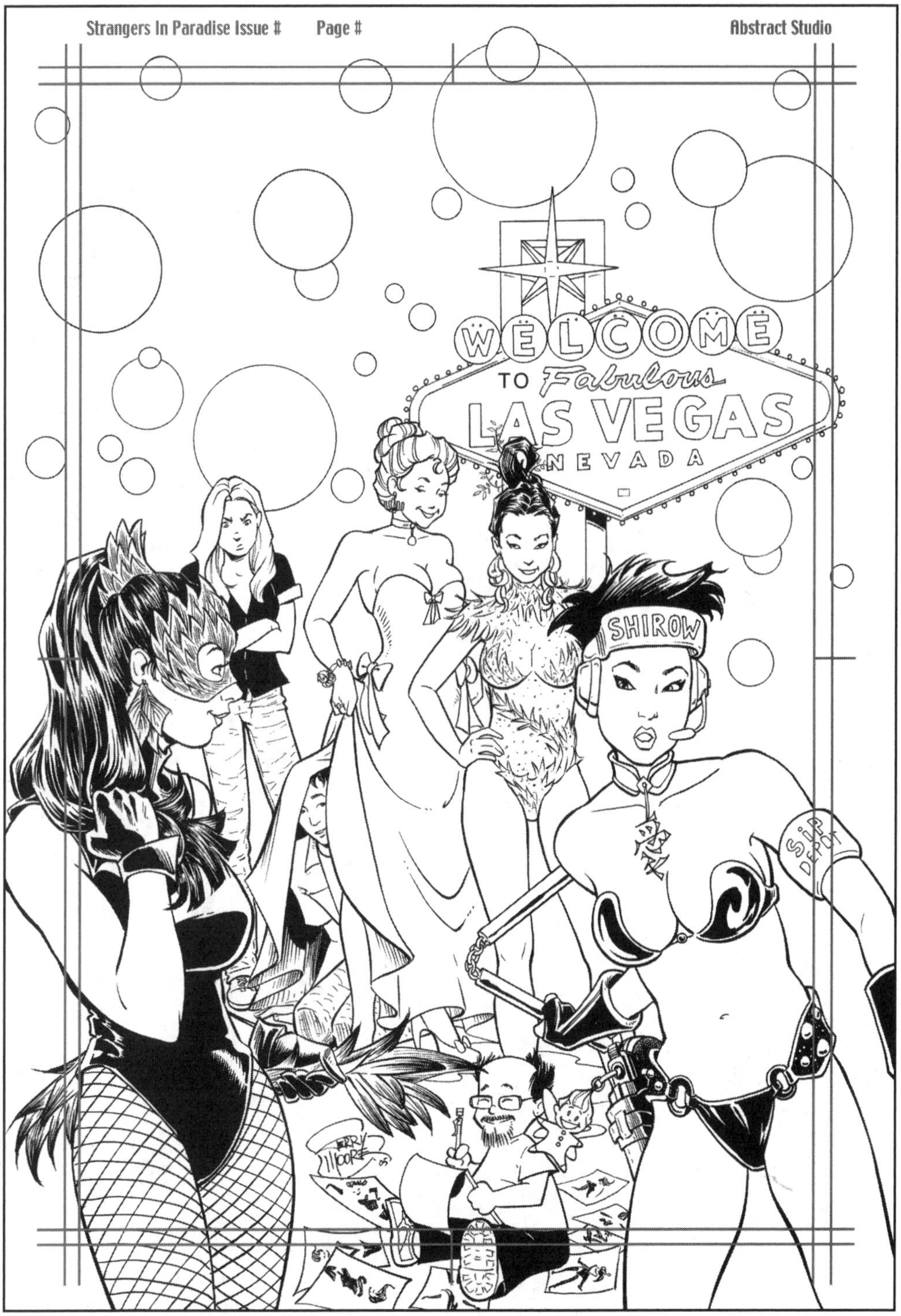

Strangers In Paradise Issue #
Page #
Abstract Studio
WELCOME
TO Fabulous
LAS VEGAS
NEVADA
SHIROW

Cover Gallery

ABSTRACT STUDIO

70

STRANGERS IN PARADISE

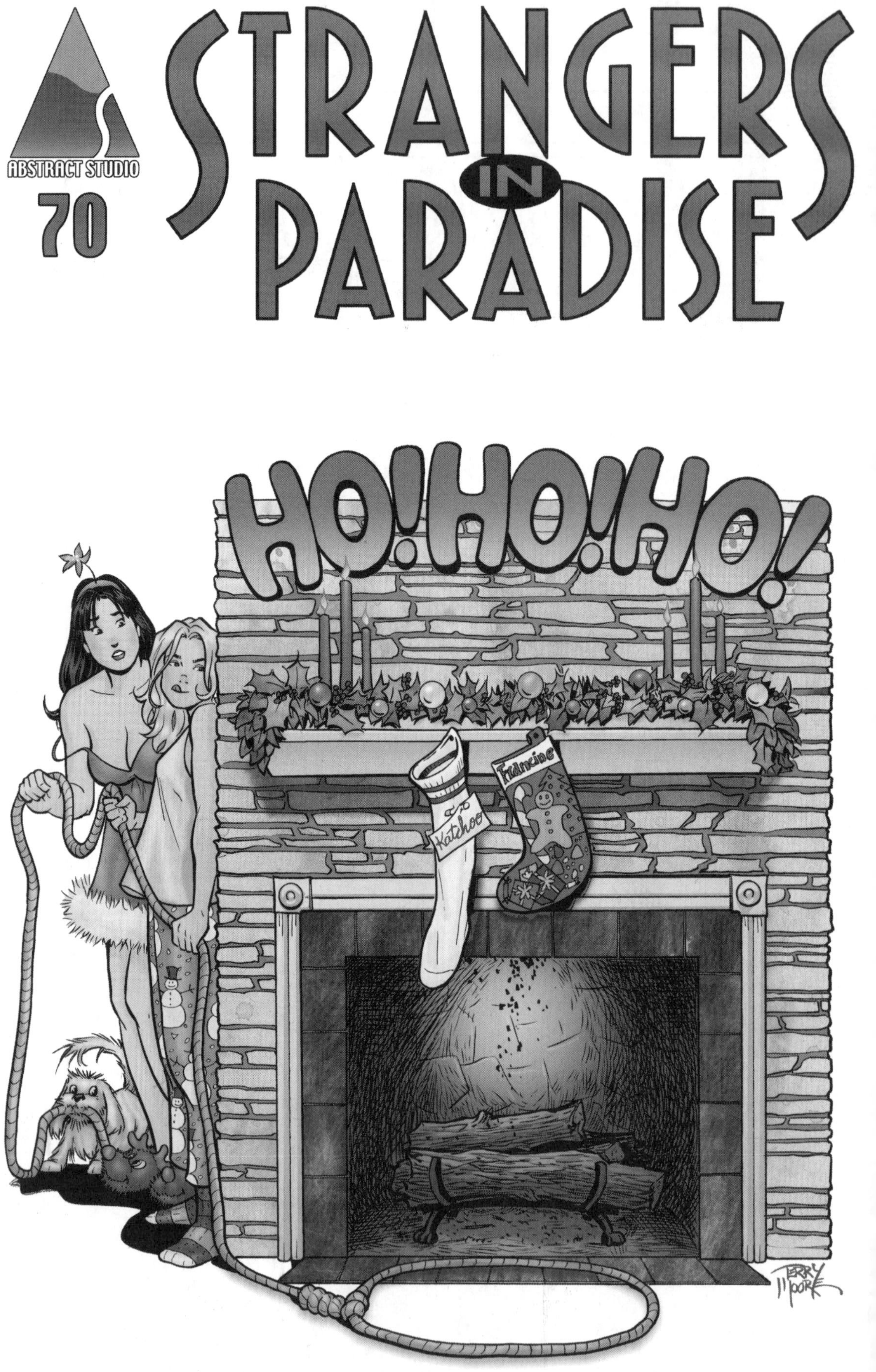
HO! HO! HO!
Katchoo
Francine
TERRY MOORE

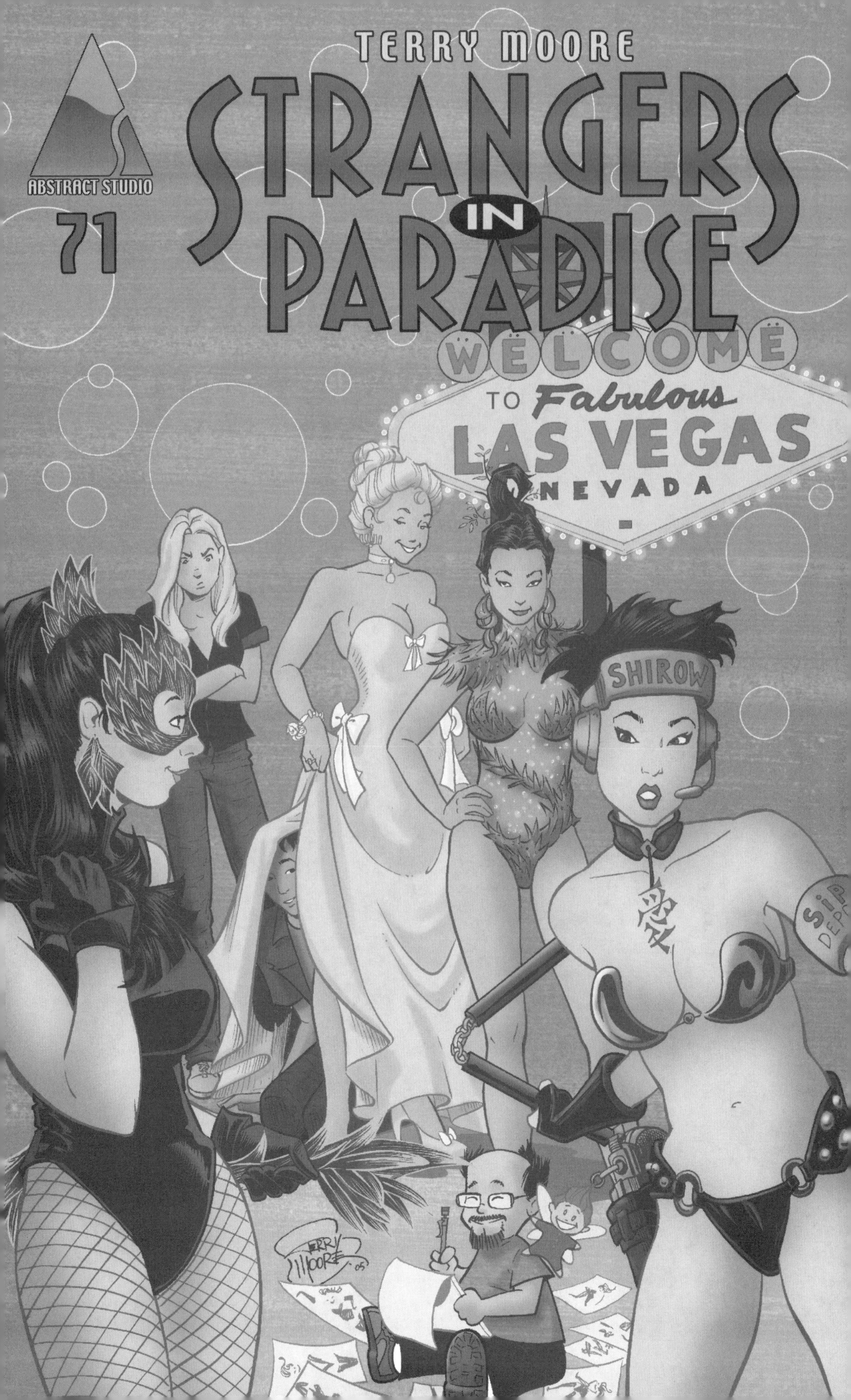
TERRY MOORE
STRANGERS IN PARADISE
ABSTRACT STUDIO
71
WELCOME
TO Fabulous
LAS VEGAS
NEVADA
SHIROW
TERRY MOORE '05

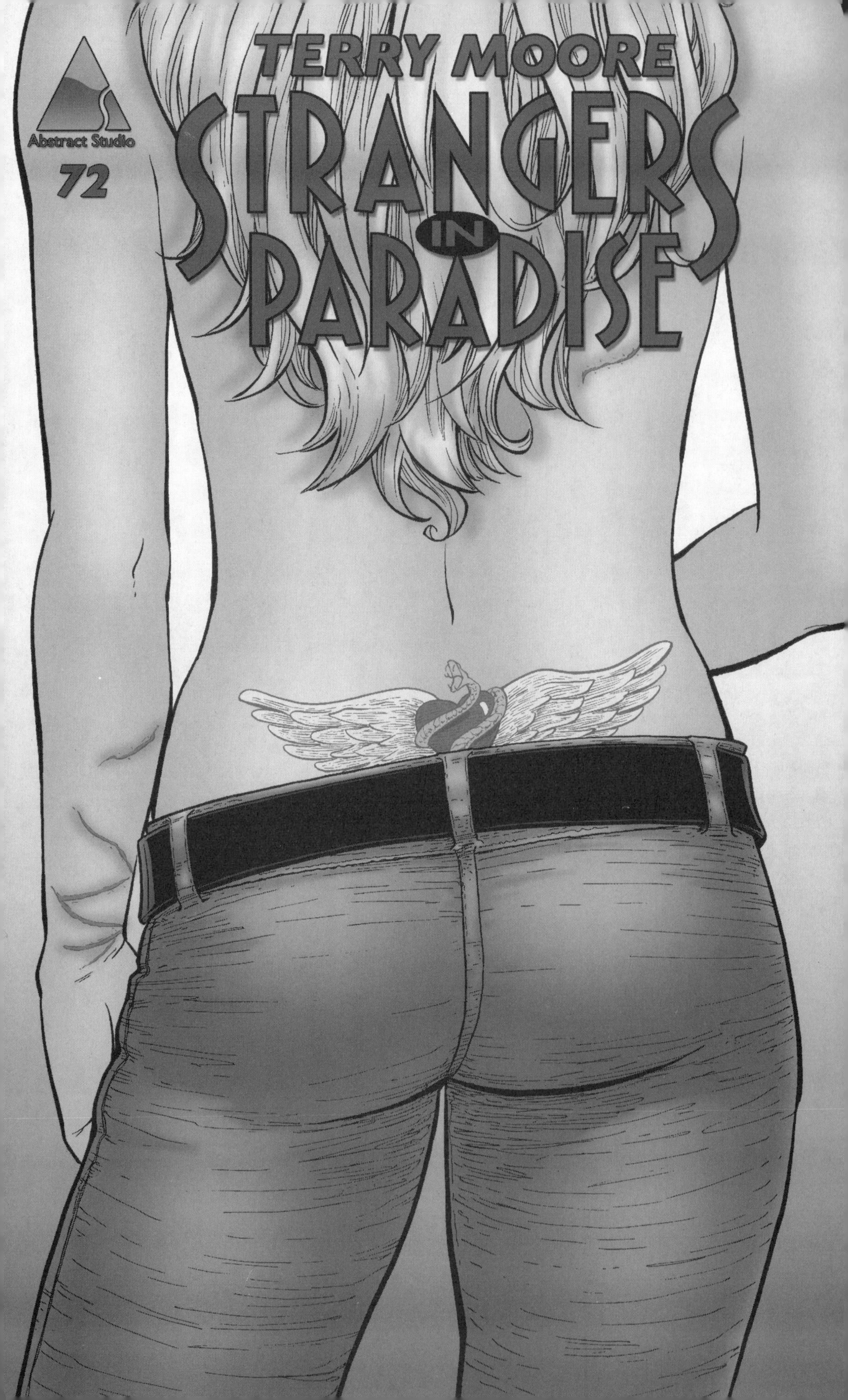

Abstract Studio
72
TERRY MOORE
STRANGERS IN PARADISE

TERRY MOORE

STRANGERS IN PARADISE

Abstract Studio

74

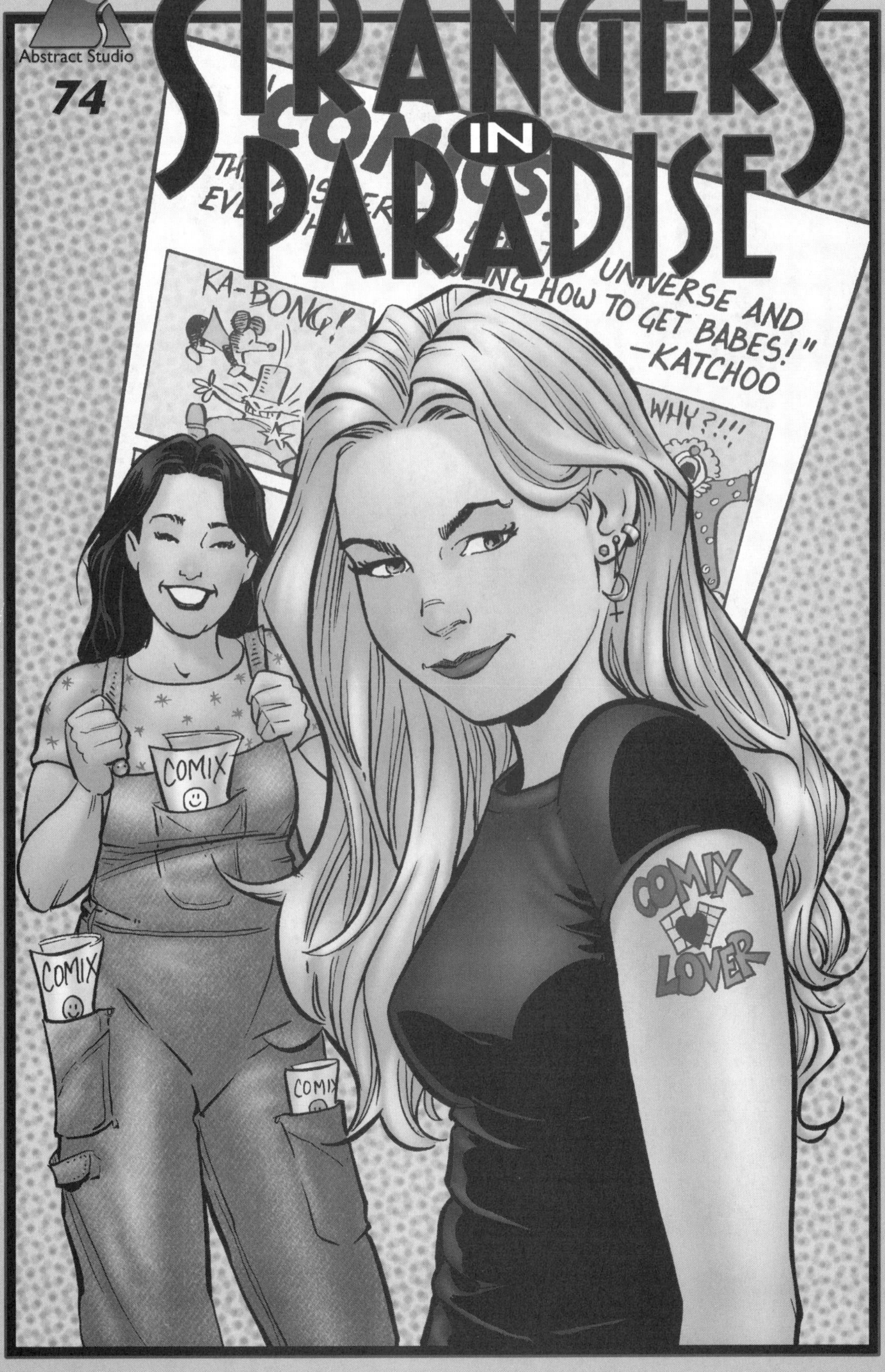

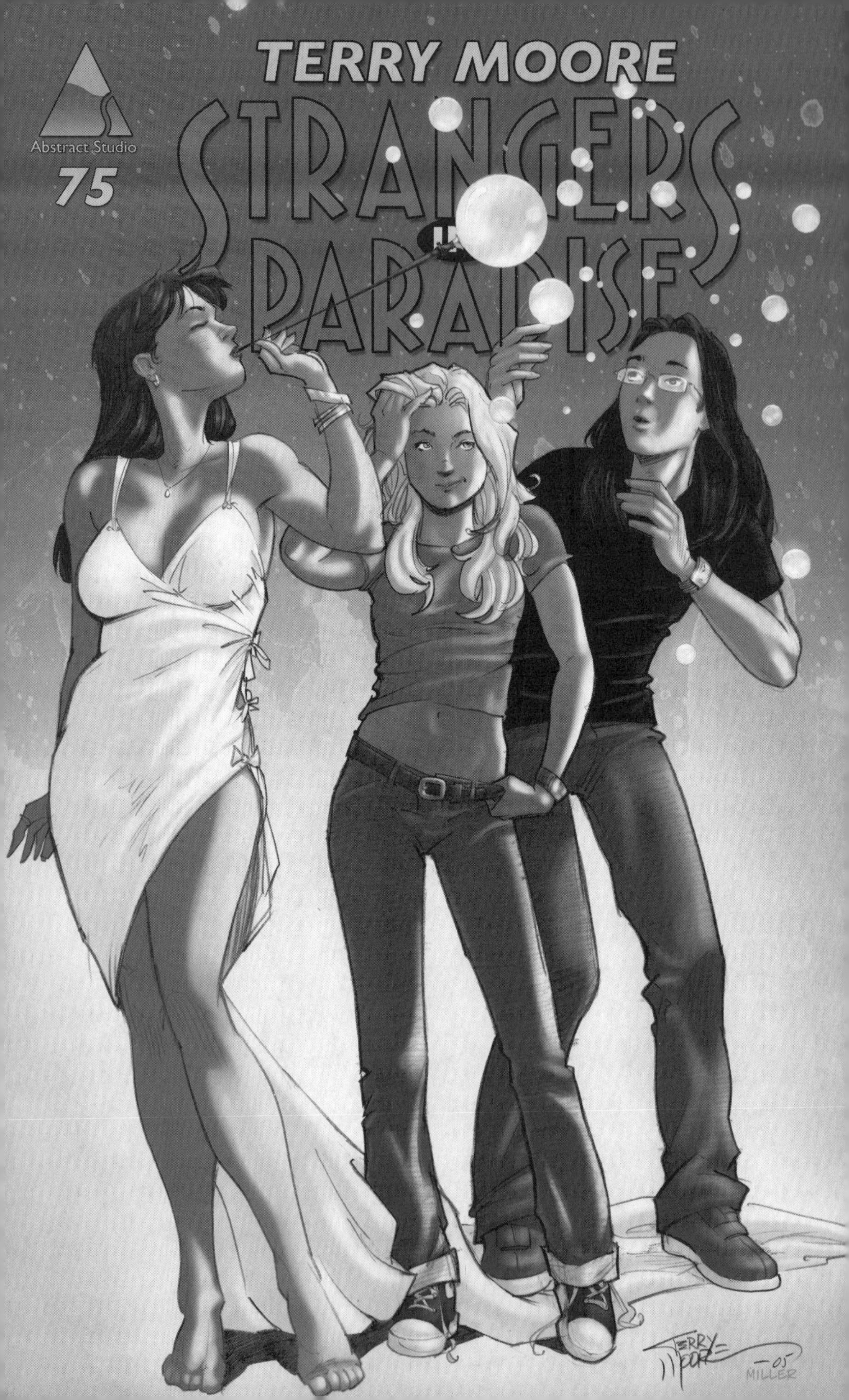

Abstract Studio
75
TERRY MOORE
STRANGERS IN PARADISE

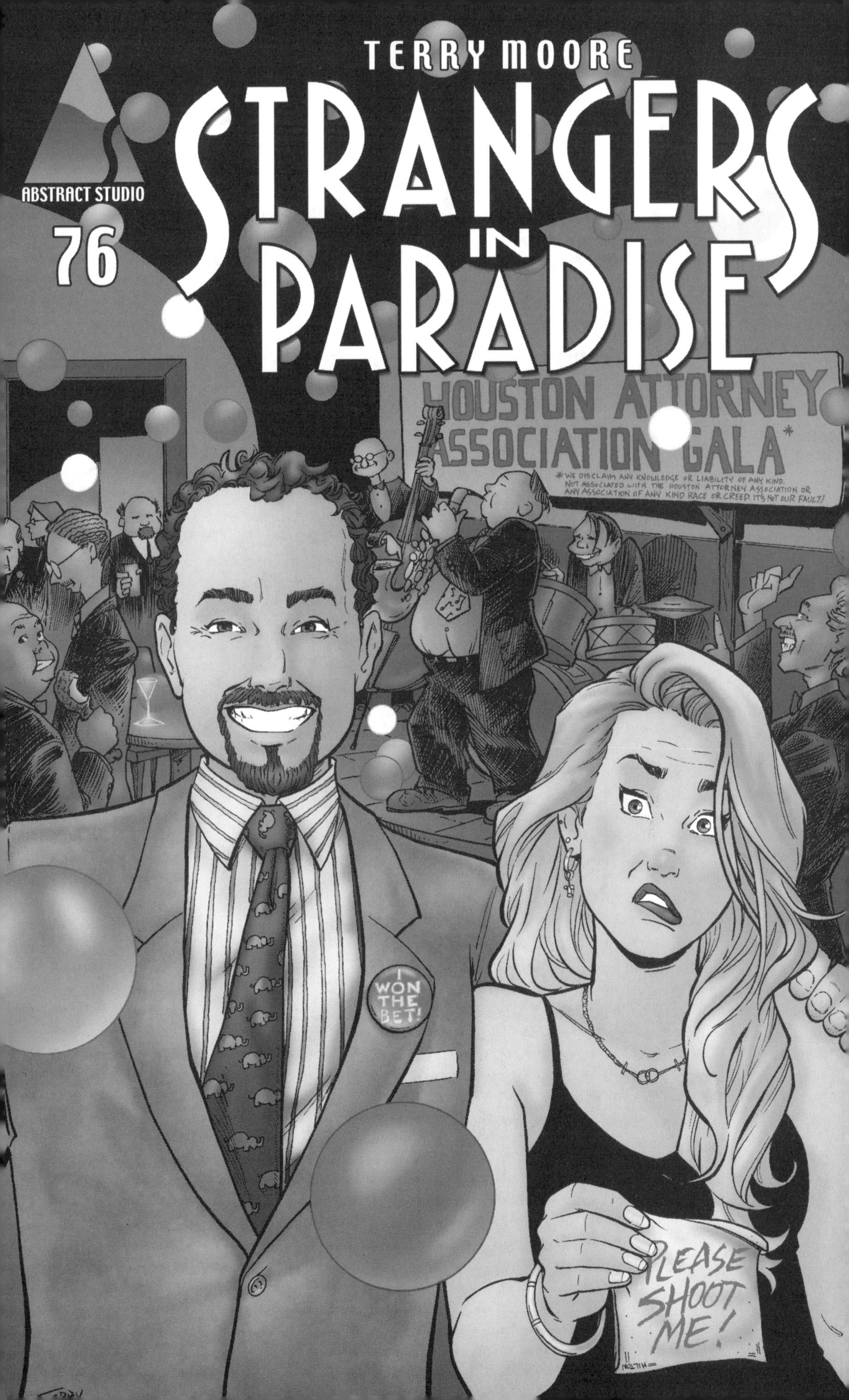

TERRY MOORE
STRANGERS IN PARADISE
ABSTRACT STUDIO
76
HOUSTON ATTORNEY ASSOCIATION GALA*
*WE DISCLAIM ANY KNOWLEDGE OR LIABILITY OF ANY KIND. NOT ASSOCIATED WITH THE HOUSTON ATTORNEY ASSOCIATION OR ANY ASSOCIATION OF ANY KIND RACE OR CREED. IT'S NOT OUR FAULT!
I WON THE BET!
PLEASE SHOOT ME!

Fan Tattoos

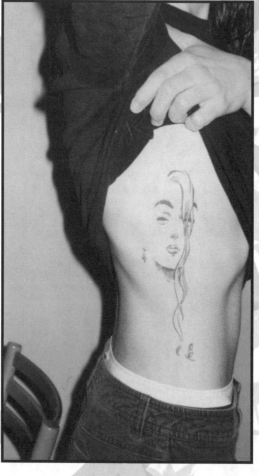

Nora Bedevion's I Dream Of You Katchoo

When I began writing and drawing Strangers In Paradise, my dream was to make story art that would end up in books. What I never expected to see was my art on people's bodies. I can't think of a higher compliment. Over the years I have seen more body art of Francine, David, Katchoo, Kixie, Plato, the polar bear —even correctly placed Darcy Parker lilies!— than I can count. Everything from cover art to story panels is now permanently engraved in public and private places on SiP fans all over the world. So next time you're talking to a SiP fan, beware: You never know what they are hiding under that shirt!

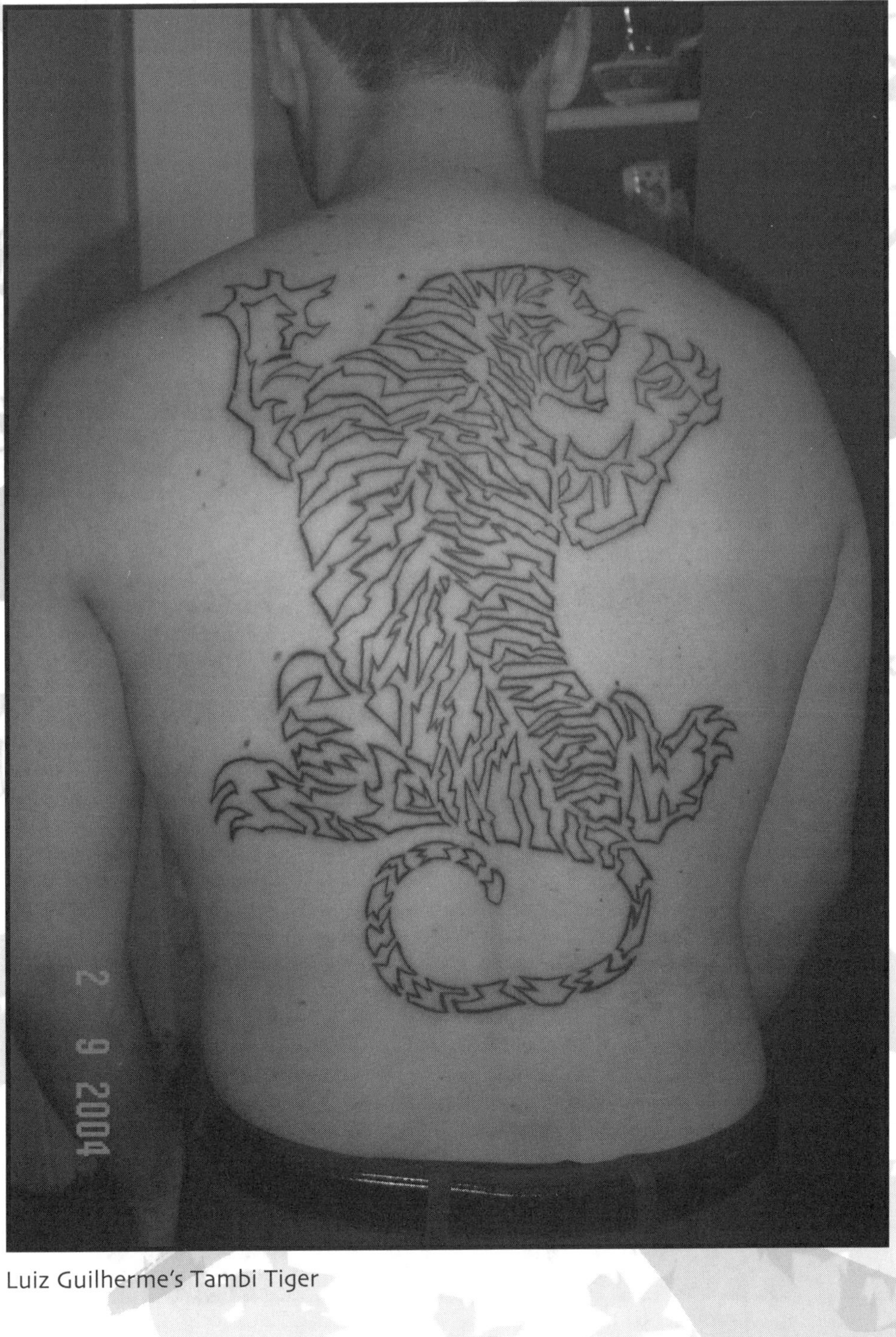
2 9 2004

Luiz Guilherme's Tambi Tiger

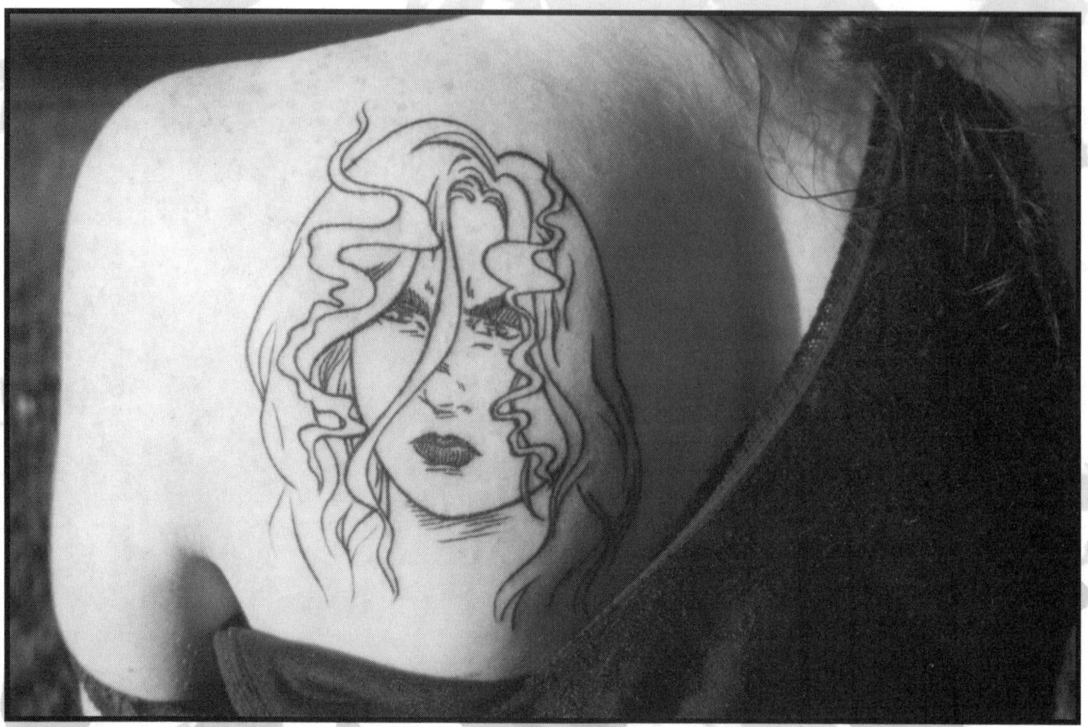

Lauren Johnson's Smoking Katchoo

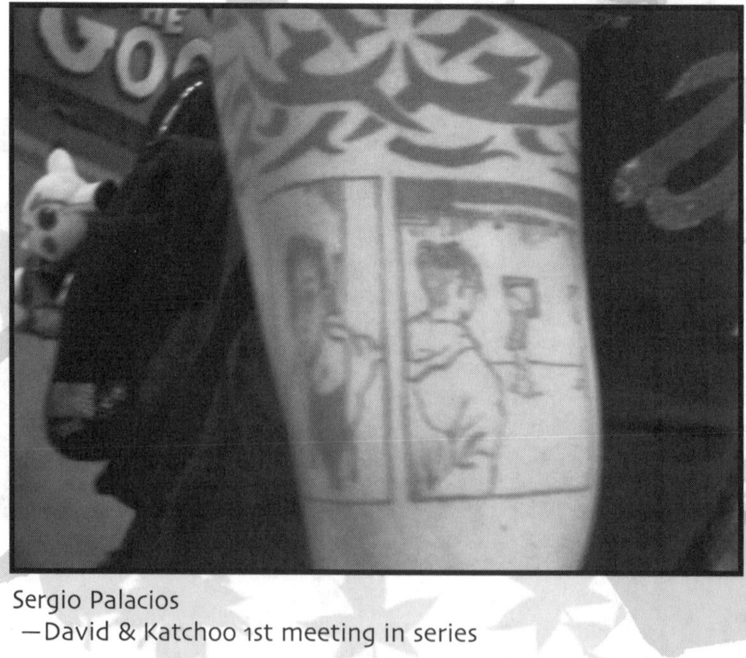

Sergio Palacios
—David & Katchoo 1st meeting in series

Eluminados Alfero's Cute One Katchoo

Tarin Lewis'
Parker Lily

Shannon Drew's Kixie

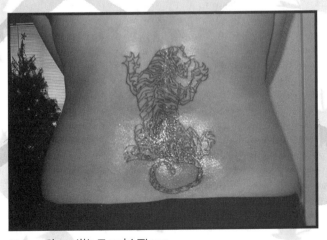

Kerry Sherrill's Tambi Tiger

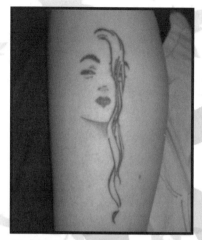

Melissa Fodor's
I Dream Of You Katchoo

Marlena Hall's Cute One

Jill Endress's painting Katchoo

Adam van Son's
Parker Lily

Carolyn Garley's Parker Lily

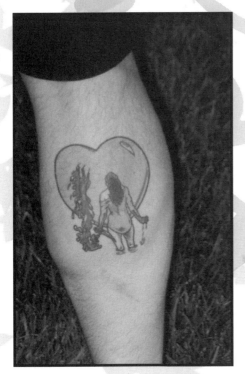

Maurice L. Poussard's SiP #3 (v.I)

Donna Hirsch's Kixie with Breast
Cancer Awareness Ribbon

Just a few behind-the-scene peeks at

Terry's Sketchbook

During The Making Of This Book

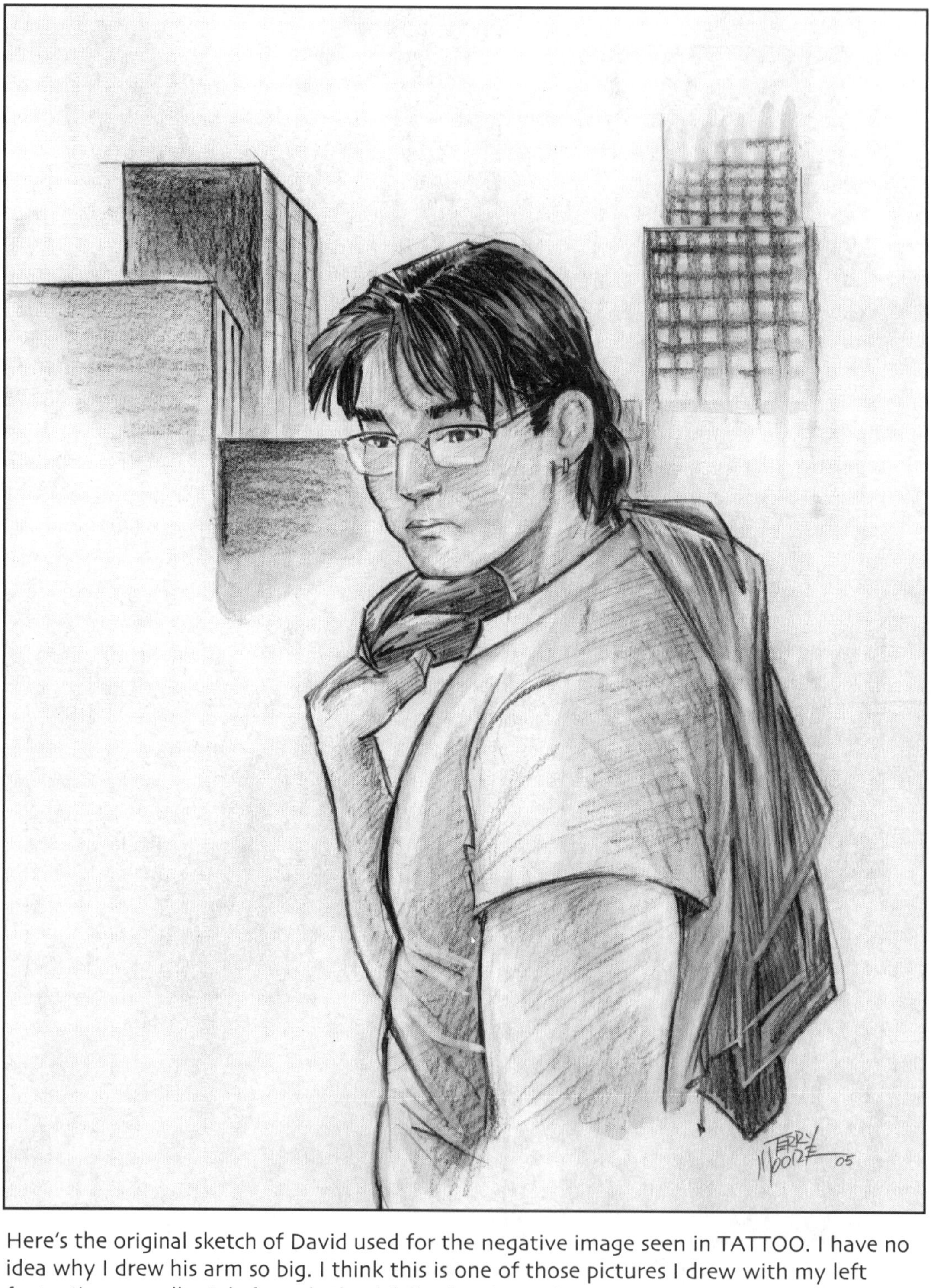

Here's the original sketch of David used for the negative image seen in TATTOO. I have no idea why I drew his arm so big. I think this is one of those pictures I drew with my left foot—I'm normally rightfooted. Thankfully they have this magic potion called Photoshop that allowed me to fix the image before it went into the book. The fix didn't really look that good though, so I decided to run it in negative, the flanger of the art world.

I thought you might like to see this. My original idea for Katchoo's first sighting of Francine back in Houston was to have them meet at The Savoy Apartments, where Francine & Brad lived, and into which Katchoo was helping David move. Below was the page where that was outlined, along with a sketch of the real Savoy, which I found on a scouting mission through the Houston Museum district. I later nixed all this in favor of the party scene, but I still think it's funny. It's not easy being Katchoo.

back to get groceries. Brad comes around the SUV and heads for the apt. next door to
16 Katchoo's. Then Fran comes around SUV, smiles and says "Hi David." David feezes like a deer in headlights. He replies weakly, "Hi Francine." Just as Katchoo is coming back out onto the balconey. She stops in mid-step and drops to the ground spilling the drinks all over herself, hiding just inside the doorway, eyes wide. Fran freezes in her step and realizes what she has just
17 said…and seen.
"This isn't happening. It's just a dream. I bumped my head on the tailgate, I'm lying on the ground, hallucinating." Francine says.
Brad comes back out. He stops when he sees Francine frozen and staring at David on the
17 balconey. "Hey, what's up?" he asks.
"What are you doing here"? Francine asks.
"Moving in." David replies. "What are you doing here? I thought you were in Nashville"
"We moved here last week. Brad got a job at the medical center."
"Congratulations," David says weakly.
19 "Thanks," Brad replies. "Excuse me, what's going on? Am I missing something here?"
"Hi Katchoo." Francine says.
A long pause. David stares at Fran. Finally, "Hi" replies Katchoo from out of sight.
David pulls Katchoo up by the back of her collar. She is drenched in soda and looking a mess.
She stares at Francine wide-eyed.
"Oh, you have got to be kidding me." Brad says in disgust.
"Small world…isn't it?" Katchoo smiles weakly.

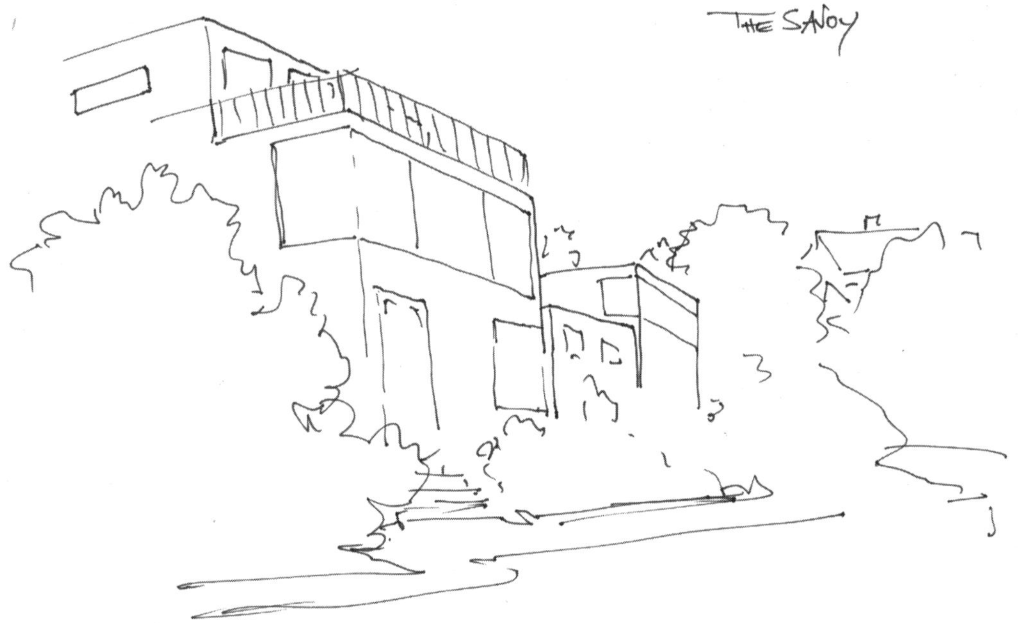
THE SAVOY

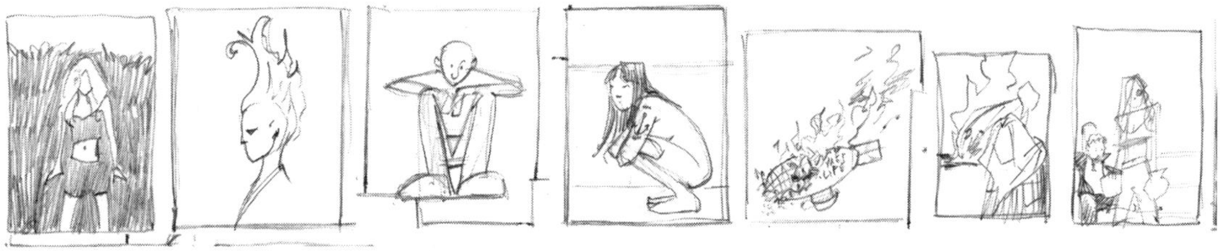

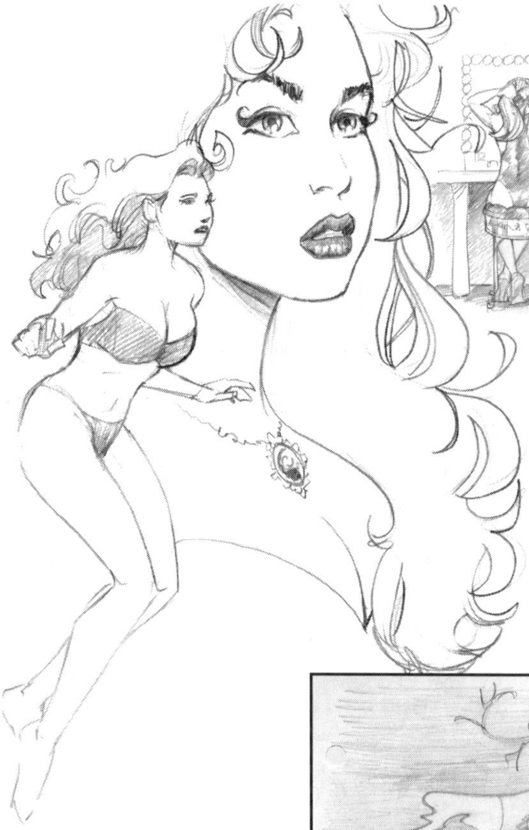

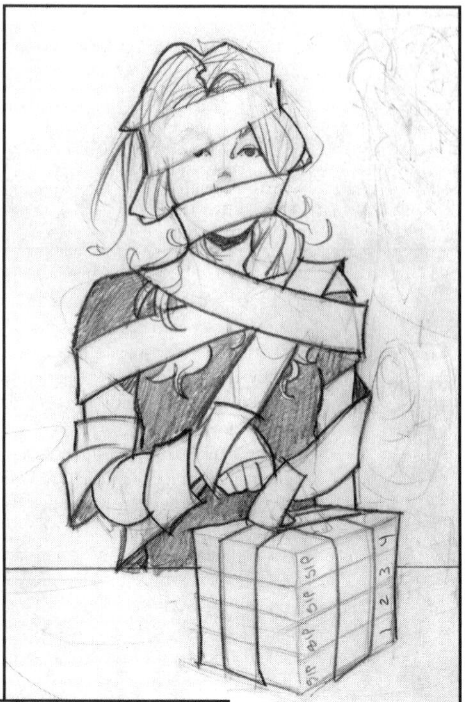

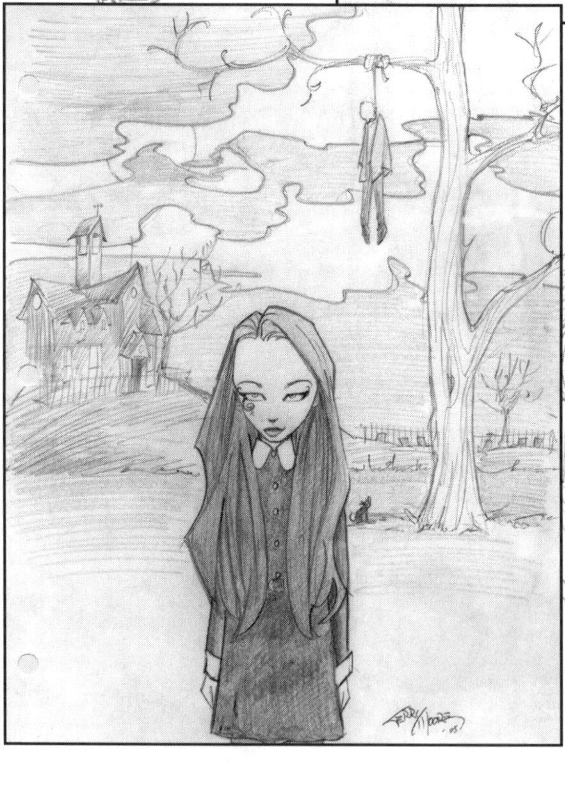

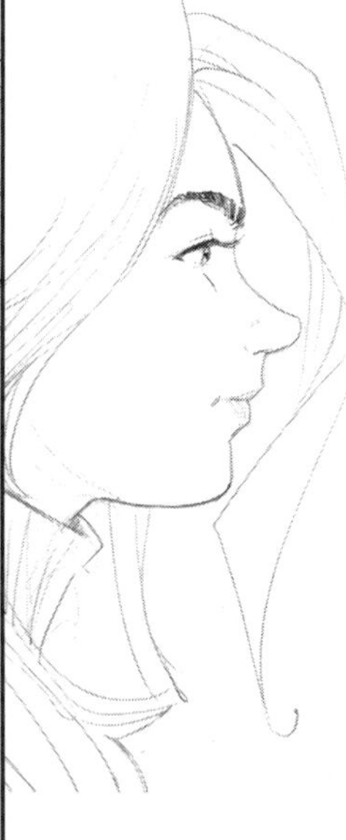

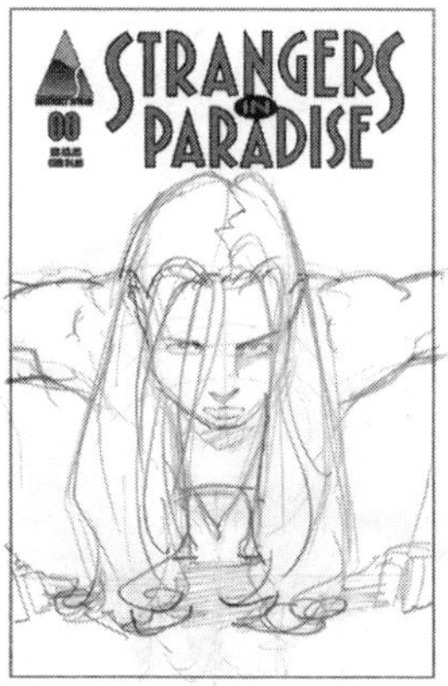
STRANGERS IN PARADISE
00

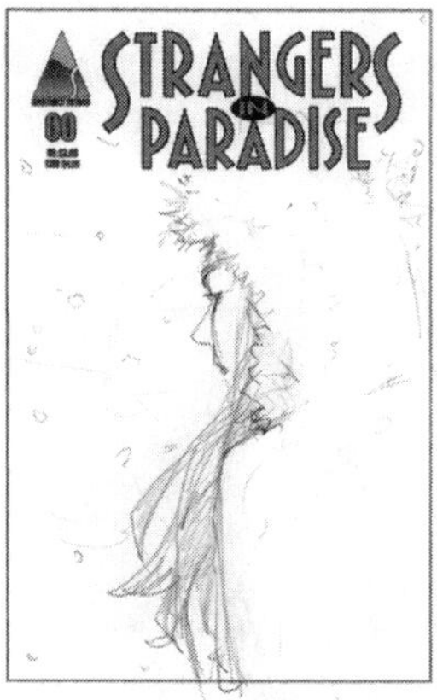
STRANGERS IN PARADISE
00

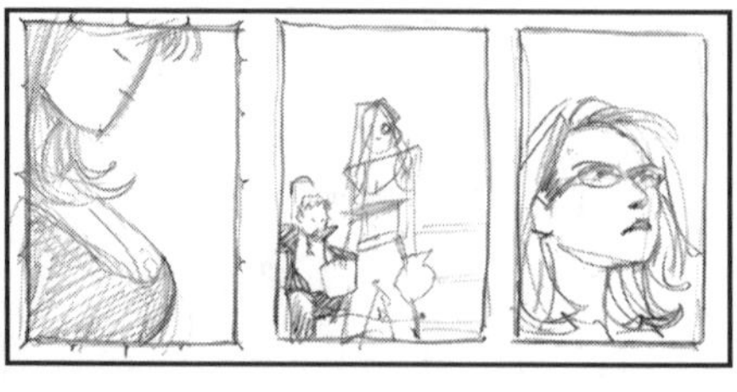

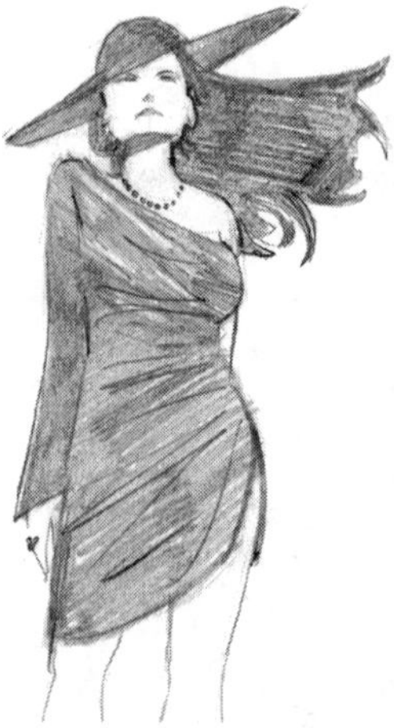

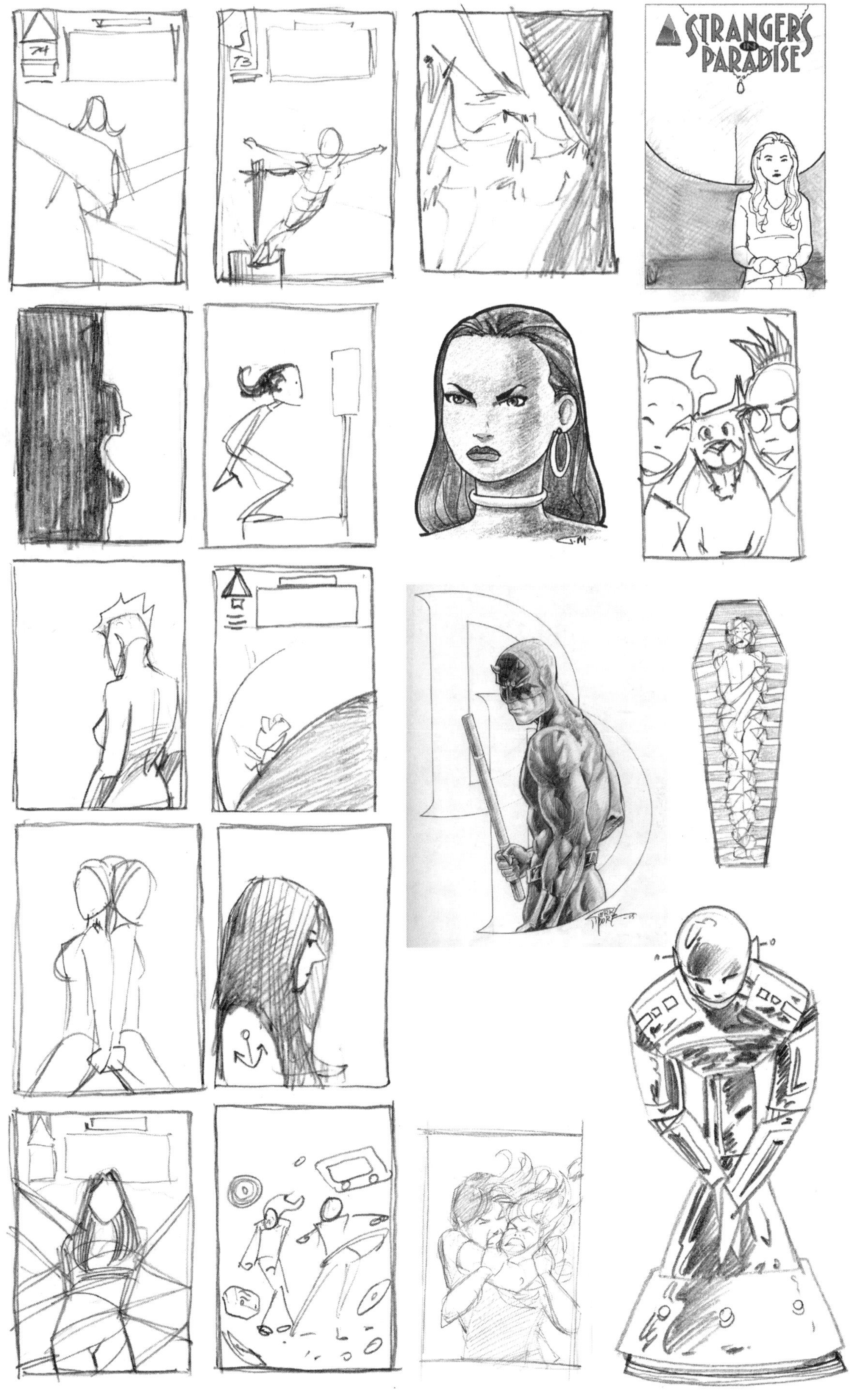
STRANGERS IN PARADISE

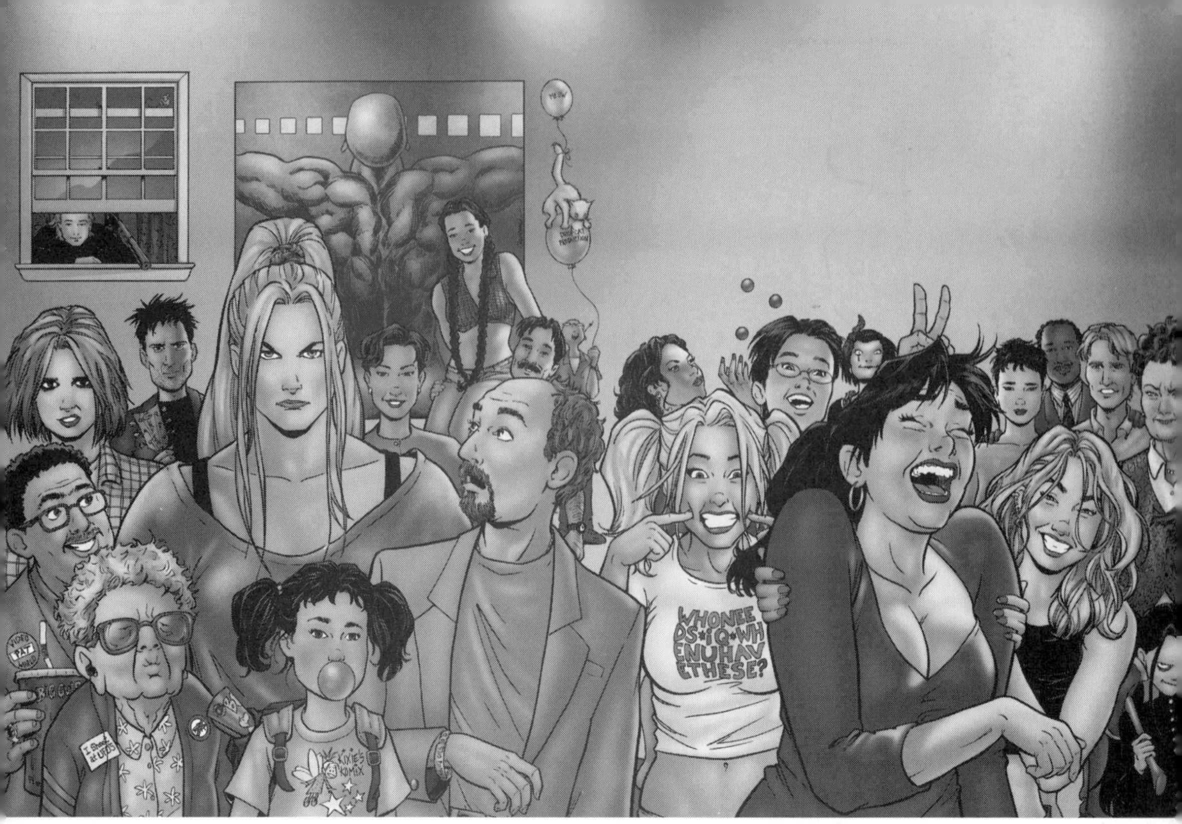
WHONEE
DS*IQ*WH
ENUHAV
ETHESE?

Other Strangers In Paradise Graphic Novels by Terry Moore

The Collected Strangers In Paradise

I Dream Of You

It's A Good Life

Love Me Tender

Immortal Enemies

High School

Sanctuary

My Other Life

Child Of Rage

Tropic Of Desire

Brave New World

Heart In Hand

Flower To Flame

David's Story

Tomorrow Now

Molly & Poo
